P&O *at* 175

Produced and designed by Ferry Publications trading as Lily Publications Ltd

PO Box 33, Ramsey, Isle of Man, British Isles, IM99 4LP

Tel: +44 (0) 1624 898446 Fax: +44 (0) 1624 898449

www.ferrypubs.co.uk E-Mail: info@lilypublications.co.uk

Printed and bound by Gomer Press Ltd., Wales, UK +44 (0) 1559 362371

First Published: January 2012 Second Edition: May 2012

Contents

Acknowledgements 4

Introduction 6

1 Iberia, the Mediterranean and early passages to India 8

2 Out East and Down Under 20

3 Through two World Wars and a Great Depression 34

4 Decades of Revolution 90

5 The Sterling Era 124

6 Dismantling the Empire 154

Epilogue 176

Fleet Lists 182

References 185

Bibliography 188

Index 190

Acknowledgements

The authors and publishers would like to express their sincere thanks to Susie Cox and Stephen Rabson of P&O Heritage for all their assistance and advice with the manuscript. Their attention to detail and co-operation with the book has been very much appreciated.

The publishers would like to express their sincere thanks to Phil Neumann and Jon Wheeler of FotoFlite for all their assistance with the research of historical photographs and images. The curator and staff at Barrow Museum should also be thanked in allowing us to use a wealth of their historical pictures.

Thanks must go to Caroline Hallworth and Mick Lindsay for copy editing the manuscript and Sara Jayne Donaldson for indexing the publication. Ferry Publications is indebted to the following for allowing us to use photographs from their personal collections, for background information on P&O and for general assistance and support: John Hendy, David Buri, Jim Davis, Ann Glen, Ann Haynes, Donald E. Meek, Trevor Jones, Andrew Kilk, Chris Laming, Kai Levander, Sarah Lockie, John McNeece, Stephen Macey, Matthew Murtland, Ken Neil, John Peter, Sandy Stirling, David Trevor-Jones, Tage Wandborg, Lawrence Rennie, Ambrose Greenway and Paul Woodbury.

Finally, our thanks goes to Nicola Cowsill for undertaking all the Photoshop work for the book and to Nicola Green, Ferry Publications, for all her assistance.

Above: The British India East Africa liner ***Kenya*** *operated the P&O Group's last scheduled liner voyage in 1969. Here, she is seen dressed overall in the Port of London. (Mick Lindsay collection)*

Run away to sea!

P&O

WORLD WIDE SERVICES

P&O Heritage collection

Introduction

The name P&O is synonymous with the development and success of Britain as the pre-eminent mercantile and military power of the nineteenth and early twentieth centuries. The Peninsular and Oriental Steam Navigation Company grew rapidly to become the world's largest and greatest shipping enterprise whose liners – often among the finest of their day – bound the British Empire together, carrying its administrators, dignitaries and troops, as well as tourists and general cargo.

From the outset, the P&O fleet was steam-powered – a relatively recent technology in the 1830s which transformed the world, unleashing new forces of modernity and leading to what we nowadays call 'globalisation' – the spreading of modern industry and manufacturing value chains around the world. The first sea-going steamship, Henry Bell's *Comet*, first sailed on the River Clyde in 1812. So great was progress with steam power for ships that, not much more than a quarter-century later, steamship services were beginning to spread from Britain to the Mediterranean, across the Atlantic and, a short while thereafter, to the Red Sea, the Indian Ocean and beyond.

With the modern steamship, Western values also were spread worldwide as never before, while cultural traditions and ways of life from elsewhere were brought back to Britain. P&O's liners connecting the Middle East with the Indian Subcontinent, South-East Asia and Australia were, notwithstanding their relatively compact dimensions, intensely culturally diverse environments. Under the command of British officers, crew members and passengers of many nationalities voyaged in confined, yet highly structured environments in which very different lives could be observed in close proximity. No doubt, a voyage by P&O in the latter nineteenth century would have been a fascinating and exotic experience for those Victorians privileged enough to travel 'Out East'.

Modern steam-powered ships must equally have been perceived as otherworldly and 'exotic' by peoples elsewhere in the world when they made their initial 'deep sea' voyages to far-flung ports. Equally, in both their merchant and military forms, steamships projected British (and European) power overseas and this fact must have led foreign observers to view them paradoxically. On the one hand, ships brought new commodities and wealth but, sometimes, they brought less welcome cargoes – such as opium to China – and, occasionally, their presence signalled military oppression. This notwithstanding, in developing steamship routes from India, P&O required all of the great ingenuity we nowadays associate with engineering and

The P&O liner ***Strathnaver*** *is seen arriving at Tilbury. Both she and her 'white' sister ship* ***Strathaird*** *originally appeared with three funnels, the dummies being re*

entrepreneurship in the Victorian era. Simply supplying coal for these vessels was a major logistical challenge, as was the provision of replacement mechanical parts and cuisine appropriate to British tastes.

By the Edwardian era, P&O had re-equipped with larger, comfortably appointed vessels, fitted with more fuel-efficient compound engines. When in 1911 the *Medina* was chartered as a Royal Yacht to carry King George V and Queen Mary to the Delhi Durbar, the British Raj was at its height – but the remainder of the twentieth century was to prove much more turbulent as, through two world wars, the global centre of power and innovation gradually shifted from Europe to America and a great deal of British tonnage was lost as a result of enemy action. With admirable foresight, during the economically unstable years of the 1930s, P&O invested in notably advanced new liners – the famous white 'Straths', which gave the Company's passenger services a new identity as the operator's gleaming white tropical ships, rather than the dull black and ochre used hitherto. The Second World

ng their post-war refits. Latterly involved in the emigrant trade to Australia, the ***thnaver*** *was scrapped in Hong Kong during 1962. (FotoFlite)*

War, alas, devastated the P&O fleet once again – but the Company's liners and their crews took part in heroic actions in fields of conflict around the world.

When peace returned in 1945, once again P&O needed urgently to build anew and it is the liners of this period which will remain within living memory for many of the older readers of this book. Vessels such as the *Chusan*, the *Himalaya*, the *Arcadia* and the *Iberia* were regarded as being among the finest and best run of the post-war British merchant fleet. The subsequent *Canberra* and *Oriana* were even more iconic – and much has already been written about them and, indeed, P&O's wider history.

In this context, being commissioned to write a new history of P&O was, for the authors, a tall order. Where David and Stephen Howarth's authoritative 1987 work concentrates primarily on P&O's corporate history, we have decided here to focus on the Company's ships and shipping operations. We have also attempted to convey something of the experience of sailing on liners and cruise ships in various periods of P&O's lengthy history.

We have carried out extensive archival research to find vivid newspaper accounts of P&O voyages and we have interviewed former P&O directors and passengers who can account for the P&O experience in more recent times. Above all, we are greatly indebted to Stephen Rabson and Susie Cox at P&O Heritage who have been unfailingly kind, diligent and generous with their knowledge and time to assist and enhance our research and writing.

Existing observers of P&O's history tend to view the Company's 'golden age' as spanning a period from the latter-nineteenth century until the early 1960s, reaching an apotheosis with the commissioning of the *Canberra*. Thereafter, many previous accounts tell a tale of gradual decline. In contrast, we strongly argue that, after the revolutionary 1960s and 70s, the 1980s represented a further – though unfortunately all too brief – 'golden age' when, under the shrewd Chairmanship of Lord Sterling, P&O grew once again into Britain's premier shipping company. Sterling invested boldly and imaginatively in new ferries, cruise ships, container ships and bulk carriers, as well as in the construction, real estate, catering and maritime service industries on *terra firma*. Sadly, at the behest of certain institutional shareholders and other interests in the City of London during the ensuing decades, Sterling was forced to dismantle this empire until only a handful of supposedly 'core' activities remained. Lacking the size and strength to survive on its own following Sterling's retirement, P&O was sold to DP World in Dubai.

One may speculate – as many have – that P&O's fate could have been very different had a longer-term view been taken by its major shareholders and that the Company's recent history merely reflects the decline of Britain's wider industrial sector in recent years, being chopped up and sold overseas to make quick profits for a privileged few. As this book shows, however, the story of modern shipping is one of constant flux and change and so the recent story of P&O is actually reflective of this wider historical narrative.

The authors and the publisher hope that you will enjoy this 175th anniversary history of P&O's ships and of their shipping interests.

Bruce Peter
Glasgow, December 2011

Chapter 1

Iberia, the Mediterranean and early passages to India

The Peninsular and Oriental Steam Navigation Company, better known simply as P&O, was formed in 1837 at the dawning of an age of great human accomplishment, social development and commercial prosperity. In the early nineteenth century the age of steam meant that the whims of the winds were replaced by the preciseness of a direct line cut through the sea. Distances shrank rapidly and Britain – the first industrial nation – became the era's global superpower. In 1844, the German cultural commentator Friedrich Engels, wrote vividly of his experience of arriving by ship into the Port of London, which appeared to him to represent one of the greatest spectacles of modernity:

'This colossal centralisation, this heaping together of two and a half millions of human beings at one point, has multiplied the power of this two and a half millions a hundredfold; has raised London to the commercial capital of the world, created the giant docks and assembled the thousand vessels that continually cover the Thames. I know nothing more imposing than the view which the Thames offers during the ascent from the sea to London Bridge. The masses of buildings, the wharves on both sides, especially from Woolwich upwards, the countless ships along both shores, crowding ever closer and closer together, until, at last, only a narrow passage remains in the middle of the river, a passage through which hundreds of steamers shoot by one another; all this is so vast, so impressive, that a man cannot collect himself, but is lost in the marvel of England's greatness before he sets foot upon English soil. But the sacrifices which all this has cost become apparent later.'[1]

Engels' commentary reveals many things about shipping and modernity. Firstly, ships and the Port of London represented to him a sublime and enthralling aesthetic experience, initially pleasuring his gaze. He subsequently modified his recollection, however, when his initial enthusiasm for the visually captivating qualities of the port had been tempered by his knowledge of its social consequences on *terra firma*. Secondly, ships appeared to him to represent one of the iconic visible faces of a powerful and dynamic political and economic system, on the one hand linked to imperial expansion and on the other related to the emergent class system. Thirdly, the development of ship design was progressive; at the time he was writing, sail power was still the standard form of propulsion for deep-sea vessels on longer routes such as those to India and the Far East. Steam had first been tried in small river and lake craft, both in Britain and elsewhere, and 'was already being adopted with great success, to the east by P&O in the Mediterranean and westwards across the Atlantic with the Cunard Line.

An oil painting by T.F. Dicksee showing P&O's co-founder and Chairman Arthur Anderson in 1850. (Ferry Publications Library)

Brodie McGhie Willcox, also painted by T.F. Dicksee in 1850. (Ferry Publications Library)

Captain Richard Bourne, owner of the William Fawcett, who collaborated with Anderson and Willcox in creating P&O. (Ferry Publications Library)

British industrialisation in the eighteenth and nineteenth centuries was characterised by a *laissez-faire* approach whereby entrepreneurs usually did only what was necessary to make money. Thus, the British 'deep sea' merchant fleet was slow to convert from sail to steam in the second half of the nineteenth century, let alone from steam to diesel in the first half of the twentieth. Indeed, notwithstanding the country's lead in developing and refining the steam engine – the world's first sea-going steam-powered ship, Henry Bell's *Comet*, had her maiden voyage on the River Clyde in 1812 – by the 1860s Britain still had 3.66 million tons of sailing ships and only 185,000 tons of steamships. In the 1840s, the use of steam beyond Great Britain's own territorial waters was still severely limited by the availability of sufficient quantities and quality of coal further afield on routes other than the North Atlantic. Early steamship services to Gibraltar and the Mediterranean became possible thanks to British control of Gibraltar and Malta, which became coaling stations.

As P&O's routes began to spread eastwards around the globe, in 1840 a second important British liner company, George Burns' and Samuel Cunard's British and North American Royal Mail Steam Packet Company, known subsequently as the Cunard Line, began to open up the North Atlantic trade to Canada and the United States. The creation of the joint Burns and Cunard venture was indicative of a growing inter-reliance between steamships and the British imperial project, which was soon to embrace the Middle and Far East. The imperial project harnessed the shipbuilding expertise of the Clyde, Thames, Tyne and Mersey and the keen competitive and organisational enterprise of merchant venturers and shipowners who were readily enticed to the Orient.

Both in mercantile and military applications, steam power enabled Britain to project power abroad and so, when they appeared in foreign ports, P&O's vessels were potent symbols of modernity, the shrinkage of distance and an increasingly obvious British hegemony overseas. From the time of its establishment in 1837, P&O was at the vanguard of the development of Royal Mail-carrying steamship services. Such Government contracts provided a reliable source of steady income that enabled steamship companies then to build up their fleets' services and loyal passenger clienteles through the formative periods of their development and well on into the twentieth century. P&O and its younger North Atlantic compatriot are without doubt among the greatest names in seaborne transport, and both continue trading today in the third century of their illustrious existences.

THE PENINSULA

Although 1837 is traditionally accepted as being the birth year of P&O, its roots can actually be traced back to a modest *naissance* of sorts as early as 1815. It was then that Arthur Anderson (1792-1868), an amiable and resourceful Shetlander later acknowledged as being one of the founders of P&O, was engaged by Brodie McGhie Willcox (1786-1862) as a clerk in his ship brokerage business at 46 Lime Street in the City of London, at that time the commercial heart of British merchant shipping activity. Neither Willcox nor Anderson were men of means with the resources to buy ships of their own when they started out and so instead they chartered tonnage as needed and paid these ships' owners out of revenues from each voyage on an ongoing basis.

While little is known of Willcox's background, he appears to have been something of an entrepreneur and a self-made man who took the opportunity to establish himself in business as a shipbroker to expedite the transport of cargo and passengers. After escaping being press-ganged into the Royal Navy in his youth, Anderson later joined of his own accord, serving for ten years before being honourably discharged from his ship following Napoleon Bonaparte's exile to Elba. Like many of his shipmates at the time, he was left virtually destitute and ended up allegedly walking from Portsmouth to London where he eventually found employment with Willcox.

In 1823 Anderson was made a partner in what then became the firm of Willcox and Anderson, providing a cargo service with available passenger accommodation under sail from London to the Portuguese and Spanish ports of Vigo, Oporto, Lisbon and Cadiz on the Iberian Peninsula, with some voyages also continuing on to Gibraltar and later South America. Within little more than a decade, Willcox and Anderson had progressed from ten small sailing vessels, with their dependency on prevailing winds to the scheduling reliability of steam propulsion. They had chartered steamships on occasion since 1830 from the General Steam Navigation Company and other owners. The wooden paddle steamer *William Fawcett* was chartered in 1835 from the Dublin and London Steam Packet Company owned by Captain Richard Bourne and his Irish associates, who were already running a successful scheduled steam packet service between Dublin and London, and employed by Anderson and Willcox to run a regular service to the Iberian Peninsula.

The *William Fawcett*, named for her engine builder and part owner, was a modest ship of 208 tons completed in 1828 by the Liverpool shipwrights Caleb and James Smith and powered by a 140 hp engine made by Fawcett and Preston. The ship was originally owned by Joseph Robinson Pim and William Fawcett, who sold her to Bourne and his colleagues in 1831 for service between Dublin and London until 1835 when she was first chartered by Willcox and Anderson for their Peninsular trade.

The success of the *William Fawcett* and a second steamer, also chartered from the Dublin & London Company, led to the revival in 1835 of the name Peninsular Steam Navigation Company which Willcox and other London and Iberian businessmen had first coined in 1834. The working arrangement for the new Peninsular company was that Bourne and his associates would build three new ships and Willcox & Anderson one (though they also supplied a small steamer for use on the Spanish coast and a coal hulk at Gibraltar). Existing Dublin & London ships were chartered in as necessary. As the first of this latter group to be employed by Peninsular Steam, the *William Fawcett* has been traditionally accorded the status of the 'first P&O ship'.

More than a century later in 1961, P&O's ultra-modern flagship, the *Canberra*, had her Tourist Class main lounge named the William Fawcett Room in honour of P&O's pioneering ship, with the room also being adorned by a detailed model of the *William Fawcett* in a glass case. There is now also a William Fawcett suite on the current-day P&O Cruises ship *Aurora*, introduced in 2000 (see below).

One of the underlying reasons for Richard Bourne's interest in Willcox and Anderson's Iberian Peninsular operation was to secure a government contract to carry the Royal Mail on this route. The Post Office had up to this point been dispatching overseas mails aboard merchant ships loosely under its control, which on the North Atlantic, for instance, were also permitted to engage in other trade to their own account. Service was erratic and unreliable and crews were suspected of seeking to be captured by privateers leaving them free to profit from bogus insurance claims for the losses of non-existent revenue cargoes. There were rampant complaints that the mails from the UK sent aboard Post Office packet ships were often taking as long as three weeks to reach Spain and Portugal, while Willcox and Anderson were regularly covering the route between Falmouth and Cadiz in less than a week. With similar concerns regarding other overseas postal routes there was a widespread public demand for the Admiralty to be given ultimate responsibility for overseas transport of the Royal Mail.

As an honorary Naval captain himself, and coming from a family that held a government commission to carry overland mails by coach in Ireland, Richard Bourne believed that he was in a sound position to offer reliable sea passage to the Iberian Peninsula for the Royal Mail through his business arrangement with Willcox and Anderson. The Admiralty was at first unreceptive to the proposal made in October 1836, eventually relenting, though insisting that they would need to call for tenders from others. A rival bid from the Commercial Steam Navigation Company failed to satisfy the Admiralty that it actually had the ships and infrastructure needed to provide the service, and ultimately Bourne's proposal was accepted and signed on 22nd August 1837. This is generally acknowledged to be the date of P&O's birth, though the Company's full name was yet to be coined.

With the Royal Mail contract came the assurance of a constant trade with the whole business of carrying passengers and cargoes by sea being less risky and susceptible to seasonal fluctuations in demand. The advent of steam propulsion led to ships costing considerably more to build and to operate. Their machinery's cost was in addition to the expense of still having to outfit the vessel with a complete sailing rig. This was still needed as a back-up resource for times when the boilers and machinery might need to be serviced while underway, or in case of their outright failure when the ship would have to proceed under canvas. There was also the issue that early steamers were too small to carry the large amounts of coal that their primitive fuel-hungry boilers needed for longer sea passages. Later, as larger iron- and steel-hulled vessels were built and engined with more fuel-efficient machinery and screw propellers, an entire crossing could be made under power and the sailing rig became an auxiliary in case of mechanical failure or depleted coal bunkers. In either case, complete sailing and engineering crews both had to be carried, significantly increasing crewing costs. On top of all that, where Mother Nature provided the winds *gratis* for sailing, the greater reliability and speed of steam propulsion came at the cost of large quantities of coal that had to be paid for and which also reduced the amount of on-board cubic and deadweight capacity otherwise available as revenue-earning cargo space.

The steamship business was clearly getting to be beyond the means of the independent owners who had built up much of the sailing packet trades of the early nineteenth century. At the time of P&O's birth, steam was still a newfangled technology of unknown potential in which many speculators would have been hesitant to invest large sums of money. There were no State master plans, Government grants or subsidies for things such as transport and infrastructure development as there are today. The Government postal contract was to all intents and purposes the steamship owner's best, and only, option. Where Willcox, Anderson and Bourne already had their ships and services in place, Samuel Cunard secured his Royal Mail contract for North Atlantic service as the basis for building the ships to start up his Cunard Line.

The Peninsular Steam Navigation Company's Iberian mail service was inaugurated on 1st September 1837 with the *Don Juan*. She and her similar sister ship *Tagus* were designed and built for the Peninsular service, and at the time were claimed to be the world's largest and fastest steamships. Both provided a relatively high quality of passenger accommodation and ample cargo capacity by the standards of their day. The slightly larger *Tagus* had cabin berths for 86 passengers, a cargo capacity of 300 tons and could make a speed of 9.5 knots. The scheduled steamship service they provided operated with departures from London on Fridays and from Falmouth the following Monday. Steaming times from Falmouth to Vigo were two days and six hours and an additional 30 hours onwards to Lisbon, where a 24-hour stop was scheduled. Gibraltar could be reached in seven days with a brief additional stop at Cadiz.[2]

The inaugural outbound passage to Gibraltar, with stops made at Vigo, Oporto, Lisbon and Cadiz, was entirely successful and otherwise uneventful. Most unfortunately, shortly after making a mid-afternoon departure on the homeward voyage from Gibraltar on 15th September, the *Don Juan* ran aground and held fast in fog near the lighthouse at the southern Spanish town of Tarifa. Anderson, who was aboard for the voyage, chartered a local fishing boat that had chanced upon the incident to get himself, his wife, Mary Ann, two gentlemen passengers, Lieutenant Roupel, the Royal Naval courier responsible for the mail and the mail itself to Gibraltar from where the HMS *Medea* was sent to the stricken ship's aid. At Tarifa, HMS *Medea*'s master, Captain Austin, had a fractious argument with the local governor regarding who now had control of the stricken *Don Juan*. At one point, Captain Austin reputedly threatened to call in a large Royal Naval fleet from Gibraltar to batter down the town's walls. The threat apparently persuaded the governor to co-operate, and so the *Don Juan*'s remaining crew were rescued by HMS *Medea*, along with a consignment of $21,000 in cash. This was only one of many

*The wooden paddle steamer **Tagus** was built in 1837 at a cost of £28,000. (Ferry Publications Library)*

occasions when British gunboat diplomacy was to prove effective in bullying others into submission. The *Don Juan* was declared to be a total constructive loss, abandoned and eventually broken up where she lay. Thanks largely to Arthur Anderson's exemplary handling of the emergency and to the Royal Navy's personnel at Gibraltar, there was no loss of life and the ship's valuable cargo was saved with only minimal compromise to the fledgling Peninsular Steam Navigation Company's reputation.

The *Don Juan*'s master, Captain John Engledue, was technically culpable for the accident, though never blamed for it. As a seafaring man himself, Anderson understood the perils of navigating in fog and the reality that error in judgement can occur. Engledue was exonerated by his employers and continued his career with the Line, later becoming P&O's fleet superintendent and ultimately a member of the Board of Directors. Public opinion regarded the *Don Juan*'s loss with 'sympathy and consolation' while the Admiralty recognised the efforts of Anderson, Engledue and the ship's crew in expeditiously carrying out their duty of securing and dispatching the Royal Mail.

ONWARDS TO THE MEDITERRANEAN

Gibraltar was the Mediterranean terminus of the Peninsular Steam Navigation Company's original postal route. From there, mails, passengers and cargoes bound for other destinations around the Mediterranean, as well as for India and other British possessions in the Far East, could be carried either directly by sea all the way around Africa or by way of the ancient Red Sea route with an overland portage having to be made from Alexandria to Suez. The Honourable East India Company served the sea route around Africa to Calcutta over which it operated a fleet of magnificent sailing ships. The time taken to make this voyage was so great that only one round trip per year was possible, with this being arranged for the outbound and inbound passages of the Indian Ocean to take advantage of the steady seasonal monsoon south-westerly winds from May to September and the north-easterlies from October to April[3]

The great sailing ships that first undertook these long commercial voyages between Europe and India, and beyond to South East Asia, China and sometimes to Australia, were known as the East Indiamen, with the largest, fastest and most prestigious of these being operated by or under charter to the English and Dutch East India Companies. The first British ship was the *Red Dragon* of 1601 and the last was the *Repulse*, whose ten-year career ended in 1830. Many of these vessels came from the Blackwall shipyard on the River Thames adjoining London's East India Docks, with others being built in India. These latter vessels had hulls and masts of remarkably robust Burmese teak construction.

The original Indiamen were succeeded by the Blackwall frigates, built between 1837 and 1875. Characteristically, these were given a single stern gallery, as opposed to the double galleries of the East Indiamen and had a more refined underwater hull form to achieve greater speeds on a par with the China clipper ships against which they competed for the East India Company's share of the lucrative Chinese opium trade. The Blackwall clippers had a deftly rounded above-water hull form for which they were said to be 'apple cheeked'. Both these and the earlier East Indiamen were remarkably safe and comfortable ships with a notably high standard of passenger accommodation, ideal for the very long trading routes over which these served. While their officers and some crew were British, their deck crews often also included Muslim men, recruited from ports on the Horn of Africa, such as Aden in Yemen, or from the Indian Subcontinent. They were highly valued for their absolute sobriety, reliability and willingness to work hard for a basic salary and so, even in the era of sail, there began a British shipboard tradition of recruiting staff from destinations served in the Middle East and India. This tradition continues even today on P&O Cruises' ships, whose hotel staffs are Goanese and whose deck and engine crews typically come from rural India and Pakistan being known as Lascars. Back in early nineteenth century Britain, the crews of the East Indiamen established the country's first Muslim communities in the great port cities.

To speed up the existing service for diplomatic and other priority post going to Alexandria, an overland route through France by coach to Marseilles and from there by sea to the Eastern Mediterranean was inaugurated. With its Peninsular postal service already successfully established, Willcox, Anderson and Bourne were asked in 1839 to advise the Admiralty on how its existing mail service to Alexandria might be replaced by a commercial operation that would connect with the East India Company's steamers already plying between Suez and Bombay (now Mumbai). When tenders were invited for the service, it was hardly surprising the contract was awarded to the Peninsular Steam Navigation Company for the services using newer, larger and faster steamers sailing directly from British ports to Alexandria, with calls en route only in the possessions of Gibraltar and Malta they had already recommended. The new service was to begin in September 1840 at a cost of £34,200 per annum for five years as an initial step towards establishing an onwards steamship route to India via Suez and the Red Sea.

For so great and rapid an expansion, the company needed to be re-constituted as a limited liability company, enabling it to raise capital through the participation of outside shareholders. With the words 'and Oriental' added to its name, the Line was incorporated under Royal Charter in December 1840[4] in the City of London, becoming The Peninsular and Oriental Steam Navigation Company, though far more widely known as P&O. Prior to the Companies Acts of 1862, a company's liability could only be circumscribed by Royal Charter or by a special Act of Parliament, as used for example by the General Steam Navigation Company. Despite its title, a Royal Charter did not mean that either HM Government or the Crown had any involvement in the finances of any such company, but only that it had satisfied the authorities that its people were deemed acceptable to be permitted to raise a certain amount of capital to conduct their business. This authorised P&O to raise a starting capital of one million pounds. Richard Bourne, Arthur Anderson and Brodie McGhie Willcox were all appointed to the newly incorporated company's board of directors. All of this happened so quickly that, by the time P&O actually received its charter, the Company had already commenced the Alexandria service, with formal acquisition arrangements for its newly acquired ships only being completed subsequently.

In the short time span available before the new Alexandria service was to be started, P&O opted to purchase existing tonnage of suitable size and speed rather than building to their own specifications. Two suitable ships were acquired through the City of Dublin Company from the Transatlantic Steamship Company, in exchange for £80,000 in P&O shares. One was the *Liverpool*, then already in North Atlantic service, and the uncompleted second vessel was the *United States*, purchased 'on the stocks' for £60,000. The business arrangement also included Transatlantic Steamship Company executive officer Francis Carleton being appointed to a position on the P&O Board of Directors and as one of the new Company's three Managing Directors, together with Willcox and Anderson. With the arrangement for tonnage secured, the mail contract was finally signed with Bourne in August 1840 only weeks before the service commenced.

As there was already a *Liverpool* in the P&O fleet, the first of their two new acquisitions was renamed the *Great Liverpool*. This vessel had cabin accommodation for 98 passengers but unfortunately, had proved far from successful in Atlantic service due to her poor sea-keeping characteristics and reputation for being slow and mechanically temperamental. She was re-boilered and substantially refitted for P&O's Alexandria service. The second purchase, the *United States* had been planned as the *Liverpool*'s transatlantic fleet mate and was of similar overall dimensions, though seemingly without her near sister's shortcomings. For P&O, she was completed as the *Oriental* and was in fact the first of the two ships actually to enter their service, sailing from Southampton on 1st September 1840. No doubt as a gesture of confidence and even forgiveness on P&O's part, the *Oriental* sailed under the command of Captain John Engledue, three years to the day after the *Don Juan* had left London on her ill-fated first round-trip Royal Mail sailing to Gibraltar.

The *Great Liverpool* made her maiden P&O departure for Alexandria a month later, following difficulties with the ship's conversion and the Admiralty's surveys for acceptance to fulfil the Royal Mail contract. At the time of their debut, these were the largest, fastest and most comfortably appointed steamships sailing to Egypt. The Alexandria service was also significant and prestigious in its own right, as the city was a crossover point between the Occidental domains of Great Britain, Europe and the Mediterranean and the Oriental world of India, Singapore and China. These two domains were then detached one from the other by a 241-kilometre (150-mile) overland crossing of arid desert terrain that lay between Alexandria on the Mediterranean and the port of Suez at the northern tip of the Red Sea, where the Isthmus of Suez joined the African and Asian continents.

This was a formidable barrier between the deep-sea trading routes of the East and West over which all passengers, cargo and mails had to be portaged prior to the completion of a rail route in 1859 and the Suez Canal's opening a decade later. It also provided the logical next step in P&O's development as the Alexandria mail contract specified that the Line's services were to be extended to India within two years.

*A lithograph by J.I. Herdman depicting the Mediterranean service liner **Great Liverpool**, ex **Liverpool**, as she appeared in 1840. (Ferry Publications Library)*

EARLY CRUISING

The Royal Mail service between Southampton and Alexandria was the most prestigious P&O route in early days. Meanwhile, the original Iberian Peninsular sailings to Portugal and Spain continued to be maintained and feeder services were established to and from various places around the Mediterranean, including Athens, Beirut, Constantinople (now Istanbul), Jaffa (now Tel Aviv) and Valetta. Apart from augmenting P&O's Admiralty postal operations, these also carried passengers and general cargo from place to place around the Mediterranean as well as to and from Britain. From Gibraltar, P&O ships sailed to Valetta and Athens, with that route later extended to Constantinople on a speculative basis. By combining these routes, passengers could make a contiguous journey from Southampton or Falmouth all around the Mediterranean and back again in a sequence of four connected P&O sailings.

While Arthur Anderson, in particular, was keenly focused on P&O's development of core Royal Mail routes to India and beyond, he also saw the opportunity to broaden and diversify the Company's passenger services. Prior to establishing P&O, back in Shetland, Anderson had founded his own newspaper, the *Shetland Journal*, which was first published in 1835. It would appear that, even then, he had ideas about cruising. At the beginning he wrote much of the paper's copy himself and even resorted to running fake advertising to fill blank spaces on its pages. One of these was for a two-week cruise from the Shetlands to the Faroe Islands and Iceland. While the advertisement served to fill the paper, Anderson could also rest assured that there were unlikely to be any takers for such excursions in these cold and often stormy waters. Yet the idea of cruising was already in his mind, and some ten years later, thanks to P&O, he would see it ultimately materialise in the far more hospitable climate of the Mediterranean.

By 1844 P&O's network of mail and cargo operations round the Mediterranean, along with various ancillary experimental and promotional feeder services, most of which offered passenger accommodation, provided opportunities for travellers to arrange round-trip leisure travel with the chance to visit various places of interest along the way by booking aboard a series of connected sailings. The Company's Peninsular postal services could be used to ferry passengers directly between Southampton or Falmouth and the principal Mediterranean transfer points at either Gibraltar or Alexandria. Deep-sea steamship travel was then still a privilege of the wealthy, and for those taking pleasure voyages for their own enjoyment and enrichment, having the leisure time to travel for two or more months was an additional luxury. P&O's largest ships of the day, the *Great Liverpool* and the *Oriental*, each offered only about 100 passenger berths that were typically otherwise lightly booked, with those taking voyages for pleasure usually travelling individually or in very small groups of no more than a half-dozen or so people with like-minded interests and aspirations.

Early pleasure travel was, for the most part, still rooted in the tradition of the classic Grand Tour. This was a pleasurable journey through Southern Europe to view the cultural treasures of classical and Renaissance art and architecture. Since the early seventeenth century, young aristocratic men had made the Grand Tour for the purpose of enlightenment, discovery and personal enrichment. It was considered to be a prerequisite also for seriously aspiring artists and a sound preparation in the language skills, fashion sense and social etiquettes needed for a career in government or in the diplomatic service. The Tour was made on a more or less prescribed standard itinerary, usually escorted by one's own servants and a *Cicerone*, serving as an informed local guide and tutor. With the mid-nineteenth-century advent of the railways and ocean-going steam navigation, the Grand Tour gradually became less elitist and more widely available to a greater cross section of the upper and professional classes, while at the same time a wider variety of destinations could be visited within shorter time frames.

The British traveller of the mid-nineteenth century would usually have begun his journey by crossing the Dover Strait to Ostend or Calais and making his way by carriage to Paris. After taking some time to absorb the French capital's language, art, fashion and social culture, he might then go on to Switzerland, or alternatively travel to Madrid and Barcelona. Either crossing the Alps by way of the St Bernard Pass or sailing from Barcelona, Italy would be reached, with extensive visits to Naples and nearby Pompeii and Rome, then onwards to Padua, Bologna and Venice. Crossing the Alps once more, the Tour's homeward leg would be made through German-speaking central and northern Europe, staying at Vienna, Dresden and Berlin en route with some university study time taken at Munich or Heidelberg, and perhaps final visits to the Netherlands and Belgium before heading back across the Channel to London. Variations of the itinerary also included Greece, Egypt, The Holy Land and Turkey.

P&O's Mediterranean services and sailing schedules already offered an opportunity for a self-contained alternative Grand Tour

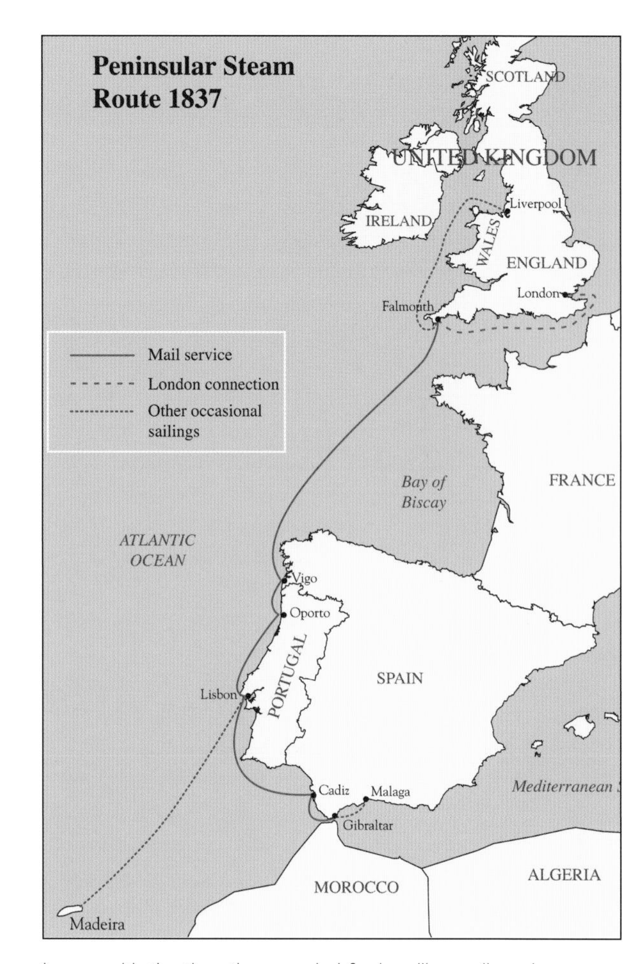

by sea, with the time then needed for handling mails and cargo, provisioning and coaling of their ships allowing passengers a stay of a night or sometimes longer at most major port calls. With its key ports in the eastern Mediterranean being served by two ships operating on alternative itineraries to and from Alexandria, longer inland travels could be arranged to Jerusalem and to Cairo from where Nile excursions were made to the Pyramids of Giza. In 1844, P&O gave the popular London satirist, novelist and author William Makepeace Thackeray (1811-63) tickets for a connected series of voyages around the Mediterranean in return for which he wrote a short book telling of his experience as an enticement for others to also make the tour.

By the time he had made his voyage with P&O, Thackeray was already well known to readers of *Fraser's Magazine*, for which he wrote art critiques and various short fictional pieces, and was making his mark with the then newly created 'Punch' magazine with his socially satirical Snob Papers, later assembled as *The Book of Snobs*. He also wrote two moderately successful travel-themed works, *The Paris Sketch Book* and *The Irish Sketch Book*, though he remains best known for his satirical portrayal of British High Society, *Vanity Fair*, published shortly after his P&O voyage chronicle *Notes of a Journey From Cornhill to Grand Cairo*, which appeared in 1846.

Travel writing, as we know it today, sprang from a genre of popular literature originating in the late seventeenth century with works such as *Oroonoko*, penned by the pioneering English lady author Aphra Behn in 1690. Then, before the advent of modern fiction writing, works of this sort were written to be taken as being true stories. As in the instance of Thackeray's P&O voyage, these were based on actual accounts of the author's own, or perhaps other people's travels and adventures without necessarily being biographical or autobiographical *per se*. This left a certain amount of latitude for fantasy in creating the circumstances and settings of the story, often with mystical depictions of distant and foreign shorelines, lush vegetation and fabulous pleasure domes in the sky that added to the charm of these stories.

Thackeray was obviously thrilled to have an opportunity to make such a trip as he relates in the opening passages of his narrative:

> 'The Peninsular and Oriental Company had arranged an excursion in the Mediterranean, by which, in the space of a couple of months, as many men and cities were to be seen as Ulysses surveyed and noted in ten years. Malta, Athens, Smyrna, Constantinople, Jerusalem, Cairo were to be visited, and everybody was to be back in London by Lord Mayor's Day.'[5]

Writing under the *nom de plume* M.A. Titmarsh, Thackeray apparently gives an accurate account of his adventures, though the genre of his work afforded him the latitude to be fairly creative in his depiction of fellow passengers, ship's company and other personalities he would have encountered along the way. And so, as Thackeray's story relates, Mr Titmarsh sailed from Southampton on 22nd August 1844 aboard the P&O steamer *Lady Mary Wood*, bound for Vigo, Lisbon and Gibraltar. There he transferred to the *Tagus* to continue his journey eastwards across the Mediterranean, calling at Valetta, Athens, Smyrna (now Izmir), Constantinople, Rhodes, the ancient ruins of Telmessus, Beirut and Jaffa, where he left the ship and made his first of two overland excursions, this one to Jerusalem and the Holy Land. Mr Titmarsh then sailed aboard the *Iberia* from Jaffa to Alexandria, where he made his second overland tour to Cairo, the Nile and the Pyramids at Giza. He then sailed back to Southampton aboard the *Oriental*, and was home again in London by Lord Mayor's Day on 9th November.

While much of his overall published oeuvre satirises the institutions of high society, the aristocracy and other social snobs, his own rather superscalar British Victorian outlook on the people and things he saw in the Mediterranean tended to cast his Mr Titmarsh as something of a snob himself. He made references to various non-British and hence foreign 'locals' encountered along the way as being malodorous and ill-mannered folk eating 'horrible messes cooked in filthy pots' with their bare and dirty hands and sleeping in unclean old bedding. He conveyed a sense of being disappointed and even blasé about some of what he saw and experienced. Yet he described other things with enthusiasm and even with affection. He described in considerable detail how a small caravan was assembled to take his tour party on the overland trip from Jaffa to Jerusalem in some detail and how the ladies in the group were carried on a litter slung between two black mules fore and aft, with 'mahogany coloured' native male grooms walking at either side to balance the litter as it swayed

The 349-ton ***Canton*** *of 1848 was built for P&O's Hong Kong and Canton River service. (Ferry Publications Library)*

from side to side and to offer their backs for the ladies to ascend and descend from their conveyance.

At several points in the story Thackeray expresses his wish to have been able to pen verse or sonnets to do justice to what was being seen and experienced. He was greatly moved by the ancient Greek city of Telmessus's ruins in what is now the Turkish city of Fethiye, writing of it:

> 'After you have once seen it, the remembrance remains with you, like a tune from Mozart, which he seems to have caught out of heaven, and which rings sweet harmony in your ears for ever after! It's a benefit for all after life! You have but to shut your eyes, and think, and recall it, and the delightful vision comes smiling back, to your order!–the divine air–the delicious little pageant, which nature set before you on this lucky day.'[6]

As a routine sanitary precaution, the *Oriental* was thoroughly cleansed and fumigated at Alexandria for its journey back to Southampton. The voyage home would also include 17 days in quarantine at Fort Manuel in Malta, which as Thackeray explained, 'was almost agreeable after the incessant sight-seeing of the past two months.' It would have been a time to collect one's thoughts and reminiscences, commit these to the diary or perhaps to sketch one's impressions on paper while still fresh in the mind.

Thackeray's published story of Mr Titmarsh's adventures in the Mediterranean during the autumn of 1844 was with its flights of fantasy, humour and satirical touches in the style that would have been expected of him at the time, and there would no doubt have been plenty among his readership quite eager to go out and also experience such things for themselves. The essence of the Grand Tour was far easier and more attainable with P&O, its ships, offices and agents, both at home and around the Mediterranean where obliging Company and port agents could help with transfers, local accommodation and travel arrangements for passengers. The Company's cruise passenger-carrying feeder service continued until 1854 when Britain and France declared war against Russia, and ships were urgently needed to carry troops and armaments to the Crimea. It was later resumed in the 1880s at which point, fortuitously for P&O, the *British Medical Journal* recommended sea travel as being therapeutic. P&O's first dedicated cruise ship appeared when the *Rome* was converted for this purpose in 1904, becoming the *Vectis*.

Apart from times of war and the immediate aftermaths of World Wars I and II in the early 1920s and the late 1940s, P&O has continued to offer leisure cruises ever since. A wide variety of Mediterranean cruises from Southampton, calling at many of the same ports that Thackeray had visited in 1844, are now made within the time span of as little as three weeks. Shore excursions to the Holy Land and the Pyramids are offered within a day's port call, thanks to the use of convoys of air-conditioned touring coaches.

EASTWARDS TO CALCUTTA

The early pleasure voyages taken by Thackeray and others keen to make the Grand Tour by sea were a means of selling otherwise unoccupied passenger berths at a time when the demand for sea passages was still relatively low. The *Tagus*'s call at Telmessus for sightseeing and exploration was the only concession to the ship's regular commercial itinerary made for the benefit of Thackeray and other excursion passengers, who otherwise amused themselves. With but few exceptions, P&O's principal focus otherwise was its deep-sea line services and the ships built for them right up to the time of the *Canberra*'s delivery in 1961. Thereafter, line service for passengers continued only until 1973, after which passenger operations under the P&O flag were focused solely on cruising and ferries.

As P&O started its mail services to Alexandria in 1840, its rival in the Eastern trade, the Honourable East India Company, seemed content to maintain its links with the British homeland under sail on the long deep-sea route around Africa via the Cape of Good Hope, if perhaps for no other reason than that the long and slow passage supported a degree of isolation and independence of its affairs from the Imperial homeland. From the passengers' standpoint there were no doubt some who still preferred the serenity of the contiguous deep-sea voyage under canvas over passage aboard noisy, hot and occasionally smelly steamships and the discomforts of the overland trek through Egypt by Nile steamer and by horse-drawn omnibus across the desert between Alexandria and Suez.

At that time, the East India Company had extensive governing and administrative powers over India as a whole, though it had forfeited its monopoly on shipping services to India in 1813 and to China in 1833, though it continued to carry mails in its own ships until the 1850s. The Company was in fact already operating its own steamship services between Suez and Bombay and was unwilling to share the route with P&O, agreeing instead to allow the Line to operate a service from Suez and Aden to Ceylon, Madras and Calcutta.

With direct passage to Alexandria inaugurated in 1840, P&O was contractually committed to developing an onwards mail service from Suez to Calcutta within two years. To meet this obligation, the Line would need two very large and powerful ships capable of sailing at full speed head-on into the strong seasonal monsoon winds on the Indian Ocean and with a high standard of passenger accommodation at least comparable to that of the East India Company's existing fleet of sailing ships already plying the Cape of Good Hope route to and from Calcutta. The other great concern was that P&O would have first to ferry the new steamers all the way around Africa to Calcutta where they would initially take up their services east of Suez. This would entail sending sufficient quantities of coal ahead of time by sailing ship to various points along the way to refuel the new steamships en route in a part of the world where P&O otherwise had no regular business of its own and thus few established resources. As the two new ships were being built, the coal for their delivery voyages to Calcutta was already being brought to the various ports where they would be bunkered and where potable fresh water and provisions would also be taken on board.

While the ships were being planned and built, P&O also endeavoured to improve and secure the overland passage of the mail and its passengers between Alexandria and Suez. The outbound passage involved first a transit of the Mahmoudieh Canal in horse-towed barges from Alexandria to Atfeh, where passengers and cargo continued under sail by boat along the Nile River to Cairo from where they travelled overland through the desert to Suez at the northern tip of the Red Sea, with the same process being done in reverse northbound. An alternative route involved a longer passage up the River Nile to Luxor and a marginally shorter desert crossing to the port of Cosseir (now Quseir), about 400 kilometres (250 miles) south from Suez on the Red Sea's western bank. Both routes had been used since ancient times, with the choice of one over the other being determined by the direction of the seasonal monsoon winds and the strength of the River Nile's current. As P&O was to use steam both on the Nile and the Red Sea, without being at the mercy of winds or river currents, the Line opted unilaterally in favour of the shorter overall distance between Alexandria and Suez.

Anderson started by engaging the services of Thomas Fletcher Waghorn (1800-1849) a resourceful and indefatigable courier intimately familiar with the Egyptian overland trek between the Mediterranean and Red Sea. Waghorn was an avid proponent of getting the mail across Egyptian territory in the fastest and most expeditious way possible and, in that endeavour, he had the support of Mehemet Ali (c. 1769-1849), the Pasha of Egypt. Through Captain John Engledue, who was then P&O's fleet superintendent, discussions were arranged with Waghorn and the Pasha, who agreed initially that the charge for goods transported across Egyptian soil by P&O would only be 0.5 per cent of their declared value.

New barges were acquired for P&O's Mahmoudieh Canal traffic and a prefabricated steam tug named *Atfeh* was shipped out from Britain to Alexandria at the end of 1842 aboard the *Orient* and assembled in Egypt to tow the canal barges back and forth. A lock was built at Atfeh to transfer the mail, passenger baggage and general cargo between the differing water levels of the Canal and the Nile with this no longer having to be done overland by camel. Two river steamers, the second-hand *Lotus* and the new *Cairo*, were acquired for the overnight Nile passage between Atfeh and Cairo. These were of lightweight iron construction with berths below decks for 50 men and 16 lady passengers and sleeping space for others under enclosed canvas awnings on deck.

For the desert crossing between Cairo and Suez, the Pasha did what he could to improve the desert tracks used for the crossings while P&O improved the horse-drawn omnibuses and the standards of food, drink and service at the string of rest houses along the way with a combined result of reducing the travel time to a day-and-a-half, including 12 hours of rest stops. As no rest stops were required for the mail, it was possible for this to be carried between Alexandria and Suez in as little as 64 hours using relays of donkeys and camels. Contractually, the mail was to be given top priority over everything and everyone else, with Admiralty-appointed couriers, often retired naval officers, having the authority to order a ship to sail as soon as the mail was stowed aboard, with no regard for the Line's passengers who might in these circumstances end up being stranded at either Alexandria or, worse still, Suez until the next sailing, which could be as much as a month later. Ultimately, through discussions in Establishment circles back in London, understandings came to be reached between the Admiralty couriers and ships' officers.

It was important for all concerned – P&O, the Admiralty and the state of Egypt – that the overland arrangements between Alexandria and Suez worked as well as possible. If the passage was too dangerous, uncomfortable and time consuming, and if there were too many complaints about hardship and lack of service, there was still the alternative of the Cape route. The ultimate solution came of course some 27 years later when the Suez Canal was opened and deep-sea ships could sail directly between the Mediterranean and the Red Sea.

Meanwhile, the first of the Calcutta ships was appropriately named *Hindostan*, meaning 'the land of the Hindus,' referring originally to the Ganges Plain in Northern India and, in the mid-nineteenth century, being used as the name for the whole of India. The name of her near identical sister ship, *Bentinck*, honoured Lord William Bentinck (1774-1839) who, as Governor General of India between 1827 and 1835, was an advocate of steamship services to Calcutta as part of his initiatives to modernise the East India Company's operations and to liberalise and Westernise Indian society. Completed in 1842 and 1843

P&O's new headquarters in Leadenhall Street, completed in 1859, as depicted in The Illustrated London News. (Bruce Peter collection)

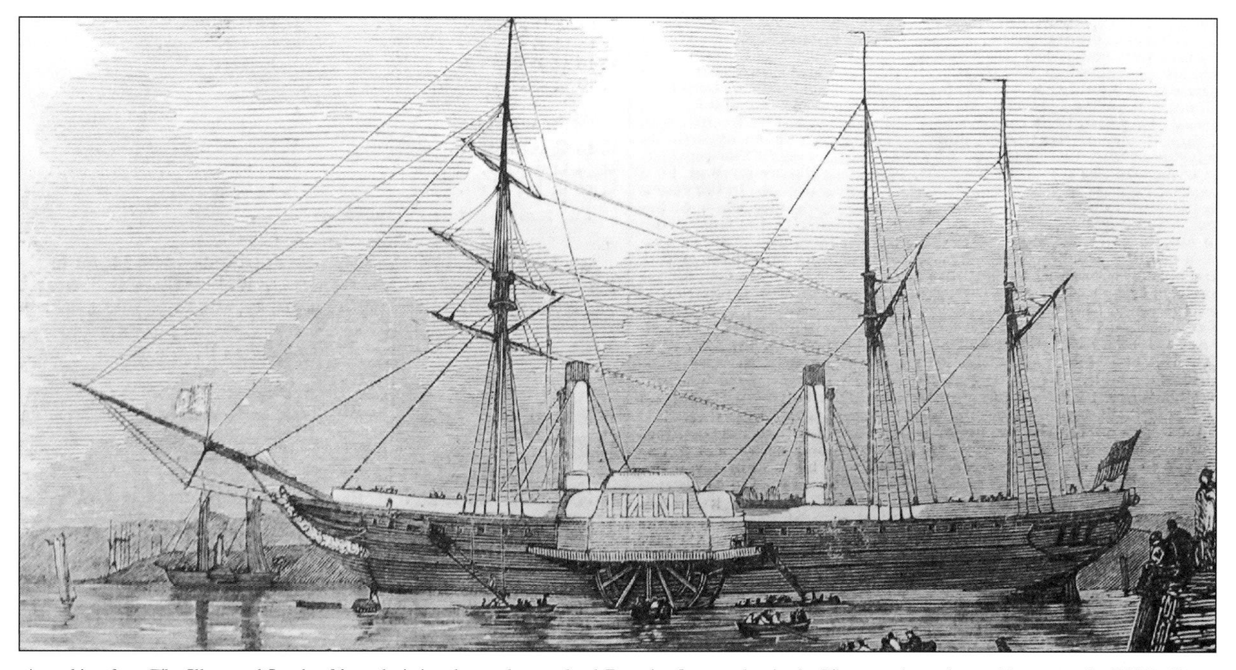

An etching from The Illustrated London News depicting the newly completed ***Bentinck*** *at anchor in the Thames prior to her maiden voyage for P&O. (Bruce Peter collection)*

The Arms granted to P&O in its centenary year, 1937. (Ferry Publications Library)

respectively, these were the largest ships yet built for P&O, each with a mail and cargo capacity of 300 tons and cabins, including single-occupancy rooms for 102 passengers with additional accommodation for 50 passengers' servants or Second Class travellers.

These were wooden-hulled paddle steamers, each with three masts, tall twin funnels and clipper bows, of fairly conventional design and engineering intended to be easily maintainable in waters so far away from where they were built and engined in Liverpool. Yet, in many regards, they were also fairly progressive for the safety precaution of having transverse iron bulkheads dividing their hulls into a number of separate watertight compartments. Rather than the then conventional arrangement of passenger cabins to either side of a central saloon, the new P&O ships had a double row of cabins along the centre of their accommodation decks that were accessed from two outer passages at the ship's sides. The idea behind this arrangement was that the passages would provide improved natural light and air circulation throughout the ship's interior from the portholes in their outer sides as well as forming a buffer zone against the heat of the Red Sea and Indian Ocean crossings and the sounds of the ship's wake churning against its sides. The dining saloons were arranged as full-beam spaces with openings at both sides admitting daylight and natural cross ventilation through their interiors.

The *Hindostan* commenced her positioning voyage from Southampton on 24th September 1842. This was undertaken as a revenue-earning commercial sailing with 150 passengers aboard, arriving on Christmas Eve in Calcutta. The voyage took 91 days, of which she steamed 63 days and spent 28 in port at Gibraltar, St Vincent (Cape Verde Islands), Ascension, Cape Town, Mauritius and Galle (Ceylon, now Sri Lanka) along the way. Her maiden voyage to Suez from Calcutta started on 17th January the following year, with passengers and mail bound for Britain arriving in Southampton aboard the *Great Liverpool* only 58 days later on 16th March. The East India Company suddenly found themselves outmanoeuvred; in terms of speed and punctuality, it was game, set and match to steam by way of Suez.

The *Bentinck* started her positioning voyage exactly 11 months later, sailing from Southampton on 24th August 1843 and joining the *Hindostan* in service between Calcutta and Suez at the year's end. Before she left Britain, she was featured in *The Illustrated London News*, which reported:

> 'This magnificent steamship is now moored off Blackwall and a more glorious burthen has never been borne by our Thames. She is the property of the Peninsular and Oriental Steam Navigation Company, whose patriotic efforts to shorten the distance between Europe and the East so thoroughly deserve the success that has attended them. The vast benefit conferred upon Great Britain and her Oriental possessions by the establishment of the mails to the Levant, and thence to India, has been most materially extended by the formation of new packet stations at Ceylon, Madras and Calcutta, and we have no doubt that ere long the commercial necessities of Great Britain will induce this company to extend the line to Hong Kong. The advantages of the new route have been now sufficiently

The P&O flag soon became a familiar sight on steamers throughout the Mediterranean and the Far East. In more recent times, P&O used it as a logo on the funnels of their ferry fleet, as shown here by the ***Pride of Winchester****. (Miles Cowsill)*

felt to obviate any necessity for commentary. By the old mode of transmission [via the Cape of Good Hope] a letter or passenger seldom reached any of the presidencies in less time than four or five months, making an interval of from eight to ten months before an interchange of communication could be effected between Great Britain and the Indian possessions; whereas now Calcutta has been brought to within less than forty, and Madras within about thirty five days' post of London.'[7]

This speeding up of communication between Britain and the Near East to within about a quarter of the time previously required had profound implications for Britain's relationship with the nations and peoples served by P&O. Their steamship services became military, business and cultural highways, not only enabling the British state to project and maintain power abroad but also bring aspects of Indian and Arab culture back to Britain.

The Illustrated London News continued, describing the *Bentinck*'s passenger amenities and the measures taken to provide optimum natural ventilation and air circulation then in days before mechanical ventilation and modern-day air conditioning, observing:

'The interior arrangements of the Bentinck are especially elegant, commodious and complete. She possesses accommodation for 102 cabin passengers, having 20 single cabins, 22 double cabins, and 12 family and general cabins. They are fitted up with every attention to comfort and convenience; and, above all light and ventilation, so desirable in tropical climates, have been abundantly provided. Each has its marble-covered basin-stand, mirrors, drawers, writing apparatus etc. Venetian blinds are inserted in the upper part of the doors, and, wherever possible, in the sides of the cabins also; and plates of perforated zinc, and all manner of contrivances, are introduced to ensure a constant circulation of wholesome and refreshing drafts of air. The spar-deck forms a magnificent walk, the full length of the ship, with convenient seats abaft. The main-deck, below, is also comparatively open and airy, and forms, with the houses on each side, a spacious and well-lighted arcade, which may be resorted to in showery or boisterous weather. The principal cabin or saloon, under the quarter-deck, is a large square apartment, well-lighted from the deck, and from the stern and side windows. It affords room for 100 persons to be seated commodiously at the tables; is lofty, and differs somewhat from those usually constructed, being nearly square; and free from the inconvenience of the several berths entering immediately into it, as it occupies the whole width of the vessel in the stern, and is upwards of 30 feet each way, having besides large stern windows, spacious ports on each side, thus giving abundance of light and air, and a full view of the sea in nearly every direction. The decorations of the saloon consist of several highly interesting views of Cabul, Ghuznee, etc., painted, or rather enamelled, on slate. The gildings are gorgeous, and all the fittings are correspondingly superb. The ladies' saloon is quite a unique apartment. It is entered by the side of the staircase, and presents a quiet, pleasing contrast to the more brilliant decorations of the grand saloon. This room, and the range of cabins adjoining it, are appropriated to the use of ladies exclusively.'[8]

Meanwhile, the Blackwall frigates continued to sail around the Cape of Good Hope on their longer routes to the Far East and China well into the late Victorian era, though in their final years mostly in cargo service as passengers sought the greater speed and creature comforts of ever newer, larger and better appointed steamships of P&O. In 1854 The East India Company finally relinquished its service between Suez and Bombay to P&O as the de facto carrier of the Royal Mail to India.

*The **Himalaya** of 1854 was at 3,438 tons one of the world's largest steamers. Greedy on coal, P&O found her unprofitable and, after only a single commercial voyage to Alexandria, sold her to the Government to bring troops to the Crimean War. (Barrow Museum)*

Chapter 2

Out East and Down Under

When Arthur Anderson first looked east from Gibraltar on the *Don Juan*'s maiden voyage, he may have been thinking about distant ports East of the Mediterranean. Indeed, within less than six years, P&O steamers would be operating from Calcutta, and continuing onwards to South East Asia two years later and even to Australia and New Zealand in another seven years. A steamer service from Europe to China would be a modern-day seaborne equivalent of the ancient trading routes for silk, spices tea and ivory through Central Asia and, more recently, those taken by sailing ships around the Cape of Good Hope. Thanks to these vessels and the merchant venturers who used them to trade, the Chinese people had developed a steady dependency on opium imported from India, a high value cargo which, like others of its kind, would soon be switched from sail to the faster and more reliable steamships of P&O. In the direction *down under* towards Australia, there was a then yet-to-materialise emigration boom that would in the next century become a further major facet of P&O's global shipping activities.

SILK AND OPIUM

P&O's new trading routes to China trace their origins all the way back to the original overland Silk Road where donkeys and dromedaries were first domesticated as beasts of burden and pack animals in the fourth millennium BCE. The Silk Road grew into a network of roads, trails, byways and passes stretching overland across the Mongolian planes of central Asia and ultimately connecting Peking (now Beijing) with Europe through the eastern Mediterranean ports of Alexandria and Constantinople. Apart from being the world's longest trading route for goods of all kinds, the Silk Road served the slave trades, and was travelled by pilgrims, soldiers and missionaries. It also served as a cultural highway passing between the Orient and the Occident through the lands of the Mongols, enabling the exchange of knowledge and ideas among the ancient civilisations of China, India, Persia and Arabia since about three thousand years ago. Few travellers of the early Silk Road would ever have made the continuous journey from one end to the other. Goods that were passed from China or India to Alexandria or Constantinople would have changed hands along the way, being traded and exchanged at various markets en route east or west.

The overland roads were supplemented by sea routes that in effect extended the Silk Road to those Western European nations surrounding the Mediterranean, and beyond to the British Isles, the North European cities of the Hanseatic League, and to Scandinavia and Russia. Other sea passages extended from the mouth of the Red River in modern-day Vietnam to southern India, Ceylon (now Sri Lanka) and the east coast of Africa, as well as the ancient Red Sea routes from Egypt to Eastern Africa and India. As early as the thirteenth century, the explorer Marco Polo (1254-1324) had brought back to Venice detailed accounts of his travels to the Far East and to China, of which he wrote in some detail, inspiring other explorers, seafarers and merchants by what he had seen and experienced. Renaissance explorers, made voyages of discovery directly from Europe to India and China, with Vasco da Gama (1460-1524) sailing from Lisbon around Africa to India in 1497 and five years later commanding a Portuguese naval armada to enforce Portugal's Asian colonial aspirations. In 1492 Christopher Columbus (1451-1506) sailed west in the hopes of reaching China by circumnavigation of the Globe, discovering instead that the continental land masses of the New World lay in between. Later on, Willem Barents (1550-97) set out from Amsterdam without success on three separate expeditions to find the North-east Passage to the Far East from 1594 to 1596.

Following the break-up of the Mongol Empire, which at its zenith included China and Russia, the overland Silk Road was eventually abandoned as the highway for commerce in favour of the deep-sea routes from China to India, around Africa or over the Isthmus of Suez through Egypt and onwards to the Mediterranean. The Russians later revitalised the overland route to China as their Great Siberian Road, known also as the Tea Road for the substantial quantities of tea imported from China by way of Siberia. It was opened in the mid-nineteenth century and ultimately succeeded by the Trans Siberia Railway, linking Moscow to China and the Sea of Japan through Vladivostok. Recently established links with the Chinese and European rail systems now provide for containerised cargoes to be carried over the entire length of the old Silk Road between China and Western Europe in as little as 13 days, against an average of 36 days by sea. There is now also a network of connected roads that form the Trans-Siberian Highway linking St Petersburg and Moscow with Vladivostok over a distance of 11,000 kilometres (6,825 miles) as well as the 1,300-kilometre (800-mile) Karakoram Highway, built between 1959 and 1979, that connects Pakistan with China.

At the time P&O started trading on the seaborne Mediterranean extension to the Silk Road in 1845, silk, teas and other expensive specialty commodities were still being exported by the Chinese, though they themselves were then importing little from Great Britain and other Western nations under China's highly restrictive foreign-relations and trade policies at that time. After the British annexed Bengal in the mid-eighteenth century, the East India Company started in 1773 to export opium from poppies grown in Bengal and processed at Benares and Patna to China as a means of offsetting the Company's trade imbalance for the Chinese teas it was importing for the British and Indian home markets. Importing opium into China was then illegal and so the drug was transferred to Chinese smugglers offshore who landed and sold it in defiance of the law. The whole matter of China's foreign trade and diplomatic relations with the outside world came to a head when opium dealers were arrested and foreign trading companies were forced to surrender their cargoes to Chinese authorities in 1838. Britain declared war on China and an expeditionary force was dispatched from India, resulting in the 1842 Treaty of Nanking that drastically liberalised China's import of goods, including opium, extending extraordinary privileges to ambassadors and other foreign nationals living there and ceding Hong Kong and other territories to Britain.

As the Chinese were understandably reluctant and slow to implement the terms of the Treaty and to uphold their side of its agreements, a second Opium War was waged by combined

British and French forces in 1856 after a Hong Kong-owned junk-rigged sailing ship *Arrow*, was arrested by Chinese Government forces under charges of piracy. First, the British attacked Canton and, shortly thereafter, seventeen thousand British and French soldiers stormed Peking where they ransacked and burned the Emperor's Summer Palace, from which they purloined enough loot to set off a new fashion trend for Chinese art in Europe and the United States.[9]

In 1845 P&O lost little time pressing on eastwards. The *Lady Mary Wood*, the vessel that had carried William Thackeray on the first leg of his Mediterranean travels in August 1844, sailed from Southampton on 27th November that year for Calcutta to inaugurate a new monthly steamship service from India to China. After her positioning voyage around Africa, the *Lady Mary Wood* set out for the Far East from Galle on 27th July 1845, arriving in Hong Kong 17 days later on 13th August, making scheduled stops at Penang for six hours and Singapore for 48 hours where coal was taken aboard. A month later, one of the *Lady Mary Wood*'s older fleet mates, the 1836-vintage *Braganza*, arrived in Galle to make the second sailing for Penang, Singapore and Hong Kong. Also built initially for the Peninsular services, the *Braganza* had been lengthened in 1844, at which point she was fitted with enlarged passenger accommodation.

An etching from The Illustrated London News showing sacks of mail and other goods being loaded on board a P&O steamer at Brindisi in Southern Italy. (Bruce Peter collection)

A night scene of navigation in progress on a P&O steamer's bridge in warm climes, also from The Illustrated London News. (Bruce Peter collection)

The Illustrated London News' depiction of an opera company performing on the deck of a P&O steamer bound for Egypt in 1876. (Bruce Peter collection)

With the transfer point between the India and Hong Kong service being made at Galle rather than Calcutta, the passage time between Egypt and India was shortened by the seven days taken to sail between these two ports in each direction so that the complete voyage between Southampton and Hong Kong could be completed under steam with P&O in as little as 55 days. Sailing from Southampton on, for instance, 20th June, one would arrive at Alexandria on 6th July, where four days were be allowed for the overland transit to Suez, sailing from there on the 10th for Galle, where a transfer would be made on the 29th to the Hong Kong-bound Steamer. Arrival in Hong Kong would be on 15th August.[10]

Larger ships were already being built for P&O's expanding operations East of Suez, the first of these being the twin-funnelled *Pottinger*, named for Hong Kong's Governor General Henry Pottinger, who had played an important role during the early 1840s in opening up Western trade with the Far East. The *Pottinger* was among P&O's first iron-hulled ships and, for her service in pirate-infested South-East Asian waters, she was armed with eight six-pounders, carried muskets and cutlasses and was fitted with hoses to repel would-be boarders with boiler steam. The *Pottinger*'s positioning voyage from Southampton brought her to Galle on 19th May 1847, from where she went into regular service between Bombay and Penang, Singapore and Hong Kong via Galle where passengers transferred to and from the Suez ships.

The *Pottinger*'s sister ship was the *Haddington*, her name honouring Thomas Hamilton the 9th Earl of Haddington and first Lord of the Admiralty (1841-46). She sailed from Southampton on 12th May 1846 to commence service between Calcutta and Suez. Meanwhile, the *Lady Mary Wood* remained on P&O's international Far Eastern services until 1850 when she was switched to a Chinese domestic route between Hong Kong and Shanghai. The former Southampton-Constantinople steamer *Achilles* also served on the Far East route to Hong Kong during the latter 1840s.

While P&O was under contract to carry the mail, it was also free to transport passengers and cargoes including silk and opium as long as these cargoes did not affect the mail contract. Yet, in the case of these, the Company was only responsible for expediting the cargo's passage from one port to another, having nothing to do with either its procurement, or its ultimate sale and use after arrival and off-loading at its destination. If opium was being carried, it got the same care as other valuable cargoes such as silks, satins, tea or spices; following *laissez-faire* principles, P&O was entirely unconcerned about who ultimately ended up wearing, drinking or smoking the stuff. Opium was delivered to P&O's bonded cargo warehouses in Calcutta in wooden crates or chests, similar to those used for tea, each of which contained 64 kilograms (140 pounds) of the substance. The operators of the fast sailing clippers that had virtually monopolised the trade since the late eighteenth century were less pleased to have competition from newfangled mail steamships. While there was little they could do to prevent their competitors from shipping opium, they nonetheless tried in other ways to make things difficult for P&O with the Chinese authorities.

Various accusations were made of P&O's ships being late with the mail, and of them being overloaded with opium carried in their coal bunkers and the coal being stowed on deck or even in the passenger accommodation. In 1850 the *Lady Mary Wood*, replaced by larger new steamers on the Galle-Hong Kong route and then trading between Hong Kong and Shanghai, was arrested, fined and banned from Cantonese waters after a small consignment of silk had been 'planted' aboard the ship by P&O's adversaries. The charges for avoidance of customs duties were eventually dropped after P&O pleaded its case with the Foreign Office in London, though by then the ship had lost nearly a whole year's revenue trading.

Whenever challenged in ways such as this, P&O was always able to substantiate its case with meticulously kept accounting and tracking of its finances, as well as with detailed logs and records of all its ships, the voyages they made, mails, passengers and cargoes carried. All of this was part of a bureaucratic attention to detail that had come from the original Anderson and Willcox ship brokerage firm in London and that had since grown with the company as it had expanded and diversified. The P&O managerial style was self-confident and self-sufficient, yet without being too overbearing. Its office culture had the sort of atmosphere also to be found in old and established family-run hotels or other businesses – an innately inspired loyalty and dedication from onshore personnel as well as ships' officers and crews. It was a sense of knowing that one was part of an organisation that was run by the best people in its field with a matching high quality of ships and the services these provided. Indeed, for its employees, being part of P&O was something to be proud of.

The characteristic P&O atmosphere has always been cordial and welcoming, without going to the higher flights of North Atlantic *grand luxe* service and social protocol. The routes served by P&O tended to attract less of the high profile wealthy and celebrity element indigenous to the express North Atlantic trade with its elitist demands and the service expectations of the European and American plutocracy. Those who sailed with P&O tended more to be the soldiers, government officials, business people, professionals and their families who lived and worked in the distant corners of the British Empire that were regularly served by P&O's ships. Where transatlantic passengers were at sea between the Old and New Worlds for a matter of days only, those travelling to and from to the Far East or Australia made their temporary homes while underway aboard ship for a number of weeks or even months at a time. There was less competition on those routes, and, while P&O never held a monopoly on any route it operated apart from its contractual obligations to carry the mail, the Line nonetheless ended up being the de-facto service provider when it alone had the necessary support services ashore to sustain regularly scheduled steamship services over such remarkably long routes to distant parts of the world.

Many of those who travelled to India, Hong Kong and later to Australia and New Zealand were on work contracts that ensured a later return voyage home, or if the duration was long enough or the contract was renewed, six-month periods of home leave might also be given. In either case, the home-leave or return-home voyages would also be taken with P&O. Therefore, passengers found themselves sailing repeatedly aboard familiar ships, and with officers and crews they already knew from the outward and earlier home-leave passages. In those days before the twentieth century Australian emigration boom in particular, the atmosphere aboard the Line's ships was remarkably club-like and, in many regards, elegantly informal.

CONSUMABLES, CAMELS AND SHIPS

By the mid-nineteenth century, P&O was maintaining some 50 ships on services east of Suez, for which sufficient quantities of coal had to be stockpiled at 14 coaling stations along the routes served by these vessels. As coal was locally unavailable in sufficient quantities, as many as 170 sailing colliers were chartered to bring coal from Great Britain around the coast of Africa to Aden and other ports in India and further East where it was needed. As the Red Sea was difficult to navigate under sail, coal needed at Suez had to be taken there by way of the Mediterranean and thence overland by camel trains until the railway was opened in 1859. Wherever possible, coaling of P&O's ships would be done at Aden, then a British colony, rather than at Suez, not least to save sailing ships having to make the difficult passage up the Red Sea. While this procedure was taking place, passengers could have time ashore to experience the local culture, as an article in *The Graphic* records:

> 'The most amusing sight in Aden is the crowd of Somali boys who swarm in their canoes round a newly-arrived steamer, all crying out "I dive, I dive, yessir me dive!" On a small coin being thrown out they plunge after it, splashing, dashing, scrambling, overturning canoes and generally seize it as it sinks. They are very dark and wear a small white band round their waist. Some have heads closely shaven, while others wear thick corkscrew curls dyed yellow. Upon landing, one hideous little imp attached himself to each of us, following us everywhere until we left, when we heard a great jabbering for "baksheesh".'[11]

With the need to feed some ten thousand people a day with the Western cuisine they were accustomed to and expected aboard ship in services east of Suez, P&O also had to run its own farms and dairies near Suez to provide sufficient quantities of milk and other dairy products, fruit and vegetables and meat. Reliable sources of fresh potable water were also needed at various ports where the Company's ships regularly called. P&O had as many as four thousands camels at its disposal in Egypt, for the transport of mail, cargo and baggage across the desert from Cairo and Suez.[12]

Until the Suez Canal opened in 1869, P&O in effect operated a two-part fleet, with its Peninsular and Mediterranean ships based and serviced in Southampton and its Oriental fleet based in India, where for the most part, the upkeep, maintenance and servicing of these ships was also handled. After being delivered by their builders, new ships destined for service east of Suez usually made at least one round-trip 'shakedown' voyage to either

Alexandria or Constantinople in an effort to identify any building or engineering deficiencies that would need to be remedied before making the long positioning voyages around Africa to start their service lives east of Suez. Periodic dry-dockings for hull maintenance, as well as general ship's repair, refitting and conversion work, upkeep and maintenance of boilers and machinery would be done in the East whenever possible to avoid the great expense and out-of-service times for these vessels to be returned to Great Britain for these purposes.

Repair and maintenance work was at first done by arrangement with the British East India Company's own shipbuilding facilities in Calcutta. Later, when P&O proposed extending its services between Galle and Hong Kong up the west coast of India to Bombay, the Line arranged to lease the Mazagon Dry Dock there as a base for its technical services. In addition to regular upkeep and repair, the shipbuilding work done by P&O in India included lengthening a number of vessels and the conversion of some from paddle to screw propulsion and of others from steamers to sailing ships for use as colliers or on other cargo services. While the Line retained its own workshops in India, large items such as boilers and engines still had to be brought by sea from Britain. Later, when the Far East services steamship *Haddington* became redundant in 1854, she was converted to a sailing barque for use as a sort of Navy-style fleet replenishment ship to transport these heavy and bulky items, as well as general-purpose Company stores to India and other destinations in the Orient. Conveniently, the *Haddington* also served as a floating officer cadet training school for P&O.[13]

Following traditions established with the East Indiamen, P&O's ships have always been staffed by British deck and engine officers, while Indian deck and engine ratings were hired locally for services east of Suez. Meanwhile, Muslim men from East Africa, Arabia and the Indian Subcontinent were recruited as deck and engine ratings on account of their willingness to work hard for a basic wage. Additionally, they were appreciated for their absolute sobriety – unlike many a British sailor – and dedication to duty. For those who toiled at stoking coal into the furnaces, life was particularly tough, as *The Illustrated London News* records:

> 'The stokers are generally short men with strong limbs and bullet heads and the very best of good nature in their disposition. Some of them will work half-an-hour in such a place as the stokehole and come up to deck again without a drop of perspiration on their dark skins. Others, when it is too hot as it often is in the Red Sea, have to be carried up in a fainting condition and are restored to animation by dashing buckets of water over them as they lie on deck.'[14]

On board a P&O liner, passengers and crew of a variety of ethnicities and religions are required to co-exist in very close proximity. For Britons travelling Out East for the first time, the experience of multi-ethnic shipboard life and of the vessels' African and Asian crews was a source of fascination. In reportage, there was however also a sense that P&O's hard-working seamen were being viewed through a prism of innate British superiority. Describing an 1875 voyage through the Red Sea to India on the P&O liner *Sumatra*, *The Graphic*'s reporter H. Johnson observed:

> 'There are many Mahommedans [*sic*] among the Lascar deck crew and deck passengers who never fail to say the sunset and sunrise prayers ordained to the followers of the Prophet. At the appointed time, off go their shoes, their faces are turned towards Mecca, their turbans and pugerees laid aside, and the enjoined genuflections performed. Their dinner mainly consists of rice, curry and meat killed by their own priest, who always accompanies them on a voyage. They sit in groups of three or four and eat out of large metal trenchers, and convey the contents to their mouths with their fingers. The carpenter's mate is a Chinaman and exceedingly clever at his trade. There is little that a Chinese carpenter will not do and the work will be faithfully executed.'[15]

Hotel staff, including cooks, pantrymen and stewards, were recruited from Goa, where thanks to the region's colonisation by the Portuguese, these people were almost all Roman Catholic and had no objections to handling and serving non-Halal foods. Later, when ships could sail directly by way of the Suez Canal between Great Britain and P&O's destinations east of the Red Sea, African, Indian and Goanese crew had become an established part of the Line's engine, deck and hotel service. Indeed, for the families of these crewmen it was considered a great honour for fathers, husbands and sons to serve as P&O crew ratings and hotel staff. The Line's Goanese, Indian, and, later, Pakistani crew were known collectively as Lascars and organised under Serangs and Leading Hands of their own nationality who had line responsibility for the day-to-day management of their duties, reporting directly to the ship's senior officers. The tradition is continued aboard present-day P&O Cruises ships.

AUSTRALIA

As mail services to Australia began to be discussed at Westminster and among the territorial capitals of the four original founding colonies, complex questions arose as to what destinations needed to be served by international deep-sea routes and from where these should originate. New South Wales was established as a British Crown Colony on 26th January 1788, a date much later to be celebrated as Australia Day, followed by Tasmania (originally Van Diemen's Land) in 1825. Western Australia followed in 1828 and South Australia in 1836. The Crown started exiling convicts to distant parts of the Empire, including New South Wales and Tasmania from 1788 onwards in an effort to alleviate intense overloading of the penal system in Great Britain's industrialised cities. This offered the added advantage that repeat and dangerous offenders incarcerated in remote places overseas were less likely to attempt escape or to return home and offend again if they survived to complete their sentences. Exile was also seen by the justice system as a more humane means of punishing lesser offences such as theft and property damage that then otherwise carried the death penalty.

Western and South Australia were founded as *free provinces*, welcoming settlers who were free to emigrate there of their own accord, though later Western Australia also landed exiled convicts. As greater numbers of free settlers arrived in Australia during the

1830s, opposition to the penal colonies increased, both on humanitarian grounds and on the basis of just payment being made for honest work. By the latter 1840s, convicts living in Australia were designated as *exiles* and were given the right to work for pay and were free to travel within Australia and New Zealand, though still barred from returning to Britain. The exile of convicts to New South Wales ended in 1840 and to Port Arthur in Tasmania which was Australia's largest penal colony in 1848, though smaller numbers of convicts continued to be landed in Western Australia until 1868. From 1788 until 1868, some 164,000 convicts were sent to Australia's penal colonies from Britain, of which 20 per cent were women.

At the time negotiations were underway in 1851 for a mail steamer service to Australia, the land's Western inhabitants still numbered more convicts than free settlers, concentrated largely along the coasts or thinly spread across the Continent's vast and largely arid interior. Although the colonies of New South Wales, South and Western Australia linked the continental land mass from the Pacific to the Indian Ocean, communication was limited – The Trans-Australian Railway would only come into being in 1917, after Victoria, Queensland and the Northern Territory Australia joined the Commonwealth of Australia in 1851, 1859 and 1911 respectively. Until then, each of the original colonies had its own view of what it alone needed from the outside world, seemingly with little reference to the concerns of the others.

The government of New South Wales favoured a trans-Pacific service from San Francisco to Sydney with an overland connection to Britain and Europe across the Isthmus of Panama and by way of the North Atlantic. (A transcontinental railway link across the United States was only to be realised in 1869, the same year the Suez Canal would open.) In contrast, Western Australia preferred a connection between either Swan River (now Perth) or King George's Sound (now Albany) and Singapore, while Southern Australia argued that Adelaide should be the Australian terminus. This was suggested because of its central location between Sydney and King George's Sound, though in fact it was too distant from either to be convenient for rapid mail delivery. Other routes discussed included Singapore to Sydney via the Torres Strait between New Guinea and the northern tip of Queensland, and an Aden to Albany service with a coaling stop in Mauritius, as well as direct passages from Great Britain around Cape Horn and the Cape of Good Hope.

No matter how one looked at it, the vast distances to be covered, coupled with the sparse and widely spread-out population of Australia along with small amounts of mail and cargo, plus the minimal numbers of passengers likely to use the service, appeared to offer only limited potential to be commercially viable. It appeared at the time to be the sort of venture that would probably end up having to be operated as a heavily subsidised mail service on a constitutional lifeblood basis with little or no potential of ultimate profitability.

Nonetheless, the Australia service contract was signed on 26th February 1852 with P&O, which against its critics and all odds, had by then proven that it alone had the experience, ships, crews and necessary supporting infrastructure ashore to service long and distant routes such as these and to make a success of them. The route finally selected for P&O's contracted bi-monthly service to Australia was from Singapore to Albany, Adelaide, Melbourne and Sydney, meeting the needs of all territories, including recently added Victoria. The Company was, however anxious to gain experience with this new route prior to its contracted start-up date on 11th January 1853 and before ordering new ships to meet its specific needs. The newly completed *Chusan*, which had been bought on the stocks and completed in March 1852 for P&O's trade between Calcutta and Hong Kong, was instead dispatched directly to Sydney. Departing on 15th May 1852 from Southampton and calling at St Vincent (Cape Verde Islands) and Cape Town en route and then steaming directly eastwards across the Indian Ocean, she made her maiden arrival in Australia at Melbourne on 29th July and called at Sydney five days later on 3rd August.[16]

A very large and diverse crowd turned out enthusiastically to greet the trim little iron-hulled, propeller-driven *Chusan* that was finally to bring regular mail, passenger and cargo sailings to their young land and the promise of ever greater things to come. Britons and Europeans living in Australia no longer would feel that they had gone to the end of the world, with regular news that would come from Europe and the opportunity to keep in touch by post and the exchange of parcels at Christmas time with families and loved ones in cherished and fondly recalled homelands that suddenly no longer seemed quite so far away.

During the *Chusan*'s prolonged inaugural stay in Sydney she, her captain, officers and crew were enthusiastically feted by the townsfolk. The high point of the celebrations was a gala evening ball and supper held in the City's Museum Great Room on 26th August. The musical programme for dancing included a piece written especially for the occasion called the Chusan Waltz and dedicated to the ship's master, Captain Henry Downs and his officers. Five days later, the *Chusan* started work on her new route to Singapore, sailing from Sydney on 31st August. She called

Stoking the boilers in tropical heat was a tough job for P&O's Lascar crews, as this illustration from The Graphic shows. (Bruce Peter collection)

at the Australian ports of Melbourne, Adelaide, King George's Sound, Swan River, and in the Dutch East Indies (now Indonesia) and at Batavia (now Jakarta) before arriving at Singapore 42 days later on 13th October. With connections at Alexandria, Suez, Galle and Singapore, the sea voyage from Southampton to Sydney was possible in about 88 days to three months.

To maintain the contracted bi-monthly Australian service, P&O transferred the *Shanghai*, also a propeller-driven steamer purchased on the stocks from her original Hong Kong-Shanghai deployment. As the time needed for necessary conversion work would be too long, the *Formosa* sailed from Southampton on 7th August to Sydney with 90 passengers aboard to take up P&O's second sailing from Sydney at the end of October to Singapore, but then continued onwards to Galle and Calcutta. With her refit work completed, the *Shanghai* sailed back from Calcutta on 26th May 1853 to Galle, Singapore and Sydney, joining the *Chusan* in regular mail, passenger and cargo service to Australia.

After successfully inaugurating P&O's Australian services, the *Chusan* and *Shanghai* were to be replaced by the larger *Madras* and *Bombay*, designed and built to meet the general purposes of the Line's various deep-sea services East of Suez. While the screw-propelled *Chusan* and *Shanghai* had been purchased during their construction for other owners, the *Bombay* and *Madras* were the first propeller-driven iron-hulled ships to be designed and built as such for P&O. After starting her service life with several Mediterranean voyages to Constantinople, the *Madras* was the first of these vessels to reach Australia, sailing from Singapore on 19th April 1854 for Sydney and, thereafter, making three consecutive round-trip voyages. The *Bombay's* place was taken by the *Norna*, a smaller new steamer designed for the Iberian Peninsular trade and transferred from the service between Bombay and Hong Kong. The change was made as an economy measure against increasing worldwide coal prices and the necessity to retain sailing schedules mandated by the Line's government contract to carry the Royal Mail.

DIFFICULT TIMES

With the addition of its steamship services to Australia, P&O had established an integral network of deep-sea routes reaching from Britain to the Iberian Peninsula, the Mediterranean and east of Suez to India, South East Asia and China. These routes would be the essence of its core trades throughout the liner era which lasted until 2006 when P&O Nedlloyd's container services were sold to Maersk Line. Yet, for P&O, the way ahead through the 1850s and 1860s would prove to be difficult for a variety of reasons outside of its own direct control.

As the demand for coal increased to meet the growing needs of heavy industry, shipping, the railways and, slightly later on, the generation of electrical power, inevitably, the fundamental laws of supply and demand would push its price significantly upwards by as much as 50 per cent. For shipping lines such as P&O, this meant that government mail contracts, agreed to on the basis of stable fuel costs, suddenly became liabilities as fuel has always been a major expense for modern shipping companies. To some degree, schedules could be rationalised, with smaller and operationally less expensive ships being deployed in place of larger ones, as was done in the Australian service. Coal could be purchased more cheaply from Borneo, though there was a shortage of sailing ships available to bring it to where P&O needed it, and so the Line ended up having to buy and operate two steam colliers of its own, adding to the operating costs of most services east of Suez.

From 1854 to 1856, the Crimean War had a substantial negative impact on the commercial operations of P&O and other lines, whose merchant ships were subject to being requisitioned by the Admiralty for trooping, and the transport of horses, stores and various war materials to the front lines. These vessels also repatriated the wounded and eventually brought troops home at the war's conclusion. Whereas the Royal Navy had been virtually self reliant until the end of the Napoleonic Wars, it had since downsized itself to the point that it no longer had the ships and other resources it needed in wartime. The Navy continued, in theory at least, to favour the traditional reliability of wooden-hulled sailing ships that could easily be patched if holed and also relied on the prevailing winds, rather than steam and the need for coal and coaling stations in distant parts of the world.

Yet, when requisitioning merchant ships in times of war, their Lordships at the Admiralty suddenly seemed to lose their prejudices against steam-powered and iron-hulled tonnage. Eleven of P&O's largest and most technologically up-to-date steamships, amounting to a third of the Line's total tonnage, were taken up for National Service as part of the Crimean War effort. There were no battles at sea and the merchant steamers had the manoeuvrability to stay out of harm's way from shore-based bombardment with the result that no ships were lost as casualties of war. What was lost, however, was the continuity and goodwill of P&O's regular peacetime commercial trades with, for instance, the Line's services to Australia being suspended altogether during the war, while the frequency of sailings and quality of service on other routes was reduced.

When P&O withdrew its Australian mail steamers, it forfeited the remainder of its Royal Mail contract. Following the end of the war and the return of requisitioned merchant ships to their regular commercial trades, tenders were again invited for resumed service under new and considerably more stringent terms. P&O tendered on the basis of reinstating its original Singapore-based service, under the new terms set out by the Crown. Bids for the contract were also put forward by the London-based Royal Mail Steam Packet Company, the forerunner of Royal Mail Lines, for a direct deep-sea routing by way of the Cape of Good Hope and by the European & Columbian Steam Navigation Company originating from Glasgow in 1853, which proposed a trans-Pacific passage involving an overland transit of the Isthmus of Panama. A two-year contract was awarded to the European & Columbian Steam Navigation Company for a monthly service to commence at the beginning of 1857.

The company was accordingly re-named as the European & Australian Royal Mail Company Limited,[17] and the steamship *Oneida* was purchased from the Canada Ocean Steam Ship Company to work the route. Chartered tonnage was sought as an interim measure while three additional ships were to be built for trans-Pacific service. P&O's 1854-built Mediterranean-services ship *Simla* made three voyages in 1857 under charter to European & Australian before being returned to P&O in March 1858 and transferred to the Suez-Calcutta route. Meanwhile, European & Australian had run into financial difficulties and, after a proposed merger with the Royal Mail Steam Packet Company failed, the company was liquidated in 1858 and the Australian service was operated by the Royal Mail Steam Packet Company until the contract expired.

A new contract for mail services to Australia was signed with P&O to commence in early 1859 on a new and more direct route between Suez and Aden, by way of Mauritius to King George's Sound, Adelaide, Melbourne and Sydney. The passage time between Britain and Australia was set in the contract at 55 days, the same time taken for the mails, passengers and cargo to reach Hong Kong when that service had opened some 14 years earlier. The overland connection in Egypt was by this time greatly simplified with the opening of a direct rail service between Alexandria and Suez in December 1858. Where four days was previously scheduled for passengers to make the overland crossing between Alexandria and Suez, with it then being possible for mail and cargo to be transported without rest stops in 64 hours, the rail journey for the mail, passengers and cargo alike took only about eight hours.[18]

Operationally, the new Australian routing was in fact an extension of a recently inaugurated service between Suez and Mauritius, launched in 1858. The long open sea passage between Mauritius and King George's Sound would take 14 days. Even with the Line's larger new ships *Salsette* and *Benares* that would operate between Australia and Egypt, an additional 250 tons of coal would need to be stowed on deck for use on the passage between Mauritius and Western Australia.[19] As this service made no regular contact with P&O's bases of operation in Bombay or Calcutta, there was also the issue that these ships would have to make positioning voyages or be deadheaded to and from India for regular maintenance and servicing.

On 1st November 1858 the *Salsette* sailed from Southampton on her positioning voyage to Australia by way of the Cape Verde Islands and the Cape of Good Hope, arriving in Sydney on 15th January the following year, from where she set out on 12th February with mail, passengers and cargo bound for Aden and Suez. She was joined by the *Benares* at the end of the year, while the *Emeu*, one of the P&O ships chartered by European and Australian Royal Mail Company, was retained on the Line's new Australian mail route. The Suez to Sydney route proved to be a difficult service to maintain owing to its very long sea passages, the cost of fuel needed to cover these, the effects of prevailing winds and currents and the inevitable need for additional ships to maintain the required frequency of sailings.

When the time came for the mail contract to be renewed in 1864, P&O was the only contender and ended up retaining the service by default. The line suggested an alternative direct service to Galle, eliminating the need to trans-ship at Singapore, though this was rejected by the Crown no doubt on the basis of the passage time for this being greater than 55 days. The Australian service remained much the same, despite the continual reallocation of ships to and from the route until the Suez Canal was opened in 1869.

The crew of the ***Candia*** *rescuing a man overboard. The steamer served P&O from 1854 until 1874. (Bruce Peter collection)*

THE SUEZ CANAL

The great French visionary Ferdinand Marie de Lesseps (1805-94) and his Compagnie Universelle du Canal Maritime de Suez (Suez Canal Company) meanwhile had been busy digging a 164-kilometre (102-mile) sea-level canal across the Isthmus of Suez, joining Port Said on the Mediterranean and the Red Sea at Port Tewfiq a short distance east from Suez. The Company had been incorporated on 15th December 1858 and construction of the Canal had actually started on 25th April 1859. Formerly the French Consul in Cairo, de Lesseps was the Canal's principal developer, who had been licensed by Sa'id, Pasha of Egypt (1822-63) to build and operate it. He arranged its financing and was advised on its construction by a panel of 13 leading experts of various scientific and technical disciplines from seven different nations, including the president of the Institution of Civil Engineers from London.

Upon completion, the Isthmus of Suez Maritime Canal, as it

Workmen load dromedaries during the construction of the canal through the Isthmus of Suez, as recorded by The Illustrated London News. (Bruce Peter collection)

In this 1875 etching from The Graphic, the captain of P&O's ***Sumatra*** *is leading a Sunday religious service on deck as the steamer progresses through the Red Sea. Her British passengers appear to be making no concessions whatsoever to the hot conditions beneath the deck awnings. (Bruce Peter collection)*

was properly called, would provide a through-passage for ships of all nations between Europe and Asia, the Far East and the Antipodes that would be financed by the fees paid by shippers for its use. The Canal was cut through flat arid desert terrain where virtually nothing stood at the time of its building. The towns of Port Said and Port Tewfiq at its Mediterranean and Red Sea ends had risen from the sands to support the Canal's building and operation and serve the traffic following its completion, with the headquarters of the Suez Canal Company located at Port Said.[20]

The canal's construction was a daring project of unprecedented scale that by its very nature attracted criticism, scorn and even ridicule. The official government stance in Britain was to dismiss the whole thing as being a physical impossibility with the hope that, one way or another, the French would fail. Success for de Lesseps was bound to be seen as a blow to British maritime supremacy that would beg the question of why Britain itself had failed to take the lead in building the Canal in the first place. There were also those who argued that, even if the Canal were to be completed, the Suez Canal Company would fail to be able to operate it on a sustained basis or, worse still, the desert winds would blow sand into it and simply fill it back up again. The Canal was nonetheless duly completed and opened with great fanfare at ceremonies held on 18th and 19th November 1869.

At the time, P&O had little or no interest in the Canal, as the terms of their mail contracts explicitly called for the mail to be

P&O's ***Mongolia*** *of 1865 at anchor in the Grand Canal at Venice in the latter 1870s. The steamer served the Company until 1888. (Bruce Peter collection)*

carried overland between Alexandria and Suez. As the Line had no more faith than many others did in the success of Monsieur de Lesseps's great ditch across the Isthmus of Suez, it had continued building new ships for its divided operations in European waters and East of Suez. The Line had also invested heavily in a vast supporting infrastructure for its existing operations that supported the livelihoods of literally thousands of P&O people, both at sea and ashore in Egypt, India and other places.

P&O had secured mail contracts, often by default as it alone had the supporting facilities to provide services to distant parts of the world. The Line had embraced new technical development in shipbuilding and marine engineering cautiously. This was partly a matter of being obliged to follow the Admiralty's remarkably conservative approach to these things until the Post Office took over responsibility for overseas mail contracts in 1861. There was also the entirely practical consideration of providing reliable service in distant waters far from the places where the Line's ships were built and those where they could be serviced. Accordingly, P&O's growth and development had always been driven more by the expansion of its trades with little exposure to the rigours of commercial competition from other shipping lines or the challenges of newer and more progressive directions in ship design and the march of progress in marine power and propulsion on other trading routes.

When P&O started sailing to Mauritius it carried the French mails to the nearby island of Réunion, but lost this contract in

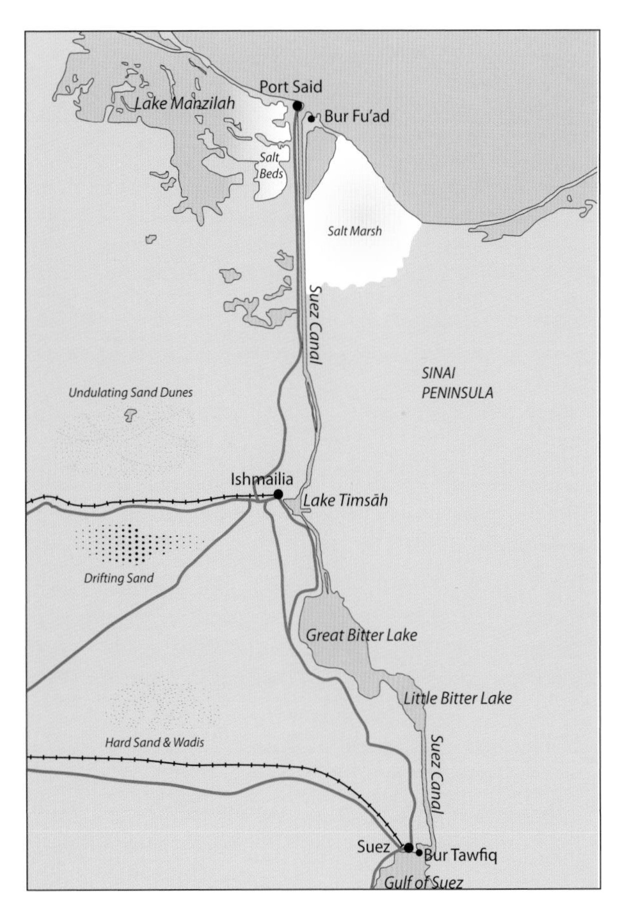

*The **Poonah** at anchor in the Grand Canal at Venice, the first large steamer ever to visit the city. This etching from The Illustrated London News makes a fascinating comparison with the frontispiece view of the cruise ship **Arcadia**. (Bruce Peter collection)*

The newly delivered steamer ***Poonah*** *pitches through a choppy sea. (Bruce Peter collection)*

1864 to Messageries Impérial, founded in 1851 as Messageries Nationale and in 1871 renamed as Compagnie des Messageries Maritimes. As this company was also providing services to France's colonial possessions in the Far East, the suggestion was put forward in Parliament three years later that perhaps this Line, subsidised by the government of France, should also be invited to tender for British mail contracts, though the idea was quickly dropped in the face of angry media reaction and hostile government opposition. The express overland Continental mail service through France to Marseilles, where it was transferred to P&O ships bound for Alexandria, was redirected during the Franco Prussian War in 1870-1 to the Italian Adriatic port of Brindisi, and there put aboard ships of the Italian-flag Adriatic & Oriental Company. As the European railway networks developed and the Mont Cenis rail tunnel was opened a year later making this route more favourable, all British mail to and from the eastern Mediterranean and points east of Suez, including parcel post introduced in 1873, was carried by rail across the Continent to Brindisi. P&O was contracted to pick up and drop off its eastern mails there, rather than at Southampton.

The Line also had a mail contract with the Italian government that allowed it to carry general cargo between Venice and Alexandria as well.[21] In Venice, P&O's ships docked at the Riva degli Schiavoni opposite the Doge's Palace and near St Mark's Square, and made stops at Ancona and Brindisi, making this service very attractive to passengers making Mediterranean cruises or doing the Grand Tour. *The Illustrated London News* of 31st August 1872 reported on the *Poonah*'s maiden Venice call:

> 'Noble buildings, the grandest monuments of Venetian glory and prosperity in the past, are seen with unimpaired beauty, looking upon a scene in the harbour of Venice which none of the Doges could have foreseen. Iron and steam power, which Great Britain possesses most abundantly, are now the rulers of the sea. Many of the townspeople came on board the *Poonah* at Venice, where so large a steamer had never been seen before.'[22]

Meanwhile, passenger fares and cargo rates were falling as other lines offered a less exclusive service aboard more efficient and agile newer ships powered by modern high-pressure boilers and compound engines that burned up to 40 per cent less coal than the older low-pressure boilers and side-lever or oscillating engines largely favoured by P&O. These new boiler and engine types reduced operating costs and freed more hull volume for revenue-earning cargo. The principle of the compound engine was to feed exhaust steam from the engine's initial high-pressure cylinder to one or more additional low-pressure cylinders of progressively greater diameter to equally absorb the exhaust steam power passed on from the preceding higher pressure cylinder. For this to work, steam has to be raised at considerably higher pressure in newly developed fire-tube-type Scotch boilers.

P&O's divergent network of deep-sea routes had become something like the old land-based Silk Road, a series of connected trails with few travellers making a continuous journey from one end to the other. By the late nineteenth century, increasingly larger numbers of passengers and greater quantities of mail and cargo did in fact need to move along the full extent of P&O's sea routes from one end to the other, for instance between Southampton and Bombay, Calcutta, Singapore, Hong Kong or Sydney. P&O's newfound French and Italian competition was already sailing direct passages between Europe, Asia, the Orient and Australia by way of the Suez Canal. The Canal transit could be made within two days, about 16 hours for the passage between Port Said and Port Tewfiq in addition to the time needed to take on Canal pilots and to be placed in a convoy for the direction of the transit. P&O had no choice but to follow suit with its own ships, though it would have extensively to rebuild much of its fleet to do so.

The *Nubia* was P&O's first ship to transit the Suez Canal on 1st to 3rd April 1870 while on her way home to Britain from Bombay with engine trouble. The Line's first round-trip by way of the Canal was made by the *Delhi*, passing from Port Said to Suez on 14th to 15th July outbound to Bombay and continuing on to Hong Kong, making the return northbound Canal transit on 17th and 18th December. In September the same year, the new liner *Australia* was the first P&O ship to make her positioning voyage to the East via the Canal instead of having to sail around Africa.[23]

While passengers could now travel by liner through Egyptian territory via the new Suez Canal, the Royal Mail contract

The ***Mooltan*** *of 1861 was the first P&O steamer fitted with compound engines. Thanks to this innovation, the amount of coal she consumed was half that of earlier vessels. (Bruce Peter collection)*

*Designed for naval service in time of war, the **Australia** of 1892 and her sister, the **Himalaya**, brought enhanced safety through her many hull divisions and also grand hotel-like interiors to the P&O fleet, in which she served for 12 years. (Bruce Peter collection)*

continued to stipulate that the mail must be sent overland by rail. In theory at least, this was the faster way, though in reality it was landed upon arrival at either Alexandria or Suez and dispatched by train to the other port and, there, stowed back aboard the same ship a day or so later. This illogical situation was resolved in 1874 when P&O was finally given permission to carry the mail through the Canal aboard ship.

FLEET DEVELOPMENT AND DIVERSIFICATION

The last surviving among P&O's founding directors, Arthur Anderson, died in 1869 while still holding the position of Managing Director. Of his old colleagues, Richard Bourne had died in 1851, and Brodie McGhie Willcox had resigned as Managing Director in 1854, remaining on the board of directors and serving as Chairman from 1854 until his death in 1862. Thomas Sutherland (1834-1922), who had risen quickly through the ranks to become P&O's Hong Kong Superintendent where he worked enthusiastically to develop the Line's business in the Far East and had also founded the Hong Kong and Shanghai Banking Corporation, was appointed as Managing Director three years after Anderson's death. He became Chairman in 1881 from which point he ran P&O virtually single-handed for the ensuing 33 years. It was thus on his watch that the Line's fleet was greatly updated and rationalised so as to prosper as never before through the latter years of the Victorian era.

The Pacific Steam Navigation Company had been the first to adopt the compound engine for its services along the west coast of South America where coal was prohibitively expensive. In 1861 P&O introduced a compound-engined liner of their own, the *Mooltan*, introduced first for an extended period of service between Southampton and Alexandria before being sent around the Cape of Good Hope to sail between Suez and Calcutta. Compared with earlier tonnage, ships such as the *Mooltan* were remarkably complex and 'high tech', with steam superheaters, surface condensers, centrifugal pumps, hydraulics and other auxiliary machinery, resulting in various initial difficulties with their operation.[24] Yet with the *Mooltan*'s fuel consumption reduced by half, the added complexity was well worthwhile. The ship was returned to Britain in 1866 for replacement of her boilers and machinery with new and improved equipment of greater reliability. The *Mooltan* was later switched between services east and west of Suez in 1871 and 1873, making both her north- and southbound positioning voyages by way of the Suez Canal.

The *Mooltan* was an especially attractive ship, reflecting an almost yacht-like aesthetic in her exterior profile and was the epitome of on-board opulence and luxury for her time. She was enthusiastically described in the 3rd of August 1861 edition of *The Illustrated London News*:

> 'She is ship-rigged, and her appearance in the water gives one more the idea of a costly yacht of immense size, so exquisite are her fine lines and her graceful buoyancy. Light, however, as she looks, the hull is of enormous strength, and broad diagonal stringers of iron so cross the ship in both sides and deck in all directions that she may be considered, of her size, as strong as the *Great Eastern* herself. Inside she is fitted up with a solidity and splendour, which have not been seen in the finest vessels of this company. Everything even on the upper-deck which is not of polished mahogany, is of polished teak, and the expenditure in ornamental fittings would appear to be carried to an

Top: The ***Himalaya*** *built in 1892 was the second ship in the fleet to carry this prestigious name. (Barrow Museum)*

Above: The ***Gwalior*** *of 1873 served P&O for 21 years. (Bruce Peter collection)*

Right: The newly completed ***Australia*** *of 1892 in the River Thames, as depicted in The Illustrated London News. (Bruce Peter collection)*

extreme, if they were not also all solid and serviceable. The decorations of the state saloon might be pointed to as a model for good taste and elegance of what a ship's fittings would be in this respect.'[25]

During the closing decades of the nineteenth century, P&O's route network was consolidated and simplified under Thomas Sutherland's direction. He was one of the first Britons to visit Japan, travelling privately to Nagasaki in 1859, and subsequently succeeded in inaugurating an extension of P&O's Far Eastern services to Yokohama in 1864. The Line's fleet was greatly expanded with larger and faster ships that brought a wealth of technological advancement, ensuring greater safety and reliability, as well as added creature comforts for passengers and crew alike.

In 1878 the iron-hulled *Kaisar-I-Hind*, the name meaning Empress of India in the Hindi and Urdu vernacular in honour of the title having been bestowed upon Queen Victoria the previous year, introduced refrigeration for the first time aboard a P&O ship. Two years later the *Ravenna* was delivered in 1880 for Far Eastern service as P&O's first all-steel ship, with her lifeboats also being made of the same metal. The reduction of weight compared with a similarly dimensioned vessel built of iron, gave the ship a considerably lighter displacement. Her hull's cellular double bottom compartments could be filled with ballast water to maintain the ship's trim under various load conditions. Her two

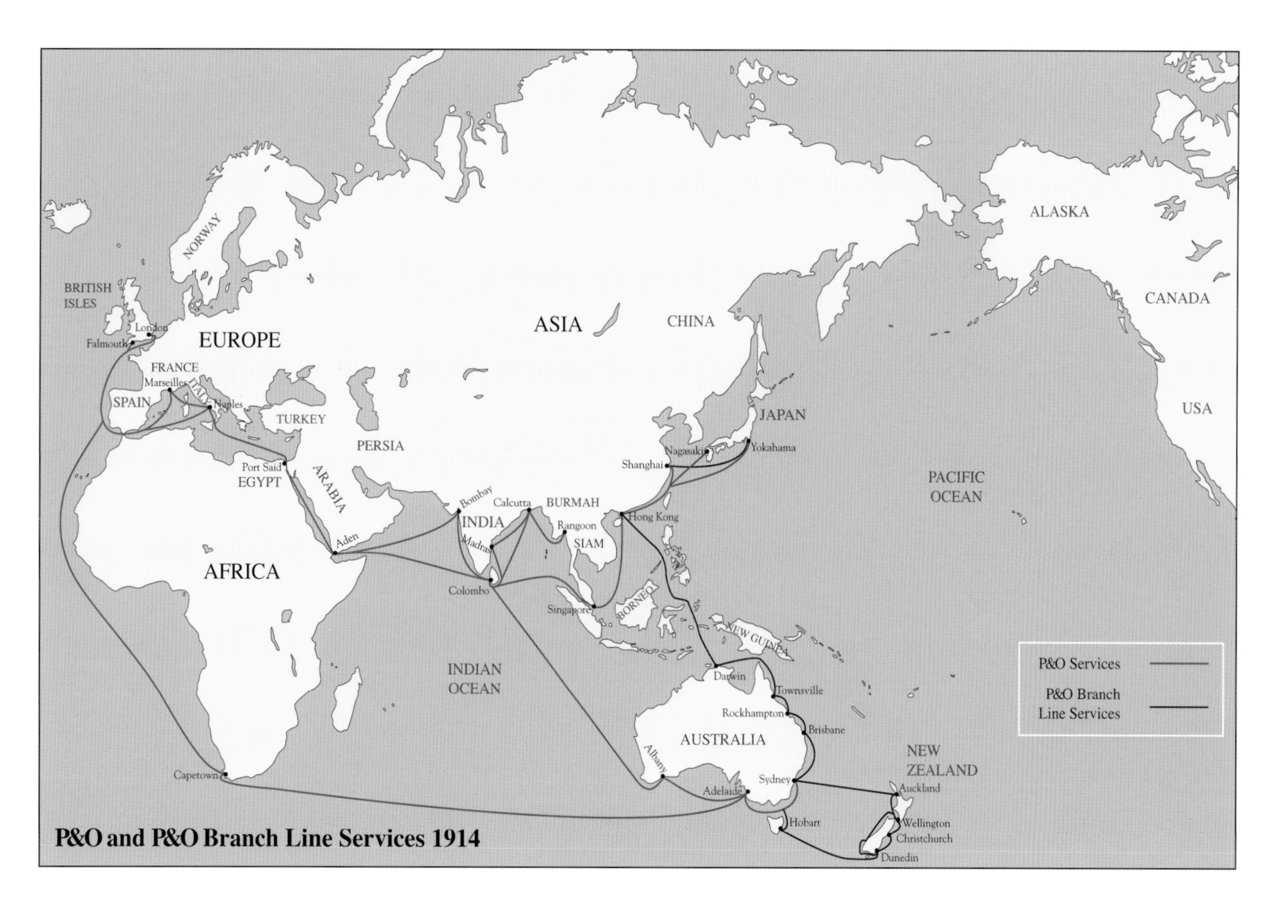

P&O and P&O Branch Line Services 1914

sister ships, *Rohilla* and *Rosetta*, were, however, completed at the same time with iron hulls.

The *Rome* and *Carthage*, delivered the following year, were the first P&O ships to break with the sailing-ship tradition of having the best passenger cabins located aft in favour of the more modern steamer approach of arranging the First Class cabins and suites amidships on the upper decks, with Second Class relegated astern. The *Rome* was refitted in 1904 as a cruise ship with single-class accommodation for 150 passengers and renamed *Vectis* in response to a revived interest in cruising brought about by recommendations made in the *British Medical Journal* during the 1880s that sea travel offered curative and therapeutic benefits to one's health. Electric light, albeit then only in the First Class saloon, was first introduced aboard the *Valetta* in 1884, while the progression from two-cylinder compound machinery to the triple expansion engine was made with the *Coromandel*, completed a year later. By this time, the voyage time to India was as little as two weeks.

P&O's greatest shipbuilding triumphs of the Victorian era were its magnificent Jubilee ships *Victoria*, *Britannia*, *Oceana* and *Arcadia*, completed in 1887 and 1888, and marking the jubilees both of Queen Victoria's reign and of P&O's founding. Larger by half than anything in the P&O fleet that had preceded them, these remarkably elegant and comfortable ships were a foretaste of even greater things to follow in the early twentieth century. They were followed in 1892 by the slightly larger second *Himalaya* and *Australia* that were, in essence, a continuation of the Jubilee series. As both ships were also designed to serve as naval auxiliaries in times of war, they also met the Admiralty's high standards for internal subdivision of their hull spaces with watertight bulkheads.

The London-based architect Thomas Edward Collcutt (1840-1924), who had already designed part of P&O's London offices in Leadenhall Street, was also commissioned to design the passenger interiors of the *Himalaya* and *Australia*. *The Illustrated London News* was impressed by the *Australia*'s considerable speed and fine appointments:

> 'Launched on July 29 from the yard of Messers. Caird and Co. at Greenock, the speed trials have fully realised all the expectations that had been formed, the steamer attaining a speed of nineteen knots an hour… She is elaborately fitted up, and the different saloons, library, music-room, and smoking room are ornamented with beautiful carvings by Signor Cambi, of Siena, and designs by Mr T.E. Collcutt, the architect of the Imperial Institute… A special feature is the large number of deck cabins. The bathrooms, which are fitted with douche, spray, wave and needle baths, will prove a great luxury in the tropics.'[26]

As part of an emerging trend towards bringing the luxury of the Grand Hotel ashore to sea, steamship companies began to commission professional architects to design and decorate the passenger accommodation and public spaces of their newest ships. These were done in the romantic arts and crafts, period revival or beaux arts styles then popular in the design of country houses, private clubs and luxury hotels on *terra firma*. P&O's newest vessels were at the forefront of such splendid innovations in passenger comfort.

P&O Heritage collection

Chapter 3

Through two World Wars and a Great Depression

The twentieth century's dawning decade was a time of continuing fleet expansion for P&O, with the five sister ships *India*, *China*, *Egypt*, *Arabia* and *Persia* being completed between 1896 and 1900. The again larger M-class *Moldavia*, *Mongolia*, *Marmora* and *Macedonia*, that were the Line's first twin-screw liners and featured an added superstructure deck compared with the earlier *India* class, followed in 1903-4. Built for the long deep-sea routes to India and Australia, these were all a direct progression from the Line's highly successful Jubilee ships of 1887-8 in their overall design characteristics, layout and facilities. With the M class, of which ten ships were built prior to World War I, P&O began to change the superstructure colour from dark khaki first to a light ochre grey and later, between the wars, to white. Following his success with the *Himalaya* and *Australia*, Thomas Edward Collcutt was commissioned to design the interiors of the *India*- and M-class ships in the popular beaux arts idiom of the time.

The M class was extended with a further four slightly larger ships added later in the decade, including the second *Mooltan* in 1905, the second *Malwa* in 1908, the *Mantua* in 1909 and the *Medina*, completed in 1911. Before going into commercial service for P&O in June 1912, the *Medina* was first used as a Royal Yacht for King George V and Queen Mary's 1911 tour to India, for which the ship's hull was painted white with a blue band beneath its uppermost line of portholes and a third mast temporarily added amidships to carry the Royal Standard. Once in regular service, the *Medina* rounded out an essentially similar series of M-class ships servicing the Australian mail route with sailings every two weeks, all year round. By this point, P&O had also extended its services to New Zealand, with occasional sailings onwards from Sydney to Auckland. It was then found that the service could be operated using only nine ships, with the *Morea*, the sixth M-class ship, being transferred to full-time cruising as a replacement for the *Vectis*, dating from 1881. The *India* and *China* were moved to India and Far East services.

The same Jubilee-class design approach was also adapted to a number of smaller cargo/passenger ships designed for various intermediate (non-mail carrying) and auxiliary services, including various routes based in India, from London to the Far East, and the express Aden-Bombay mail run. Many of these were also used to carry large numbers of troops that would be accommodated dormitory-style in their cargo spaces. Most notable among them were the five-ship *Sicilia* class, including also *Soudan*, *Syria*, *Somali* and *Sardinia*, built between 1901 and 1902. Apart from their regular non-mail commercial service with P&O, these were also chartered to transport Indian troops as needed. The most attractive and fastest of the smaller ships was the 20-knot *Salsette* of 1908, built for the Aden-Bombay express mail service on which she sailed almost continuously until 1914. With the visually remarkably well-balanced massing of her all-white hull and superstructure and her substantial twin yellow funnels, this ship had the stance of a luxury cruise yacht, and indeed her maiden voyage was a cruise from London to Amsterdam, Copenhagen, Helsinki and Kiel, followed by a Mediterranean excursion to Gibraltar, Algiers, Corfu, Cattaro, Venice, Sicily and Marseilles.

GROWTH BY ACQUISITION

As P&O continued to carry the mails to and from Australia and maintained its policy of catering exclusively to the First and

*The **Persia** of 1900 was built on the Clyde by Caird & Company of Greenock. In December 1915, a German U-boat torpedoed her off Crete, killing 343 of the 519 on board. (Mick Lindsay collection)*

*The **India** of 1896 was a near sister of the **Persia**. While serving as an armed merchant cruiser, she was sunk by a German torpedo off Western Norway in March 1915; ten officers and 115 ratings lost their lives. (Bruce Peter collection)*

Second Class passenger trade, emigrant traffic was left to others. In addition to its own First and Second Class trade, Orient Line had started carrying Third Class passengers to Australia via the Cape of Good Hope in 1877. The London-based Blue Anchor Line had been running a cargo and emigrant service to Australia since its founding by Wilhelm Lund and his family in 1869. Originally passengers were carried under sail from London by way of the Canary Islands and Cape Town to Sydney. Vessels continued from there in ballast to China from where tea was carried back to Great Britain. After the Suez Canal was opened, the Chinese tea trade became less attractive to Blue Anchor which then changed its operations to a direct monthly service between London and Sydney, later making the transition from sail to steam. During the 1890s, Blue Anchor took delivery of the purpose-built steamers *Narrung*, *Wakool* and *Wilcannia*, with the *Commonwealth* added in 1901, its name commemorating the Commonwealth of Australia's incorporation as a Dominion of the British Empire at the beginning of that year. These cargo/passenger ships were fitted out with cabins for 50 passengers each and used portable accommodations for several hundred emigrants

*The first duty for the newly delivered **Medina** was to perform the role of Royal Yacht, carrying King George V and Queen Mary to India for the Delhi Durbar in 1911. This pageant was a high point of the Raj. She too was torpedoed by a U-boat in February 1917 sinking off the Devon Coast. (Ambrose Greenway collection)*

The ***Osiris*** *of 1898 was built for the Brindisi-Port Said mail service. She is pictured here moored at Port Said. (Ambrose Greenway collection)*

assembled in the cargo holds for the outward voyage and dismantled so that dry cargoes could be shipped on the return passage.

While the Orient Line's First and Second Class passenger services in particular were viewed as a source of competition, the two companies shared this trade from 1888. P&O faced the obstacle that, under Australian Merchant Shipping Act regulations, British ships transporting emigrants to Australia were required to be operated by all-white-skinned crews. Since P&O's passenger ships employed deck and engine ratings, hotel and passenger service staff from the Indian subcontinent, East Africa and the Middle East, they would be categorically barred from landing emigrant passengers in Australia. Therefore, the Line would either have to build up or acquire a separate fleet of ships for this trade.

In 1909, tragedy befell the Blue Anchor Line's newest ship, the *Waratah*, a considerably larger vessel with accommodation for 128 cabin passengers and 300 emigrants, which was lost at sea on the return leg of her second voyage. After sailing from Durban for Cape Town on 26th July with 92 passengers, 119 crew and 6,500 tons of cargo on board, the *Waratah* encountered a gale the following day and, after exchanging greetings with the British cargo vessel *Clan Macintyre*, disappeared without a trace. Despite rigorous searches of the area where she was last seen, nothing was ever found of her; there was no wreckage, flotsam or dead bodies. Some observers who had seen the ship during her maiden and outward-bound second voyages alleged that she appeared to be top-heavy. Maybe she was or perhaps, as some recent commentators have speculated, she was hit by a rogue wave of the kind known to be encountered on the South East coast of South Africa which have caused substantial damage to ships in more recent years.[27]

The Lund family was devastated by the loss and ultimately decided to sell the Line. For P&O, this was to provide a remarkable opportunity to, in effect, purchase a ready-made Australian emigrant operator with the established goodwill, ships and onshore support facilities of a viable and functioning business. The assets of the Blue Anchor Line were offered for sale later in 1909 and acquired along with its five remaining ships by P&O in January 1910 to be retained as an entirely separate operation to serve the emigrant trade to Australia. The Blue Anchor funnel colours were also kept and the thin white band of P&O's livery painted around the hull, with the P&O and Blue Anchor house flags flown on the main and forward masts respectively. The operation was officially branded with its own separate address in London as P&O Branch Line in June 1910.

P&O immediately endowed its new subsidiary ships, as the older Blue Anchor tonnage was sold. The new B-class *Ballarat*, *Beltana*, *Banala*, *Berrima* and *Borda* were delivered for P&O Branch Line between 1911 and 1914. These were a larger improved rendition of their Blue Anchor predecessors, each with cabins for around 300 passengers and portable dormitory accommodations for an additional 750 in 'tween-deck spaces otherwise usable for cargo on return voyages to the UK. With the latter two of these ships, *Berrima* and *Borda*, P&O reverted to the black funnel as with the Line's mail ships. By 1914 P&O was offering the best and most complete services to Australia, using

*The **Macedonia** was built in 1904 for P&O's Australia service. She survived until 1931 when she was scrapped in Japan. Her sister, the **Marmora** was less fortunate, being torpedoed off Ireland in July 1918. (Bruce Peter collection)*

16 ships, none of which was more than 11 years old, with its *India-* and M-class sailing via the Suez Canal and the Branch Line operation by way of the South Atlantic and Cape Town.

P&O depended on various other feeder services to and from its own mail services in much the same way that today's major airlines rely upon various domestic and regional carriers that connect with their long-haul international and intercontinental services through key airport hubs. P&O had maintained a long-standing collaboration with the British India Steam Navigation Company, universally known throughout the Indian Subcontinent and the Orient simply as the B.I.

The B.I. originated as a development from a trading company established in Calcutta during the 1840s by Robert MacKenzie (1814-1853) and William MacKinnon (1823-93). Hailing from Kintyre, Argyll, MacKinnon, has been described as 'a shrewd and dapper, yet colourless and puritanical Highlander.' Returning to Glasgow following MacKenzie's death on 15th May 1853, he used his sharp talent for business to rescue the failing City of Glasgow Bank and to establish the Calcutta and Burmah Steam Navigation Company in 1856. In 1862, this became the British India Steam Navigation Company, being contracted to operate a mail service between Calcutta and Rangoon. Following the opening of the Suez Canal, MacKinnon succeeded in creating a vast commercial empire, centred on the Indian Subcontinent and dominating the sea routes from there to the Persian Gulf, East Africa and the Far East.[28]

Like the Blue Anchor Line, B.I.'s strength was its great ability to operate basic transport at low fares for the masses, rather than endeavouring to compete in the luxury market sector. B.I.'s vast numbers of smaller ships, with absolutely basic low-fare accommodation, carried generations of migrant Indians seeking better lives for themselves and their families in East and South Africa, Burma, Mauritius and Fiji. B.I. also engaged other similar trades for Hong Kong and Chinese migrants travelling to the Malaysian Peninsula and elsewhere. Thanks to its frequent sailings and reliable schedules, B.I. was also regularly contracted by the governments of various nations and territories to provide mail services and the movements of troops as needed.

While B.I.'s ships had a limited amount of comfortable First Class accommodation, the great majority of the Line's clientele travelled as deck, or 'unberthed' passengers, with shelter provided by overhead canvas awnings and side curtains when monsoon rains appeared. Later, they were also accommodated under cover on the shelter decks or below decks aboard larger ships, where portable sleeping platforms were suspended on cables from the deckhead above. The standards of safety and sanitation were relatively high, with wide access stairways to the lower decks and ample ventilation, latrines and bathing facilities. Passengers could travel with or without 'diet' included in the passage fare. Families travelling together used the baggage and belongings they brought aboard to mark their claimed deck space for the voyage, while unberthed women passengers travelling alone were accommodated in a separate enclosed space for their comfort and protection.[29]

The unique character of B.I.'s ships and its services were in many respects complementary to P&O's operations in the Eastern world, extending its reach to places beyond its own route network and serving a broader spectrum of the local and indigenous populations. P&O's Thomas Sutherland and B.I.'s James Lyle Mackay (1862-1932) were like-minded in their business aspirations. While in India, Mackay had also become Sheriff of Calcutta, President of the Chamber of Commerce, and a Commercial Member of the Viceroy's Council and was even considered for the position of Viceroy of India. In 1911, Mackay was created Lord Inchcape of Strathnaver and in 1913, he succeeded to the Chairmanship of B.I. In complete secrecy, one-on-one, he and Sutherland negotiated a takeover of the B.I. Company by P&O with B.I. retaining much of its autonomy under P&O ownership. Both companies were to share the same board of directors meeting consecutively and their marketing, booking and administrative operations in Great Britain were coordinated. The fleets and day-to-day operations of each Line otherwise remained entirely separate.

The City of London was taken completely by surprise when the takeover was announced *fait accompli* at a special general meeting of both Lines' proprietors on 22nd May 1914. Apart from the complete confidentiality in which the takeover was negotiated, the element of surprise had much to do with the fact that British India was less familiar in London as few of its ships ever returned west of Suez after their delivery voyages to India. The fusion of these two great British shipping companies was accomplished by the interchange of stock, without so much as a single ship's funnel colours and markings being altered or one house flag being lowered and replaced by another. The move brought together 64 P&O ships with an average of 7,847 tons and 133 B.I. vessels, averaging 4,934 tons apiece, in the creation of a new enterprise owning 197 ships with a total of 1,158,506 gross register tons.[30]

Sutherland remarked on the takeover:

> 'It means that we command the employment of a capital of 15 million...and this capital and this tonnage will be working with a common aim and purpose for the prosperity of a great national enterprise...in the interest of British commerce throughout our Eastern Empire.'[31]

Sutherland sprang a second complete surprise on his audience that day by announcing his own imminent retirement at the age of 78 years, and the appointment of Lord Inchcape to succeed him as Managing Director in October 1914 and as Chairman in the New Year.

The ***Kaisar-I-Hind*** *of 1914 was a famous liner on P&O's India service. She survived the First World War and was broken up in 1938. (Bruce Peter collection)*

The magnificent three-funnelled ***Naldera*** *was completed in 1920 by Caird & Co of Greenock for P&O's Australia service. (Bruce Peter collection)*

THE FIRST WORLD WAR

Within 24 hours of Great Britain's declaration of war against Germany on 4th August 1914, the first P&O ships were requisitioned by the Admiralty for wartime service. Among the first to be 'called up' were those that since the late 1880s had been built with government subsidies to be readily convertible as armed merchant cruisers to serve the dual role of carrying troops and war materials, and for general patrol and convoy protection duties. P&O, Cunard and other British merchant steamship lines had all reaped the financial benefits of this scheme with the full understanding that these ships would be requisitioned as needed in times of war or other national emergencies. P&O's *Himalaya*, one of the Line's first ships to be built under such subsidy, along with the later M-class *Mantua* and *Macedonia* were the first to be converted and engaged in national service.

The government also had, and readily wielded, the authority to seize other ships as needed. A large number of B.I. ships were quickly requisitioned for wartime service, their unique style of mass passenger accommodation already being ideally suited for bringing 30,000 Indian and Ghurkha troops and their officers to France. The Branch Line's services via Cape Town were curtailed altogether early during the War as its ships were requisitioned by the Australian government for deployment, like those of the B.I., as troop carriers. Each of the five Branch Line ships then was readily adapted to carry between 50 and 70 officers and around 1,500 troops. The *Borda* was converted to accommodate 26 officers, 550 other ranks and 260 horses.

With many of its captains and senior officers being in the Royal Naval Reserve (RNR), P&O has always been willing and able to cooperate in wholeheartedly providing the necessary ships and services to Crown and Country in times of War. Non-RNR P&O crews who continued to serve with their ships during the war did so on a voluntary basis, with the Line making up the difference between their service pay and standard wage and with their regular posts and levels of seniority preserved until their return to peacetime duty after the War. Yet, apart from this, the Line was also left to continue providing contracted mail deliveries and at least a basic level passenger and cargo service on its regular commercial routes, retaining as best it could the sustained patronage and goodwill of its regular passengers and commercial shippers. This had to be accomplished using whatever un-requisitioned tonnage could still be mustered and against considerable increases in operating costs, especially for coal. While passenger numbers were considerably lower, there was a ten-fold increase in the volume of mail, reducing available cargo space and thus any advantage to be gained from the higher freight rates prevailing at that time.[32]

The ***Mongolia*** *of 1923 was a one-class liner for the Australia service. A long-lived vessel, she was only sold by the P&O Group in 1951 and, after serving Incres Line as a cruise ship, she was scrapped in 1965. (Bruce Peter collection)*

Top: The ***Narkunda*** *was the* ***Naldera****'s sister in the Australia service. She continued until 1942 when she was sunk by German bombers, having landed troops at Bougie in Algeria. (Bruce Peter collection)*

Above left: The ***Naldera****'s swimming pool, ingeniously fashioned by her crew through filling a hatch opening with a canvas lining. (Bruce Peter collection)*

Above right: The ***Moldavia*** *of 1922 operated alongside the single-funnelled* ***Mongolia*** *in P&O's one-class Australia service. Unlike her fleet mate, her career was short as she was sold for scrap in 1938. (Bruce Peter collection)*

Left: The ***Naldera*** *at Valetta, Malta in the latter 1920s. (Bruce Peter collection)*

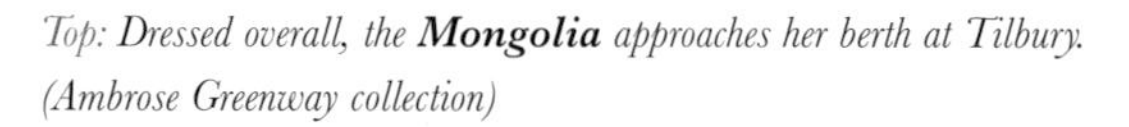

Top: Dressed overall, the ***Mongolia*** *approaches her berth at Tilbury. (Ambrose Greenway collection)*

Above left: The launching of the ***Cathay****, a new liner for P&O's Australia service, at Barclay, Curle's Clyde shipyard in 1924. (A. Ernest Glen)*

Above right: The completed ***Cathay*** *leaves the Clyde on her delivery voyage. As with the* ***Narkunda****, in November 1942, she was sunk by German bombers at Bougie in Algeria. (A. Ernest Glen)*

Right: The P&O cargo liner ***Lahore****, built in 1920, typified freight-carrying members of the fleet in the 1920s. (Bruce Peter collection)*

Line services to India and Australia were considered to be of greatest importance, with the Bombay and Sydney routes being combined to make the most advantageous use of available ships. The routing was from London Tilbury via Suez to Bombay, Colombo and by way of the Torres Strait to Sydney and vice versa, with the new route being taken up by the *Mooltan*, sailing from Tilbury as early as 7th August 1914. Four ships – *Khyber, Karmala, Kashgar* and *Kashmir* – of a new K class 'superior intermediate steamers', intended for service to the Far East and Japan, were deployed for about four round-trip voyages each to Bombay and Sydney from 5th September 1914 until 22nd December 1916 when the *Kashmir* started her first of only two voyages. These helped to maintain a basic service, despite their considerably lower passenger capacities. As ever, more ships were requisitioned later during the war; this operation was by 1915 reduced to a bi-weekly cargo service only as far as Bombay.[33]

In addition to its great array of tonnage that served as armed merchant cruisers, troop transports, stores carriers, depot ships and mine layers, P&O and B.I.'s passenger ships *China, Devanha, Sicilia, Soudan* and *Syria* served as hospital ships throughout the war, providing life-saving medical facilities to the injured at Scapa Flow, Mesopotamia, East Africa and Gallipoli. Also converted as a hospital ship, B.I.'s *Rohilla* suffered the misfortune of being wrecked off the British East Coast near Whitby on 1st November 1914 with the loss of two lives while on her way to Belgium.

In 1917 the *Borda* was requisitioned by the Shipping Controller for additional services and, after the War's conclusion, used to repatriate 900 German women and children from the former German East Africa colony of Dar-es-Salaam. Towards the War's end, the *Kalyan* provided support for the campaign against the Bolsheviks in northern Russia and became mired in ice at Arkhangel'sk through the winter of 1918-19.

Almost half of P&O's fleet was requisitioned immediately after the outbreak of the First World War, that number later peaking at 41 ships, or nearly two thirds of the fleet. Fourteen P&O ships were sunk by enemy submarines and a further three by mines, with 586 crew and civilians losing their lives. A total of 334 deaths occurred aboard the *Persia*, torpedoed 70 miles south of Crete on 30th December 1915 while carrying a large number of passengers. Despite such dangers, P&O played a key role in keeping open the vital lines of supply and communication that are Britain's lifeblood. Addressing the Line's Annual General Meeting a month after the Armistice on 11th December 1918, Lord Inchcape opened with characteristic understatement, saying, 'Ladies and Gentlemen, the old business of the P&O Company for some time past has not been what it was.' He concluded by observing that: 'the old prestige of the P&O Company must and will at all costs be maintained' (Cheers).[34]

REBUILDING

The return of P&O's 'old prestige' was slow, with some requisitioned ships retained in Government service until as late as 1920 to complete various war-related services, such as the repatriation of demobbed military personnel. Time was needed also for tonnage returned to the Line after up to four years of near-constant service to undergo extensive overhaul and reconditioning before being returned to civilian service. The opportunity was taken for some ships to be converted from coal to oil-firing of their boilers, eliminating the filthy and labour-intensive process of coaling and doing away with manual boiler-stoking on board.

As an immediate interim replacement for its wartime losses, P&O bought six standard-design cargo ships out of a class of 196 such vessels built for the Government, along with a further two cargo ships from former German and Austrian tonnage seized as war reparations; these latter vessels were put into P&O service as the *Padua* and *Perim*. Lord Inchcape, who with Sir Owen Philipps of Royal Mail Lines, was given the responsibility of selling the remainder of this tonnage was, however, generally unimpressed by German passenger liners and declined to purchase any of these for P&O's use, though a few were operated on a temporary basis. The Line's first priority was to re-establish essential mail and cargo services on its core routes to India, Australia and the Far East. Many of the freighters used on these routes were fortunately also able to accommodate small numbers of passengers.

P&O had a number of ships in various stages of construction at the War's outbreak, when merchant shipbuilding in Great Britain was halted altogether. The completion of two refrigerated freighters for the Australian general cargo and frozen meat trade was cancelled outright, while that of others was indefinitely postponed. The *Naldera* and *Narkunda*, ordered as larger three-funnelled renditions of the Line's successful M-class liners, were eventually requisitioned on the stocks in 1917. These were first to be completed as armed merchant cruisers, then as jumbo freighters, troop carriers, hospital ships and even aircraft carriers, before the War ended in 1918 and they were returned to P&O. They were fitted out in a by then rather dated style, and still with their original coal-fired boilers, as passenger ships for the Australian and Far Eastern routes they were originally designed to serve.

The *Naldera* and *Narkunda* went into service in January and April 1920 respectively, with the *Naldera* sailing from Tilbury to Bombay and Sydney, and the *Narkunda* first sailing round-trip only to Bombay before making her first voyage to Sydney in July. Until the first post-war C-class ships were completed in the mid-1920s, these were joined by the remaining earlier M-class ships on alternative sailings either direct to Sydney or via Bombay. Two

The ***Ranchi*** *of 1925 was one of three sisters for P&O's Far East service. (Bruce Peter collection)*

additional M-class ships, the *Moldavia* and *Mongolia*, were completed in 1923 as replacements for their 1903 namesakes lost as war casualties, with the class finally being completed in 1923 with the new *Mooltan* and *Maloja*, which were P&O's first ships registered at over 20,000 gross tons. Apart from some refinement to the layout of the latter two ships, with a greater emphasis on single- and double-berth cabins with en-suite toilet facilities, none of these offered anything radically new, but rather a warmly reassuring sense of returning to normality after a terrible period of upheaval, with P&O once again apparently restored to its old prestige.

Meanwhile, P&O Branch Line emigrant services via Cape Town were re-opened mid-1920 using five surviving ships, with new replacement tonnage for these introduced as early as 1921-22 in response to increased emigrant traffic to Australia. Named *Ballarat*, *Baradine*, *Balranald*, *Barrabool* and *Bendigo*, the new vessels had much larger superstructures than their predecessors, enclosing permanent cabins for 490 Third Class passengers in addition to portable accommodations for an additional 680 emigrants on the decks below that could, as in previous emigrant ships, be used for cargo on the homeward voyage from Australia. The permanent accommodation was sufficiently comfortable that these ships actually achieved some degree of popularity with the travelling public.

In 1922, the Australian Government inaugurated its own emigrant services on the same route using similarly appointed Australian-flag ships. For a few years, there was sufficient traffic to support both operations until the trade finally began to wane later in the decade. Those still seeking low-cost travel to Australia by then had the choice of travelling with other lines offering service by way of the shorter route through Suez and, thus, the Branch Line switched its ships to this more direct passage via the Mediterranean with calls at Malta, Port Said, Aden, Colombo, Fremantle, Adelaide, Melbourne and Sydney. At the time this was being done, the B-class ships were converted from coal to oil-firing and had engine exhaust turbines fitted, thereby increasing their speed from 13 to 15 knots, while their accommodations were upgraded to carry 586 passengers, all in permanent berths.[35] The Branch line continued to sail this route, with occasional departures from Liverpool until 1936 when its operations were discontinued altogether.

P&O's post-War fleet rebuilding initiative was completed in 1925 with the intermediate ships, the *Ranpura*, *Rawalpindi*, *Ranchi*, and *Rajputana* for mail and passenger service between London and Bombay. As related by Captain D.G.O. Baillie in his autobiography 'A Sea Affair':

> 'Bombay ships in those days certainly carried a great many interesting and important people: Governors of Presidencies or Provinces of India; Maharajas and their enormous retinues, demanding special accommodation and cooking facilities in accordance with their religious faith; famous figures in politics or society going out to enjoy what was then a fashionable and popular winter pastime of the wealthy – cold weather in India.'[36]

Among those of fame to sail aboard R ships were King Albert and Queen Elizabeth of Belgium, who travelled aboard *Ranpura* in 1925, and Lawrence of Arabia (Thomas Edward Lawrence/Shaw) who, in 1929, made a passage from India to England aboard the *Rajputana*. Later, Mahatma Ghandi sailed from Bombay on 29th August 1931 on his way to join the Round Table Conference on India's future, arriving in Marseilles on 11th September, from where he travelled overland to London. The *Ranchi* was used for

The ***Mooltan*** *of 1923 in the Suez Canal surrounded by palm fronds. (Ambrose Greenway collection)*

*The **Chitral** of 1925 was one of a trio of new liners completed in the mid-1920s for P&O's Australia service. (Ambrose Greenway collection)*

cruising in the late 1920s and the *Rawalpindi* in 1930-31. From the early 1930s onwards, the R ships were transferred to the Far Eastern services from Bombay to China and Japan.

THE VICEROY OF INDIA

The *Cathay*, *Comorin* and *Chitral* followed in 1925 as the first ships entirely designed and built after the First World War for the longer mail and passenger routes to Australia and the Far East. These were in the smaller and more agile size category of the Bombay service R ships. They were of conservative design, however, with quadruple-expansion steam machinery rather than steam turbines. P&O apparently still believed this to be the most reliable approach for ships trading on such long routes and so far from home, where their technologically less sophisticated mechanical workings could more readily be serviced as needs be by their own on-board engineering personnel or with the help of local technical resources from ashore. By the time these ships were built, the performance expected of them was reaching the limits of what could be yielded by the type of machinery they were using.

A slightly larger ship that might otherwise have been the fourth vessel of the C class was ordered with turbo-electric machinery. Lord Inchcape was quick to point out that, rather than being anything experimental or groundbreaking, the new *Viceroy of India* 'would show greater economy than other types of machinery of similar power.'[37] Turbo-electric propulsion, by which steam turbines drive generators to generate electrical power to run motors to turn the propellers, was then quite new but had been already used successfully in American ships. When she made her debut on the London-Bombay service in 1929, the *Viceroy of India* was the first European deep-sea liner to adopt the system. She lived up to her claim of economical operation with lower fuel consumption as well as the need for 20 fewer engine-room ratings than would have been needed aboard ships of a similar size fitted with quadruple-expansion machinery.

So far as the passengers were concerned, the *Viceroy of India*'s quieter and much smoother running was greatly appreciated and very much in line with the luxury of the ship's accommodations and services. Despite the turbulent economic situation at the end of the 1920s, Lord Inchcape believed that there would always be a market for luxurious travel and hospitality, if for no other reason than those still on the move needed a break from the gloom of the place at one end of the journey and the uncertainty of that at the other.

The *Viceroy of India*'s interiors were designed and decorated to what would today be called 'world-class' standards of elegance, luxury and comfort. Her overall layout similar to that of the Royal Mail Line's *Asturias* and *Alcantara* of 1927, with the forward part of her lofty promenade deck likewise arranged with a glass-enclosed veranda surrounding the forward public rooms. Accommodation aboard the *Viceroy of India* was opulent by the standards of her era yet also reflected the specific needs of the India trade, with each of the First Class suites having an attached smaller bedroom for use by an accompanying valet, maid or *ayah*. The remaining First Class accommodations were all single rooms, arranged with connecting doors so that these could be joined for

Top: A rare 1930s colour image of the ***Viceroy of India*** *at Hong Kong. (Bruce Peter collection)*

Middle and above views: The ***Viceroy of India****'s ornate First Class interiors were a late example of the 'floating palace' approach to shipboard design. Each space was in a different grand idiom – ranging from a baronial smoking saloon (centre left) to a Pompeiian swimming pool (centre right), a lounge in the Palladian style (bottom left) and a Louis XV dining room (bottom right). (Bruce Peter collection)*

The stately ***Viceroy of India*** *at Tilbury. (Bruce Peter collection)*

occupancy by couples or added to additional rooms to form larger suites for families or groups travelling together. With a view also to being used for worldwide cruising, she was the first P&O ship to be fitted out with an indoor swimming pool.

Lady Inchcape and her third daughter, The Hon. Elsie Mackay (1893-1928) took an interest in the interior design and decor of the Line's ships. Previously, Elsie had launched the *Maloja* and had a hand in the interior design of the R ships. For the *Viceroy of India*, she was paid a designer's fee out of Lord Inchcape's personal *emoluments* to provide advice on the design and decoration of the liner's interiors. She was a young and fashionable woman of her time, accustomed to the glamour of stage and screen and who took her lead from the latest transatlantic liners to engender a palatial sense of grandeur in the liner's accommodations and widely varied public spaces. Quite the extent of her contribution is unclear, however and it is obvious that the spaces were rather similar to those of other prestigious British liners of the immediately preceding era. In any case, this was Elsie's last work for P&O as sadly she died in 1928 while attempting to be the first woman to fly across the Atlantic Ocean.

The *Viceroy of India* was a one-of-a-kind ship that won immediate popularity from the travelling public, both for her line services to and from Bombay and for her many cruises. During her commercial career, that ran until she was requisitioned for war service as a troopship in 1940, the *Viceroy of India* never sailed in regular service either to Australia or the Far East. In regard to this she was to all intents and purposes a magnificent and influential final addition to the R ships and the P&O service to Bombay.

AFTER THE WALL STREET CRASH

On 29th October 1929, share prices on the New York Stock Exchange collapsed. Their value continued to fall for a whole month afterwards. In the weeks leading up to the crash, the market had been unstable, with repeated waves of stock selling, rallying share prices and then renewed purchasing. By Christmas, there was a partial recovery, followed by a second, more severe decline and a new crash on 8th July 1932, from which the Dow Jones Industrial Average of shares did not fully recover for over 20 years.[38] The Wall Street Crash led to a widespread and catastrophic loss of confidence in the market which left many destitute and brought about a Great Depression.

This situation had a disastrous effect on the shipping world, especially for less efficient companies that were forced to lay up their ships, and in the worst cases ended up declaring bankruptcy. From 1930 onwards, there was a breakdown in international trade, worsening the depression's negative effects, especially in countries whose economies depended on exports. Businesses and individuals consequently defaulted on their loans and this caused banks to collapse, further compounding the problem. Britain – the world's

*The **Strathmore** is seen in the fitting-out basin at Barrow in Furness with Orient Line's **Orion** being completed to the rear. Note that the **Orion** is painted in the old Orient Line black livery and not as delivered with a corn hull and buff funnel. (Barrow Museum)*

leading imperial and maritime power – suffered terribly, unemployment reaching 2.5 million by the end of 1930 (around 20 per cent of the working population). P&O suffered along with the entire shipping sector, the company's credit balance plunging by 75 per cent from its 1924 peak of £281,000 and, with many cargo ships sailing near empty, there could be neither dividends for shareholders nor wage increases for employees.

THE 'STRATHS'

Fortunately, funds were directed to complete the first of a series of innovative new liners for the Line's service to Australia. Building upon the *Viceroy of India*'s great popularity and the satisfactory performance of her turbo-electric propulsion on these vessels, P&O decided to create a fresh outward identity and nomenclature for these new ships, adopting 'Strath' at the beginning of each ship's

*The **Strathaird** (illustrated) and her sister **Strathnaver** introduced a distinctive new look to the P&O fleet; they were the epitome of the tropical ocean liner in the 1930s. (Bruce Peter collection)*

Furniture for the ***Stratheden****'s interiors was supplied by Heal's of London, whose photographer comprehensively recorded her interiors upon completion. As can be seen, these mixed elements of 'streamline moderne' with chintz-upholstered armchairs and curtains. Her ballroom (top right) ingeniously featured folding glazed screens, enabling the space to be opened out to the surrounding promenades during warm tropical evenings. (David Trevor-Jones collection)*

*Part of the **Stratheden**'s smoking saloon, with 'moderne' furniture and fireplace, somewhat in the manner of the BBC's recently completed Broadcasting House in London. (David Trevor-Jones collection)*

Liners making lengthy voyages needed to appeal to broad ranges of passengers with different tastes and moods. This lounge on the ***Stratheden*** *mixes traditional elements of a London gentlemen's club with moderne details and some furniture displaying more of a feminine charm. (David Trevor-Jones collection)*

*The **Strathnaver** and **Strathaird** near completion in the fitting-out basin at Barrow-in-Furness. (Barrow Museum)*

Display cases filled with gifts, souvenirs and travel accessories in the ***Stratheden****'s shopping arcade. (David Trevor-Jones collection)*

name. The first was the *Strathnaver*, named in honour of Lord Inchcape of Strathnaver, a valley north of Loch Naver, and the second was the *Strathaird*, a headland of Skye and honouring the baronetcy of B.I.'s co-founder Sir William MacKinnon of Strathaird and Loup, from whom Inchcape had taken over as Chairman of that company in 1896.

The 'Straths', as these ships were known, were a bold departure from anything P&O had ever previously built, with their massive superstructures and overall white paint scheme, with red boot topping at the waterline and buff coloured funnels and masts, suggesting a sense of youthful energy, speed and beauty. While other P&O ships had been painted white for special roles, such as *Medina*'s service as a Royal Yacht, or for use as troopships and hospital ships, only the *Salsette* had worn white for her regular express line service between Aden and Bombay from 1908 to 1914. This was now adopted as the standard livery for P&O's deep-sea passenger fleet and it became the iconic identity of the modern British tropical liner. In 1930s advertising imagery, the Straths were depicted grandly aloof at anchor in far-flung exotic ports, framed by palm fronds, dockside clutter and picturesque locals in the foreground.

Interior design aboard the 'Straths' drew upon the *Viceroy of India*'s great success, though with a trend towards the more contemporary influences from the 1925 Exposition des Arts Décoratifs et Industriels Modernes in Paris, the event which subsequently gave its name to the 'Art Deco' style. Perhaps most significantly, the public interiors were less formally arranged and had a greater degree of open planning, particularly a blurring of the separation between indoor and outside areas. Folding glazed walls allowed the indoor swimming pool that would otherwise have been located on a lower deck to be given access to sunlight, as well as for a lounge to be arranged so that its dance floor likewise could be merged with an adjacent deck area where passengers could foxtrot under the stars on warm tropical evenings. All of this suited the long tropical passages to India and Australia for which these ships were designed, as well as their secondary uses for cruising in temperate climes.

The 'Straths' boasted a high standard of passenger accommodation, with the first of the series featuring large numbers of single cabins in First Class that could be joined for occupancy by couples, yet both passengers ended up with their own private bathrooms. The vessels also reflected a fundamental change from the old P&O standard of First and Second Class to a more contemporary designation of First and Tourist. In 1928, Second Class on the *Mongolia* and *Moldavia* was initially re-designated as 'Third Cabin' with both ships later being converted to a single Tourist Class with cabin accommodation for 840 passengers each. Designation of the less expensive class aboard the new 'Straths' as 'Tourist' reflected the notion that, rather than being penniless émigrés fleeing to the new world, its clientele were younger people wanting to travel more economically as tourists in less formal surroundings. The reality was that, during the depression, fewer people were willing to pay the higher cost of First Class travel and were quite happy to accept the standards of

The ***Strathallan*** *sinking off Oran after being torpedoed by a German U-boat in December 1942. (Kevin Philips collection)*

Tourist Class on P&O's newer ships.

For P&O the most prestigious 1930s passenger operations belonged to the 'Straths'. These vessels set the standards for the Line's future developments well into the post-Second World War era and, ultimately, the *Canberra*. In the wake of the first *Straths*' success, *Strathmore*, *Stratheden* and *Strathallan* followed between 1935 and 1938. Although of similar size and internal layout, these had a rather more modern appearance, as their less severe superstructure lines sported terraced open deck areas forward, and each having only one funnel instead of the three carried by the first two ships, of which the forward- and aft-most stacks were dummies. As an economy measure, the later three ships were engined with less expensive conventional geared steam turbines.

Following Lord Inchcape's death in 1932, his son-in-law, the Honourable Alexander Shaw (1883-1944), who was to succeed his own father as Baron Craigmyle in 1937, was appointed as P&O's Chairman. He had the difficult task of bringing the Company through the financially troubling Depression and the politically challenging 1930s. During his stewardship, the Company appointed professional auditors, in line with modern business practice of the day, who produced its first Group Consolidated Balance Sheet, showing all that P&O owned and owed. It was from this that the current term 'P&O Group' first came to be used. In 1938, Lord Craigmyle had to resign his position for health reasons and so Sir William Currie (1884-1961) was named as his successor in 1939, bringing to the P&O Chair a very similar background to that of Lord Inchcape. Currie, who came to P&O shortly after Lord Inchcape's death, had likewise built his career in India, becoming a partner of Mackinnon and Mackenzie, P&O's and B.I.'s agents in India. He too served as Sheriff of Calcutta, President of the Bengal Chamber of Commerce, and was a member of the Legislative Council and Council of State. At its highest level, therefore, P&O remained intimately linked to the British imperial project in India – but this phase was rapidly approaching its end.

WAR AGAIN

By the time the remaining 'Straths' were being completed and brought into service, the dark clouds of war were already again gathering over Europe. Benito Mussolini's Italian forces had invaded Abyssinia (Ethiopia) in 1935. In Germany, Adolph Hitler's National Socialist government had withdrawn from the League of Nations and repudiated the Treaty of Versailles with the limitations it imposed on remilitarisation and rearmament of his Third Reich. His army reoccupied the German Rhineland, territory west of the Rhine River that the Treaty had designated as a demilitarised zone. Two years thereafter, Nazi forces invaded Austria and an *Anschluss* (union) was consummated between Europe's two largest German-speaking nations. Meanwhile, in 1936 General Franco was elected as Spain's leader and, through the worst civil war in Spanish history, turned his country into a Fascist dictatorship. At the eastern end of P&O's liner route network, Japan began eight years of undeclared war against China.[39] On 3rd September 1939

The ***Chitral*** *in grey wartime paint while serving as a troop transport. She survived the Second World War and was broken up in 1953. (Ambrose Greenway collection)*

Britain and France declared war against Nazi Germany and its Allies, beginning six years of war in Europe. P&O's role in this conflict was inevitable as its ships, officers and crews were once again 'called up' for military service *en bloc*, rather than in the piecemeal manner as in the First World War.

In 1939 P&O had a modern fleet of 39 ships, the *Rawalpindi* being the first of these to be requisitioned for conversion as an armed merchant cruiser, ten days ahead of the declaration of war on 25th August. She was, coincidentally, one of the Line's early wartime casualties, being fired on and sunk two months later by the German battlecruisers *Gneisenau* and *Scharnhorst* while on North Atlantic patrol southeast of Iceland on 23rd November 1939. In total, 265 of the 302 souls aboard were lost, 54 of whom were former P&O officers and crew.

During the Second World War, P&O ships taken over as armed merchant cruisers steamed an estimated 1.5 to 2 million nautical miles on patrol and convoy-escort duties. Sixteen P&O liners requisitioned as troop carriers, excluding others such as the *Ile de France* and *Pasteur* put under the Line's jurisdiction, sailed some three million miles carrying a million soldiers. In early 1940, the *Strathaird* evacuated women and children from Aden to Bombay. All five of the 'Straths' participated in the Operation Torch invasion of North Africa in 1942. Among the P&O troop transports, *Viceroy of India*, *Cathay*, *Narkunda* and the *Strathallan* were ultimately lost, though fortunately with minimum loss of life.

The greatest amount of tonnage lost was among the Line's cargo ships that served in the essential task of keeping supply and communication lines open to the British Isles. With so many of P&O's larger and faster ships employed as armed merchant cruisers and as troop transports, the Line's cargo fleet continued as best it could to provide the remaining vestige of mail, passenger and freight movements. Casualties among these included the coastal steamer *Eston* and her crew that disappeared without a trace in the North Sea off Blyth in January 1940. They were presumed to have fallen victim to a magnetic mine.

P&O ships participated at Dunkirk, including pleasure vessels owned by various P&O subsidiaries, that crossed back and forth across the English Channel between 27th May and 4th June 1940, ferrying some 335,000 troops and officers home from the beaches of northern France. Later, the *Strathaird* embarked 6,000 troops, civilians including 200 children, along with specie from British banks in Paris at Brest on 17th June, bringing them to Plymouth the following day. On D-Day, the little P&O coastal steamer *Redcar*, that had spent most of the War going about her regular business under constant enemy attempts to sink her, brought troops, tanks and other equipment to Normandy, serving the Juno, Sward and Gold Beach landings and making 20 Channel crossings between D- and VE-Days. She was also the first British merchant ship to call at Antwerp on 28th November 1944 after its liberation.

Of the 123 names of those who died in active service during World War II listed on P&O's Roll of Honour, about 70 lost their

*The **Mooltan** as a hospital ship; she too returned to civilian service at the war's end and was scrapped in 1954. (Ambrose Greenway collection)*

lives while serving aboard the Line's ships. This list excludes those who died in prison camps and elsewhere ashore, as well as the many African, Middle Eastern, Indian and other Asian crew who served in wartime with the same dedication and diligence they brought to their work in regular commercial service and who subsequently made the supreme sacrifice of their own lives. By Easter 1940, B.I.'s entire fleet of 103 ships, that previously had served its 22 regular Middle and Far Eastern routes, was engaged in war operations. They moved troops, livestock, war supplies, munitions and general cargoes and gave refuge to fleeing refugees, displaced persons and the war wounded. Nearly half of B.I.'s ships were lost and the extent of its human losses was no doubt considerably greater.

A NEW ERA

By the time the War was over, great tracts of London and Berlin lay in ruins, while the entire centres of Coventry, Rotterdam and Dresden had been bombed flat. Nagasaki and Hiroshima were devastated by atomic bombs that left many of those they failed to kill outright seriously burned and dreadfully disfigured. For those surviving in Eastern Europe, the War's end meant only that they had been liberated from Fascism merely to live under Communism, as their homelands were annexed as satellites of the Soviet Union. The post-war order in Europe was changed irrevocably, Britain was heavily in debt and America was now the pre-eminent Western military, financial and cultural power. Yet, against this background, the Western World was about to enter one of its most prosperous and enlightened periods, with an expanded middle class of unprecedented affluence and privilege having the disposable income and free time to enrich their lives through, among other things, leisure travel and cruising.

As P&O weighed the options for its own redevelopment and revitalisation, the focus of its services was to be changed by India's independence in 1947, with other possessions of Britain, France and the Netherlands the world over following in pursuit of their own sovereignty. These lands would no longer require the civil service and military personnel of their imperial occupiers that had for so long made up the bulk of the 'carriage trade' of lines such as P&O, Orient Line, Messageries Maritimes and the Rotterdam

*The **Khyber** was an American-built wartime standard Victory cargo ship purchased by P&O at the war's end to help alleviate their shortage of vessels. Here, she is seen passing through the Suez Canal. (Ambrose Greenway collection)*

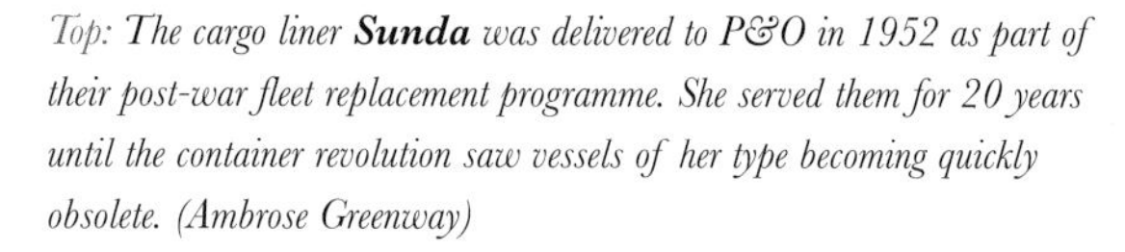

Top: The cargo liner ***Sunda*** *was delivered to P&O in 1952 as part of their post-war fleet replacement programme. She served them for 20 years until the container revolution saw vessels of her type becoming quickly obsolete. (Ambrose Greenway)*

Above left: Another P&O post-war cargo liner, the ***Somali*** *of 1948 was operated by P&O for 21 years. (Ambrose Greenway)*

Above right: The ***Salsette*** *was delivered to P&O in 1956. (Ambrose Greenway)*

Right: A second view of the ***Somali****. (Ambrose Greenway)*

*The **Sunda** arrives in Durban in the early 1970s when the Suez Canal was closed, necessitating the re-routing of P&O's liner routes via the Cape of Good Hope. (Trevor Jones)*

Lloyd. The emerging nations of Pakistan and shortly afterwards Ceylon (now Sri Lanka), Burma (now Myanmar) and Indonesia would be free to build up their own merchant marines and even to compete head-to-head against long-established European liner operators. There was also the inevitable challenge of newfound competition from the stratosphere as long-haul aircraft and air routes, developed out of the vicissitudes of war, would inevitably be adapted for civilian commercial services. Sir William Currie viewed this less as the eventual demise of sea travel, but rather took the more progressive view that each had its place and that 'air and sea can, and should, be complementary.'[40]

P&O's overall approach was to restore their liner services on a regular, though less frequent, basis with fewer but larger and faster ships. Sailing times between London and Bombay were to be reduced to 14 days and, from there, 28 days to Fremantle. There was also to be an increased emphasis on cargo, the part of the liner business least susceptible to being encroached upon by the emerging airline industry. By the early 1950s, First Class airmail was already setting new standards for worldwide postal communication. While regular mail and parcel post continued to be carried by sea, the Post Office was no longer signing long-term contracts with shipping lines.

In 1946 the P&O Group had 71 ships under construction to replace wartime losses, including the cargo vessels *Perim* and *Socotra*, which were completed during the War years. P&O's Hain Steamship Company, an operator of tramping cargo steamers, had lost its entire fleet, for example. Rather than being built as replacements on a ship-for-ship basis, the new buildings were allocated within the Group where needed to fulfil service requirements. These included the S-class general cargo ships *Soudan*, *Surat*, *Somali* and *Shillong* of 1948, followed by the *Singapore* and *Sunda* in 1951, to serve the Far East trades along with the *Cannanore* and *Coromandel* for the Calcutta route. The wartime-built Ellerman's Wilson Line vessel *Empire Paragon* was purchased under the Government's Tonnage Disposal Scheme for the Australian run, trading thereafter as the *Pinjarra*. P&O's cargo fleet was already restored to its pre-War size by the end of 1949.

Jim Davis, who joined P&O in 1952 as a management trainee straight from Cambridge University, and was shortly sent to work in the Calcutta office of their agents Mackinnon and Mackenzie, recalls that the P&O Group's post-war cargo liner new buildings showed little advance over their 1930s predecessors. Furthermore, he observed that 'The 10-12 knot B.I. cargo "liners" made an interesting contrast to their sleek 18-knot counterparts operated by Höegh and Hansa with their advanced cargo gear and cool air-conditioned accommodation.'[41] In the post-colonial era, relatively advanced West German and Scandinavian-owned vessels such as these provided P&O's liner operations with

*The **Corfu** makes a splendid sight as she is manoeuvred by tugs in the port of London in the latter 1950s. A P&O and a Brocklebank cargo liner are berthed to the rear. (Mick Lindsay collection)*

increasingly stiff competition.

Passenger shipping took longer to reinstate. Many requisitioned liners remained in Government service for a number of years following the war for the repatriation of evacuees and troops as well as the transport of war brides and their children to their new homes in Australia, New Zealand and the United States. Having served as armed merchant cruisers and troopers, the liners all needed substantial refitting before returning to commercial service, with this work being subject to delays due to inevitable post-War shortages of materials. The *Stratheden* and *Canton* restarted regular passenger sailings to Australia and the Far East in July and October 1947 respectively, followed in 1948 by the *Mooltan* and *Maloja* in the one-class tourist trade to Australia, while the *Chitral* and *Ranchi* were chartered to the

*The sleek white **Stratheden** in her post-war guise in the early 1950s. (Ambrose Greenway collection)*

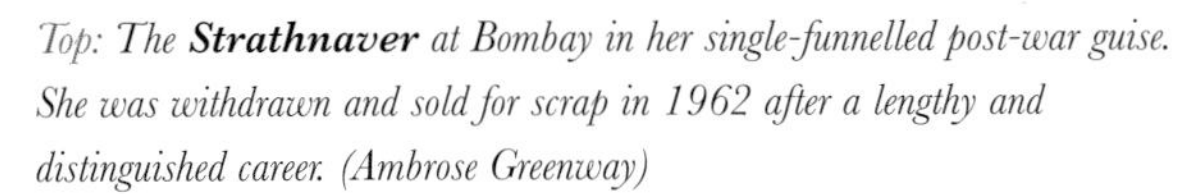

Top: The ***Strathnaver*** *at Bombay in her single-funnelled post-war guise. She was withdrawn and sold for scrap in 1962 after a lengthy and distinguished career. (Ambrose Greenway)*

Above: The ***Carthage*** *at Singapore towards the end of her P&O career; she was sold to Japanese breakers in 1961. (Ambrose Greenway)*

Above right: A 1950s colour image of the ***Stratheden*** *at sea, no doubt photographed from another P&O liner. Captains frequently altered course to enable passengers to enjoy the spectacle of a close-quarters encounter with another of the Line's ships. (Bruce Peter collection)*

Above right: The handsome ***Canton*** *of 1939 served P&O's Far East route briefly before the Second World War and regularly thereafter until withdrawal in 1962. (Ambrose Greenway)*

The launch of the ***Chusan*** *at Barrow-in-Furness on 28th June 1949. (Barrow Museum)*

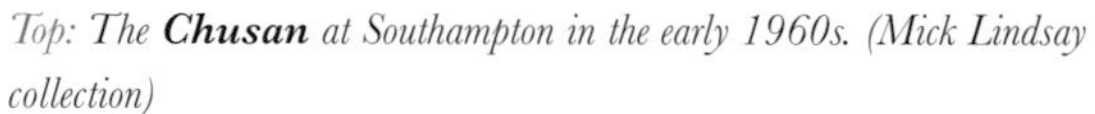

Top: The ***Chusan*** *at Southampton in the early 1960s. (Mick Lindsay collection)*

Above: The ***Chusan*** *in San Francisco Bay towards the end of her P&O career in the early 1970s. (Andrew Kilk)*

Right: Passengers relax in the shade of the ***Chusan****'s promenade deck. (Bruce Peter collection)*

Australian government for emigrant service. Among the last to return to her peacetime role was the *Strathnaver*, which sailed for Sydney in January 1950 with her original three funnels replaced by a single, broader stack amidships, giving her the more modern appearance of the later pre-War 'Straths'.

The early post-War replacement programme included only two passenger ships, the second *Himalaya*, eventually completed in 1949 for service to Australia, and the *Chusan*, delivered in 1950 for the Far East route. These and the subsequent *Arcadia* and *Iberia*, delivered in 1954, were in essence a continuation of the earlier *Strathmore* with added refinements such as fin stabilisers, introduced with the *Chusan*, and progressively extended air-conditioning of the passenger spaces. With these new ships in service, P&O's remaining pre-War passenger ships were for the most part downgraded to all-Tourist Class standards to fill the emigrant trade's needs and for cruising.

As P&O sought to expand and diversify its cargo operations, the Group decided in 1955 to engage in the bulk cargo business as operators of oil tankers. The post-War world was becoming increasingly more dependent on petroleum products needed for growing fleets of commercial ships and aircraft and by the greatly expanding automobile industry. The Group's initial tanker building programme was for 25 ships of two sizes, one batch measuring around 18-19,000 deadweight tons (dwt), the other,

The ***Chusan*** *at anchor in the Grand Harbour at Valetta on Malta. (Bruce Peter collection)*

The ***Chusan*** *at Hong Kong. (Bruce Peter collection)*

approximately 36-37,000 dwt. The first of P&O's new tankers, the *Lincoln*, was completed for its Federal Steam Navigation subsidiary in 1959. By then, unfortunately, the tanker market had collapsed, leaving some four million dwt of tonnage laid up worldwide. Confident that there would be a longer-term need, P&O revised its strategy, opting instead to build 15 larger ships of 47-49,000 dwt, and in view of the specialised nature of the oil trade, to operate them under a separate company, set up in 1962 as Trident Tankers Limited.

The Suez Crisis of October 1956 and subsequent closure of the Suez Canal until April 1957 came as a bitter blow to European liner operators trading to the Middle and Far East as it required the temporary re-routing of vessels via the Cape of Good Hope. The canal's closure followed British and French military action against Egypt, who's nationalist President, Gamal Abdel Nasser, had announced the nationalisation of the strategically important waterway in July 1956. This decision followed Nasser's refusal of American funding to build the Aswan Dam, due to America's support for Israel, and his cultivation of closer diplomatic ties with the Communist Soviet Union and China. Britain and France's failure to win back the canal demonstrated their increasing impotence as global powers and probably hastened the end of the colonialism with which P&O's liner operations had hitherto been associated.

Sydney Harbour with the ***Himalaya*** *at the famous Circular Quay. (Mick Lindsay collection)*

Above left: A four-berth cabin on the ***Chusan****. (Barrow Museum)*

Above: The ***Chusan****'s promenade deck, showing the large windows and patio doors which could be opened on tropical evenings. (Barrow Museum)*

Left: The Australia Room on the ***Himalaya****. (Barrow Museum)*

P&O-ORIENT, ORIANA AND CANBERRA

In 1955, P&O and Orient Line each announced plans for the largest, fastest and most sophisticated passenger liners ever to be built for the Australian and Far Eastern routes, or indeed for any service other than the transatlantic route. With speeds of 27 knots, these would bring the passage times between Britain and Australia down to three weeks. They were also planned with a view towards off-season use in cruising, while their sphere of liner operation extended to the Pacific Rim with the aim of joining the trans-Pacific tourist traffic from America, which the two companies were looking to develop under the Orient & Pacific Lines brand. Owing to the enormous costs of ships such as these, P&O and Orient Line would order one each. Thus, the *Oriana* and *Canberra*, as the vessels were named, would operate in a combined service.

As an alternative mode of transport on its longer routes to Australia and the Far East, P&O had in 1955 briefly investigated the possibility of building a new generation of massive flying boats with the Isle of Wight-based aircraft builder Saunders Roe (later to become British Hovercraft Corporation). The proposed Saunders Roe P192 was, for its time, a massive aircraft with a length of 96.92 metres (318 feet) and a wingspan of 95.4 metres (313 feet). Within, there would be berthed accommodation, including cabins, for as many as 1,100 passengers on five decks

ARCADIA

*The Clyde-built **Arcadia** in the English Channel in the early 1970s, by which time her rear mast had been removed. (FotoFlite)*

*Top: The **Arcadia** dressed overall during a cruise to Alaska in 1970. (Bruce Peter collection)*

*Above left: The **Arcadia**'s First Class lounge, showing the ornate carpet supplied by Templeton's of Glasgow, who commissioned the photograph. (Bruce Peter collection)*

*Above right: The First Class library on the **Arcadia**, again showing a carpet by Templeton's. (Bruce Peter collection)*

*The Harland & Wolff-built **Iberia** of 1954 was a handsome liner, but she was rather heavier than expected and, being consequently expensive to operate, so she was sold for scrap in 1973, aged only 19. (Bruce Peter collection)*

*The **Himalaya** sails under Sydney's famous Harbour Bridge. (Ambrose Greenway)*

and the cruising speed was 389 knots at an altitude of 10,000 metres (35,000 feet). It was to be powered by 24 Rolls Royce Conway jet engines, housed completely within its vast wings and working through blister openings in the leading and trailing edges of the wings.[42] Larger even than today's Airbus A380, this ultimately unrealised behemoth of the skies would then have had to take off from, and land on, water, though it would have flown a predominantly overland route between Great Britain and

*The **Iberia** at Southampton in 1973 minus the majority of her lifeboats voyage at the commencement of her delivery voyage to Taiwanese ship breakers. (Mick Lindsay collection)*

*The **Arcadia** as featured in a 1960s publicity still; frequently, P&O's white liners were pictured in tropical settings, framed by palm trees with the modernity of the ship and the picturesque setting powerfully suggesting the thought of 'getting away from it all' to potential passengers. (Bruce Peter collection)*

Australia in about two-and-a-half days each way. Progress has since brought the considerably faster Boeing 747 and Airbus A380 long-range jetliners into successful fruition as today's principal passenger carriers on this lengthy route.

As early as December 1918, P&O had already acquired a 51 per cent interest in Orient Line, its partners in the Australia mail contract, of which half was held by Lord Inchcape's firm of Gray, Dawes & Co.[43] Orient retained its own identity and much of its autonomy in an arrangement that, in effect, turned a rivalry of 40 years between the two companies into a functional partnership with a rationalisation and coordination of operations that ultimately benefited both. A tangible expression of likeness between the two companies became apparent in the appearance of their passenger fleets, where P&O's first 'Straths' and Orient Line's *Orion* and *Orcades* showing an overall likeness of form while still retaining each Line's individuality in livery, interior design and

*The John Brown shipyard at Clydebank, which built the **Arcadia**, made this submission to P&O when tendering to build the **Canberra**. An engineer's solution, rather than an aesthetic one, the **Arcadia**'s funnel has simply been glued to the rendering. (Bruce Peter collection)*

*The **Chusan** in South African waters during the 1967-75 Suez closure. (Trevor Jones)*

various structural details. Both Orient Line and P&O maintained their own fairly extensive design and technical departments which, in the post-War era, were headed by Charles F. Morris and Arthur Temple respectively. Orient's second *Orcades*, *Oronsay* and *Orsova* differed externally from their P&O counterparts *Himalaya*, *Chusan*, *Arcadia* and *Iberia* in the distinctive profiles of their superstructures. On the Orient vessels, the navigating bridge formed part of a central structure at the base of each ship's single midships funnel, whereas P&O's liners represented a continuation of their pre-War 'Strath' series.

Colloquially dubbed the *Orbustus* (for it shall 'make *or-bust-us*') and the *Strathmost* in Company circles, design of the *Oriana* and *Canberra* was done independently by the two Lines, though obviously with a degree of collaboration, and certainly the knowledge by each of what the other was doing. At a measure of 40-45,000 tons apiece and each with space for 2,000 passengers, these were designed with aluminium superstructures enclosing one more accommodation deck than would otherwise have been possible with all-steel construction. The *Oriana*, developed essentially as a larger rendition of Orient Line's existing post-war tonnage, was to emerge with a towering stepped superstructure, her navigating bridge closely grouped with her midships-located funnel and air-conditioning plant.

*The **Canberra**'s First Class Meridian Room. (Bruce Peter collection)*

Work being done on P&O's new liner *Canberra* caught the attention of John West (1927-2003), an eager young naval architect at that time working on the planning of P&O's early tankers *Maloja* and *Mantua*. Troubled that initial plans for the Line's new flagship appeared to be merely a larger 'Strath', he felt that passengers were a no less specialised cargo than crude oil and that they too should be carried aboard vessels that would accord them pride of place in uninterrupted spaces amidships with the propelling and auxiliary machinery and other services concentrated aft in tanker style and, thus, out of their way. In his own free time, West prepared an alternative design for the new P&O liner, based to some degree on the smaller aft-engined Shaw Savill liner *Southern Cross*, completed in 1955. At over twice the size of *Southern Cross* and requiring four times the propulsion power to achieve the necessary additional six-and-a-half knots of

CANBERRA

*Left: The **Canberra** shows her graceful lines as she speeds through the English Channel. (FotoFlite)*

*Top: Much later in her career, the **Canberra** arrives at San Francisco in the mid-1980s during a world cruise. (Andrew Kilk)*

*Middle: A side-on view of the **Canberra** off San Francisco, showing her well-resolved superstructure detailing and her instantly recognisable silhouette. (Andrew Kilk)*

*Above: Arriving at San Francisco on her maiden voyage, the **Canberra** receives the traditional welcome of a display of water-jets from a fire-fighting launch. (Bruce Peter collection)*

TAKE CARE
IF DIVING

*The panoramic view of the **Canberra**'s First Class Bonito Pool – a feature only made possible thanks to her aft-located machinery. (Bruce Peter collection)*

*The **Canberra's** dramatic spiral First Class stairs, as viewed from the Meridian Room. (Philip Dawson)*

*Dancing in the **Canberra's** Tourist Class Island Room. (Bruce Peter collection)*

speed, she could be no mere copy of the earlier ship.

Turbo-electric propulsion, with its inherent flexibility of the driving link between the steam turbines and the propellers being electrical rather than mechanical, was a key element of being able to achieve a satisfactorily compact aft-located machinery arrangement within the *Canberra*'s hull, with the boilers and steam turbo-alternator situated above the propeller shafts, astern of the drive motors. The *Canberra*'s distinctive slender twin side-by-side funnels specifically owed their origin to John West's involvement with P&O's tanker building programmes. The *Talamba*, a tanker originally in the 36-37,000 dwt category and to have been delivered to B.I. in 1961 but enlarged and completed in 1964 for service under Trident's management, provided the example of these elegant smokestacks that he had in mind for the *Canberra*'s crisply futuristic lines.

With her entire above-the-waterline mid-body free from the usual shipboard obstructions of funnel uptakes, engine room access hatches, ventilation shafts and other such working necessities, the *Canberra*'s interiors were designed as remarkable open-plan, inter-connected sequences of public spaces. Atop the superstructure, there were equally spectacular and spacious outdoor decks for recreation and sports, swimming, sunbathing and dancing under the stars, none of which would have been possible on a vessel with machinery amidships. Despite the care taken with her design calculations, the Canberra turned out to be about 500 tons overweight astern, resulting in some non-essential fittings being removed aft and concrete ballast added in her forward hull compartments. The resulting increase in draft and a slight degradation of speed were in time largely forgotten, though the ship had to land her passengers by tender at some ports where the *Oriana* could berth alongside.

Although the *Oriana* was more conventionally arranged, with her nonetheless ample amount of open deck space terraced at various levels forward and aft, the concentration of her machinery into a relatively compact installation amidships conveniently coincided with the vertical division amidships between her First

*The launching of the **Oriana** at Barrow-in-Furness on 3rd November 1959. (Barrow Museum)*

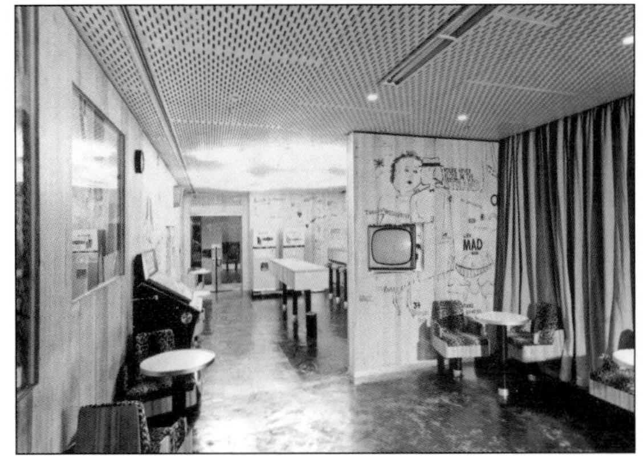

*Top: An impressive view of the **Canberra** at speed. (Mick Lindsay collection)*

*Left: A First Class cabin on the **Oriana** designed by Sir Misha Black of Design Research Unit. (Bruce Peter collection)*

*Above: The **Canberra**'s Pop-Inn, featuring 'graffiti' murals by David Hockney. These were burned into the veneer panelling using a soldering iron. Fearing a ship-wide outbreak of similar graffiti, P&O had the murals panelled over after only a single voyage. (Bruce Peter collection)*

Top: The ***Oriana*** *leaves San Francisco in evening light during the 1970s. (Andrew Kilk)*

Above: The ***Oriana****'s Assembly Room, designed by Ward & Austin with decorative panels by David Gentleman. (Bruce Peter collection)*

Right: The Tourist Class Midships Bar on the ***Oriana****, also designed by Ward & Austin. (Bruce Peter collection)*

*The **Oriana**'s elegant First Class Princess Lounge, featuring murals by John Piper. (Bruce Peter collection)*

and Tourist Class accommodation. Thus, her public spaces fore and aft of the boiler and engine uptakes were also largely unobstructed by technically determined compromises.

Both ships featured fully nested arrangements of their lifeboats above wide-open promenade decks at the bases of their superstructures. This solution was an effective means of lowering the considerable weight of the boats themselves, along with their davits and handling equipment. The *Canberra* in particular, with her main public rooms also at this lower level, made an especially attractive and functional use of this arrangement. Indeed, it has subsequently become virtually standard practice in the design of today's cruise ships, on which it is mandated by current safety rules. From the time of her planning, the *Canberra* became known as 'the ship that shapes the future' and, upon completion, she was generally regarded as being ten years ahead of her time. Indeed she very soon influenced the Italian-built liners *Oceanic* and *Eugenio C.*, completed in the mid-1960s.

High profile British modern movement architects, designers and artists were commissioned for the interiors of both ships, with the *Oriana* being handled by Professor Misha Black's firm Design Research Unit (DRU) in collaboration with Brian O'Rorke, who had served as Orient Line's own house architect ever since his trendsetting work on their *Orion* in the 1930s. Meanwhile, Sir

*The **Oriana**'s funnel, viewed from her bridge wing. (Bruce Peter collection)*

ORIANA

*The **Oriana** off the Isle of Wight with a couple of lifeboats swung out, perhaps for a crew boat drill. (FotoFlite)*

The launch of the ***Oronsay*** *at Barrow-in-Furness on 30th June 1950. (Barrow Museum)*

Top: Orient Line's first post-war liner, the ***Orcades*** *is launched at Barrow-in-Furness on 14th October 1947. (Barrow Museum)*

Left: The ***Orsova*** *takes to the water at Barrow on 14th May 1953. (Barrow Museum)*

Left: The ***Orcades*** *on the stocks at Barrow, shortly before her launching. (Barrow Museum)*

Top: The ***Orcades*** *in her P&O white livery during a cruise in the latter 1960s. She was broken up in Taiwan in 1973. (Mick Lindsay collection)*

Right: The white-painted ***Oronsay*** *at San Francisco in the early 1970s. She too was broken up in Taiwan, two years after the* ***Orcades****. (Andrew Kilk)*

Below right: The ***Orsova****'s Verandah Bar by Brian O'Rorke typifies the understated contemporary design found on Orient Line's ships. (Bruce Peter collection)*

Below: The ***Orcades*** *at Tilbury prior to one of her sailings to Australia in the late 1960s. (Miles Cowsill)*

The ***Stratheden*** *on passage from Tilbury. (FotoFlite)*

Hugh Casson's Casson Conder Partnership was given responsibility for the *Canberra*'s interiors, along with collaborating architects John Wright and Barbara Oakley. Hugh Casson, Misha Black and James Gardner, who later styled the *QE2*'s exterior for Cunard, were the three principal coordinating architects chosen for the Festival of Britain in 1951, whose work there was later to greatly influence modern British architectural and industrial design through the 1950s and 1960s.

As the *Canberra* and *Oriana* were being built, P&O finally acquired the then still outstanding 46 per cent minority share of the Orient Steam Navigation Company, with management and operation of the existing passenger and cargo fleets of both Lines, including Orient's single tanker *Garonne*, combined under a new subsidiary of P&O, P&O-Orient Lines. Jim Davis, who, by the early 1960s had been promoted as P&O Lines' Global Marketing Director, recalls:

> 'As the new Orient Line flagship *Oriana* was nearing completion at Vickers Armstrongs, Barrow, it became clear that the Orient Board were going to find it hard to raise the money necessary to make the final payment... The solution proposed by Sir Donald Anderson and the P&O board was to buy out the outstanding Orient shares for a generous sum and simply merge the companies. It proved pretty shattering for the P&O staff. With the introduction of *Oriana*, the Orient fleet consisted of only six passenger ships against the circa seventy passenger and cargo liners of P&O. This notwithstanding, no fewer than ten Orient directors and general managers, plus a mass of departmental heads and technical staff were retained by the joint company, leading to a reporting structure that was seriously top-heavy. These men came in at the top level and, in many instances, above the heads of people like myself who had worked our way upwards though the managerial ranks... The arrival on the scene of a mass of reasonably agreeable but very different and sometimes not very competent or experienced directors and managers of the small Orient Line completely changed the working environment at P&O HQ and ruined my promotion prospects. The only major visible change, apart from overcrowding on the management floor, was the decision to paint the previously corn-coloured hulls of the Orient ships in P&O white. Even this decision was long-delayed and fussed over.'[44]

The consequently enlarged fleet was eventually rationalised with older ships of both Lines being withdrawn and scrapped. The Compagnie Maritime Belge's then-redundant Congo-service cargo-passenger ships *Baudouinville* and *Jadotville* were acquired in 1961 and renamed *Cathay* and *Chitral* respectively for the Far East trade.

P&O-Orient Lines' two new superliners made their debuts to great acclaim, the *Oriana* sailing on her maiden voyage to Sydney on 3rd December 1960, followed by the *Canberra* on 2nd June 1961. As the *Canberra* approached Port Said six days later, she encountered the *Strathaird*, P&O's oldest ship, on the way home at the end of her last voyage. The *Strathaird*'s master, Captain A.E. Clay, hailed his venerable ship's younger sister with the words: 'You look magnificent and all in *Strathaird* wish you a happy and successful voyage, and from the old to the new, *Strathaird* bids you farewell.' From the *Canberra*'s streamlined aluminium bridge, Captain Geoffrey Wild replied with: 'You too look magnificent with your paying off pennant flying gaily. You look a gracious and not too elderly lady. All well here.'[45] Although the *Canberra* and *Oriana* proved to be enduringly popular and successful, alas for P&O, all was far from well with its core liner operations.

ORSOVA

*The **Orsova** in the spectacular setting of the harbour at Santa Cruz de Tenerife in the Canary Islands in the early 1970s. Not long after, she was sent for scrap in Taiwan in 1974, yet another P&O victim of the Oil Crisis and the ongoing rationalisation of shipping activities. (Mick Lindsay collection)*

Chapter 4

Decades of Revolution

The 1960s was a revolutionary decade in terms of popular culture – and it was equally revolutionary in the shipping world. Indeed, the rate of technological and cultural change was unprecedented since the age of steam in the mid-Victorian era. P&O entered the decade with the world's most comprehensive network of liner routes – but so-called 'break bulk' general cargo and passenger liners were woefully inefficient. A conventional general cargo liner spent about half of her time in port, while the average crane could handle only between two and five tons. A nine-man gang of stevedores could shift around eight tons of cargo per hour with 20 per cent of their time spent resting. Therefore, harbour expenses accounted for 70 per cent of ships' operating costs (harbour dues alone for a 'Strath' liner cost on average £2,000 a day in the late 1950s). Due mainly to rapidly increasing operating costs, P&O's profits declined markedly from £17.6 million in 1957 to a mere £600,000 in 1961. Tough competition from 'flag of convenience' vessels registered in Liberia and Panama made matters worse. Of P&O's various ship-operating subsidiaries, only its Trident Tankers division and the new passenger liners *Canberra* and *Oriana* were contributing a satisfactory profit.[46]

In 1960, P&O's Deputy Chairman, Sir Donald Forsyth Anderson (1906-73), succeeded Sir William Currie in the Chair and, during his decade-long tenure, he steered the Company through turbulent waters, ensuring that they were early adaptors of the new ship types necessary to become more competitive in the future – very large oil tankers, bulk carriers, container vessels, cruise ships and roll-on/roll-off ferries.

The increased use of oil and gas for heating, transport and petro-chemicals led to an exponential increase in the size of oil tankers. The importance of Middle East oil to Europe and North America in particular, gave shipowners involved in the oil trade significant profit potential. The 65,972 dwt *Orama* was the first ship actually built for Trident Tankers in 1964. Two sister ships, the *Opawa* and *Orissa*, were delivered in 1965, plus the larger *Ottawa*

The British India passenger and general cargo liner ***Dara*** *was one of four employed between the Indian Subcontinent and the Persian Gulf, carrying mainly migrant workers. In April 1961, a terrorist bomb set fire to the vessel, killing 238 of her passengers and crew. This event was indicative of an increasingly unstable political situation in parts of the Middle East. (Bruce Peter collection)*

late in 1964. The Trident venture culminated with the four *Ard*-class tankers of over 200,000 dwt. The supertankers *Ardtaraig*, *Ardshiel*, *Ardlui* and *Ardvar* were built to respond to Gulf-Europe trade via the Cape of Good Hope following the Suez Canal's second closure after the Arab-Israeli Six Day War in 1967 when it was blockaded by Egypt until 1973 and finally cleared and reopened to commercial navigation in 1975. The Trident fleet was later transferred to the new P&O Bulk Shipping division in 1971.

A similar phenomenon occurred in the bulk trades. Where iron ore or grain had hitherto usually been carried inefficiently in general cargo liners or in ore carriers of moderate size, large specialist tonnage of unprecedented size set a new standard for these cargoes. One reason for this was that the relatively high grade ores mined in Europe and North America, upon which the world's steel industries had been founded were running out and so, elsewhere in the world, vast new deposits of lower grade ores needed to be transported in quantity to the industrialised

Trident Tankers' ***Talamba*** *displays the obvious similarity in the design and location of her funnels to the passenger liner* ***Canberra****. The development by P&O of a tanker fleet represented an important change in direction for the Company. (FotoFlite)*

Top: Many of the P&O Group's cargo ships sailed in the liveries of subsidiary companies. Here, the Hain-operated ***Treloske*** *is seen in the St Lawrence off Quebec in the early 1960s. (Mick Lindsay collection)*

Above: The New Zealand Shipping Company's ***Hauraki*** *is manoeuvred by tugs in the Port of London. (Mick Lindsay collection)*

Right: New Zealand Shipping Company's ***Ruahine****, berthed ahead of a Shaw Savill liner in the Port of London. (Mick Lindsay collection)*

British India's ***Pundua****, one of a substantial fleet of relatively slow and old fashioned cargo vessels in the fleet. (Mick Lindsay collection)*

nations.[47] In 1964 P&O merged two cargo liner subsidiaries, Hain Steamship Company and James Nourse, using the name Hain-Nourse, to be responsible for the Group's bulk carrier programme. Simultaneously, they entered an agreement with the bulk shipping specialists Anglo Norness Shipping to market these ships through a joint venture, Associated Bulk Carriers (ABC), registered in Bermuda.[48] Four 43,000-dust bulk carriers were delivered to P&O Group companies in 1965-6 and named after British foxhunts – *Atherstone*, *Buccleuch*, *Cotswold* and *Dulhallow*. They were followed by three 73,000-dust ore/bulk/oil carriers, designed to be able to switch between bulk cargoes depending on market requirements, but managed by Trident Tankers because they were initially employed carrying oil. In these ships, the revolutions were of size and volume, leading to far greater economies of scale than in the recent past.

THE CONTAINER REVOLUTION

Meanwhile, the carriage of general cargo underwent a similar revolution. Although developments in the design of cargo liners between the end of the Second World War and the mid 1960s improved efficiency through more productive cargo handling – for example, the use of electric cranes or forklift trucks to speed up loading and unloading – and in terms of the performance of diesel engines and the introduction of automation, the cargo liner remained an inefficient ship type. One reason was that they carried goods of all kinds, from bulk cargoes like grain to pieces of heavy engineering as well as smaller items, manhandled by teams of stevedores. Merely unloading and loading such vessels was costly in terms of taxes and both ship- and shore-based labour (cargo liners had large crews and ports employed large numbers to heave and haul). A further disadvantage was that goods were

The Strick Line's modern ***Floristan*** *representing the final generation of P&O Group general cargo ships. (Mick Lindsay collection)*

The P&O Line-liveried ***Stathconnon****, one of three Japanese-built 'Super Straths' for worldwide service. (Bruce Peter collection)*

The 1956-vintage general cargo cargo liner ***Salmara****, a vessel of obsolescent design for her year of construction with a split superstructure and turned out in P&O's traditional black and white freighter livery. (FotoFlite)*

prone to damage and more valuable cargoes suffered pilferage. Therefore, faster and more secure ways of shipping general cargo were sought.[49]

Nevertheless, in the mid 1960s P&O ordered three general cargo liners for its worldwide service that were among the finest and fastest of their kind. The 12,539-ton, 24.45-knot *Strathardle*, *Strathbrora* and *Strathconon* were delivered in 1967 from Mitsui Zosen at Tamano in Japan to operate a 90-day circumnavigation, running non-stop between Northern Europe and Japan. That such impressive-looking vessels, known as 'Super Straths', were Japanese-built was indicative of the shifting of shipbuilding expertise from Britain to newer and more efficient South East Asian yards during the post-war decades. Although P&O traditionally was loyal to British shipbuilders, by the latter 1960s, the cost differentials between ordering from British yards and those elsewhere could no longer be ignored. The service was an instant but brief success and was implemented via an intensive marketing plan. Jim Davis recalls that:

'We encouraged an energetic team in Japan who regularly visited and assisted importers as well as shippers. The same applied to Europe, where our previous agents, the slightly sleepy P&O subsidiary General Steam Navigation, were

Operated by the P&O-owned Federal Line, the ***Taupo*** *was one of a series of modern refrigerated cargo liners bringing meat from New Zealand. (Mick Lindsay collection)*

The ***Dorset*** *was typical of Federal Line cargo vessels of the post-war era. (Mick Lindsay collection)*

replaced in Germany by Mareschiffahrtskontor, a new company set up by us with Wolfgang Buschorn as its excellent and fearsomely aggressive and efficient boss. Things were going swimmingly with our "Strath" service until we were struck with the hammer-blow of a second closure of the Suez Canal. We surely could not maintain our 90-day schedule if we had to route via the Cape until it occurred that the solution was to route via Panama. "If the front door is shut then go round the back.'"[50]

State-of-the art though they were when first delivered, the three 'Super Straths' lasted only 12 years in the P&O fleet – a sure sign of how profoundly and quickly liner shipping was transformed by the container revolution.

In liner shipping, containerisation provided a welcome solution to the problems of security, speed of loading and inter-modal transfer of general cargo. Rather than being shipped loose, or in crates and boxes of various shapes and sizes, stacked by hand in the 'tween decks, the introduction of metal boxes of standard sizes which could be transferred quickly from factory to rail or road modes and directly onto ships proved highly advantageous. Indeed, it is arguable that what we call 'globalisation' – the worldwide transfer of the production and consumption of consumer goods and services – is in fact a direct result of containerisation as the manufacture of high-value goods could be outsourced and businesses could more cheaply and efficiently bring their products securely to wider markets than ever before.

Although there had been experiments with containers in Denmark, Germany, Canada and America, it is the American truck owner Malcolm P. McLean (1913-2001), whose business was based in North Carolina, who is credited with inventing the modern shipping container. In 1955, he purchased the Pan-Atlantic Steamship Company, based in Mobile, Alabama. McLean then ordered a series of five ro-ro freighters from Bethlehem Steel plus two standard T2 tankers, which were sent to Bethlehem Steel for conversion so as to be able to carry containers on new raised spar decks forward and aft of their midships officers' accommodation and wheelhouse. These entered service in the spring of 1956, the *Ideal X* being the first to sail from Port Newark, New Jersey, on 26th April bound for Houston in Texas. Each could carry 58 containers, all attached directly to the spar deck (they were never stacked). The service was marketed as Sea-Land.

Next, McLean developed and patented cube-shaped corner castings with 'eyes' on his containers' three outward-facing sides, into which twist-locks could be inserted, enabling containers to be stacked and fastened into solid vertical structures. Thereafter, the American Standards Association proposed in 1958 that containers should be built to lengths of up to 40 feet, divisible by ten and this was agreed by the International Standards Organisation. Thus, 20- and 40-foot containers, known as TEUs (Twenty-foot Equivalent Units) became almost standard throughout the rapidly growing industry, American operators being the ones most likely

Representing a necessary revolution in cargo handling, the 'first generation' container ship ***Discovery Bay*** *was one of a series operating in OCL consortium service between Europe and the Far East from the latter 1960s onwards. (Bruce Peter collection)*

to want to be different. As railway flatbed wagons and lorry trailers were built to match, inter-modal transport became highly efficient and also relatively secure. With the container revolution, time in port declined to 10 per cent and handling costs dropped to below 1 per cent of the cargo's value; the number of port workers employed, meanwhile, fell by 75 per cent. It is thanks to the container that nowadays we can buy seemingly anything anywhere and at any time of the year.[51]

In the mid 1960s, P&O joined the container revolution. Being far more substantial and technically sophisticated than even the most up-to-date general cargo liners, container ships were costly investments. So, in order to spread risk, established liner operators joined forces to form consortia jointly to procure and operate container ships of standard designs. In many respects, this was merely a continuation of the well-established liner conference system whereby shipping lines operating between Europe and the wider world collaborated to fix prices and share port infrastructure.

In 1965, P&O joined forces with three other leading British liner owners involved in the UK-Far East-Australia trade – Alfred Holt, British and Commonwealth and Furness Withy – to form Overseas Containers Ltd (OCL), dedicated to containerising the

The ***Liverpool Bay*** *was one of a second batch of larger OCL-operated container ships. (Bruce Peter collection)*

Displaying design elements of ***Oriana*** *and* ***Canberra****, the Union Steamship Company's New Zealand inter-island ferry* ***Wahine*** *was among the biggest and best appointed of her type in the mid-1960s. Unfortunately, her career was cut short by a severe grounding and capsizing only a short time after entering service. (Matthew Murtland collection)*

partners' break-bulk services over the next two decades. OCL's first Chairman, Sir Andrew Crichton, was a member of the P&O Board, and initially its London headquarters was in Bevis Marks. As well as commissioning a new fleet of six 26,800-ton container ships, each with a capacity of 1,900 20-foot TEUs, OCL required also to arrange new container terminal infrastructure with associated road and rail transport. In addition, a standardised electronic management system called CAMEL was developed to track each OCL container's movement around the globe.

Initially, conventional cargo liners operated OCL's services pending delivery of the new fleet of container ships in 1968-69. Howaldtswerke Deutsche Werft (HDW) in Hamburg, West Germany, built five of these vessels – the *Moreton Bay*, *Botany Bay*, *Discovery Bay*, *Flinders Bay* and *Encounter Bay* – while a sixth, the *Jervis Bay*, was ordered from Fairfields (Glasgow) Ltd. To obtain the high service speed expected of such vessels, diesel propulsion would have required multiple engines and so OCL's initial vessels were steam turbine-powered single screw vessels, capable of maintaining a 21.5-knot service speed. Each could carry 1,500 containers.

The first OCL sailing by *Encounter Bay* left Rotterdam (in place of strike-bound Tilbury) in March 1969. The Australia and Japan service was converted in 1971 and Far East route in 1972 when the first of the 2,500 TEU 'Liverpool Bay' class was delivered. This consisted of the *Liverpool Bay*, *Jervis Bay*, *Cardigan Bay*, *Kowloon Bay*, *Tokyo Bay* and *Osaka Bay*. Also turbine-powered, these were twin-screw vessels, capable of maintaining an impressive 26-knot service speed. Operating an express service between Europe and the Far East via the Panama Canal (due to the Suez Canal being closed following war between Egypt and Israel) and therefore being dimensioned to fit the canal's locks, these so-called 'Panamax' vessels were actually of similar dimensions to the high-speed American transatlantic liner *United States* (they measured 290 by 32.3 metres). They were, however, neither as fast, nor as greedy on fuel, as their American container ship contemporaries, the *Sea-Land Maclean* and her seven sisters, which sailed at 30 knots, guzzling 614 tons per day (the 'Liverpool Bay' class consumed a mere 370 tons). This notwithstanding, as fuel prices grew exponentially during the 1970s and as more powerful, yet economical, diesel engines became available, OCL's entire container fleet was re-engined as motor ships in 1980. (Incidentally, OCL's main rival in the Europe-Far East container trade was the ScanDutch consortium, whose Danish- and Swedish-owned vessels were from the outset diesel-driven while their Netherlands-flagged fleet mates were turbine ships.)

ENTERING THE FERRY SCENE

P&O's management was equally determined that the Company should become involved in the operation of ro-ro ferries. It was through its subsidiaries, the Union Steam Ship Company of New Zealand (over which they had acquired control in 1917) and the General Steam Navigation Company (purchased in 1920), that they first began operating ferries. Not only did the Union Steam Ship Company control an international network of liner routes from New Zealand, but also a 14-hour overnight packet service linking its North and South Islands from Wellington to Lyttelton across the treacherous Cook Strait.

It was for operation on this route that in 1965 the P&O Group took delivery of its first ro-ro ferry, the 9,110-ton *Wahine*. Built by the Fairfield Shipbuilding & Engineering Company in Glasgow, upon delivery she was one of the largest and best-appointed vessels of her kind. Her stern-loading vehicle deck, which was capable of accommodating up to 200 cars, was arranged with a double-height aft section for commercial vehicles

Normandy Ferries' ***Dragon*** *operated a successful Anglo-French ferry service between Southampton and Le Havre. (Bruce Peter collection)*

and so-called 'Seafreighter' trailers. (These were tarpaulin-covered pallets mounted on wheeled trailers, which were towed aboard by special tractors.) As with P&O's passenger liner *Oriana*, her bridge and funnel were grouped together just forward of amidships, with the radar mast ahead of the bridge; this arrangement gave her officers better protection from mountainous head seas. Most unusually for a ferry, the *Wahine* was, like the *Canberra*, a turbo-electric vessel.[52]

Operating opposite the smaller *Maori*, which was rebuilt as a stern-loading ferry in 1965, the *Wahine* should have been a great success. Most unfortunately, while attempting to enter Wellington Harbour at the end of an exceptionally stormy crossing of the Cook Strait in April 1968, she ran aground on Barrett's Reef and was severely holed. Because conditions were so bad, the passengers stayed on board awaiting rescue. Eight hours later, the weather had worsened and the stricken *Wahine* capsized, ending up on her side, half submerged. In the tragedy, 53 lives were lost and, within weeks, further storms caused the wreck to break into three sections. The Union Steamship Company's inter-island service in New Zealand never fully recovered from the *Wahine*'s loss. A replacement, the *Rangatira*, was ordered for delivery in 1972. In the interim, however, P&O sold the Union Steam Ship Company to New Zealand and Australian interests at the end of 1971 and, thereafter, the inter-island ferry service was closed down altogether in 1976.

In contrast, P&O's other early ro-ro ferry venture, which involved its General Steam Navigation Company offshoot, was from the outset an outstanding and enduring success. Hitherto, General Steam Navigation's routes connected London with the near continent, carrying mainly general cargo. In 1964, they joined forces with a number of similar German, Dutch and British operators of small North Sea cargo vessels – Reederei Richard Adler & Söhne of Bremen, Phs. Van Ommeren of Rotterdam, Hollandsche Stoomboot Maatschappij of Amsterdam and Tyne Tees Steam Shipping of Newcastle – to form North Sea Ferries. The intention was to share the financing and management of a new overnight ferry route linking Hull and Rotterdam. P&O owned 45 per cent of the capital in the new company.

H. Vreedenburgh, the Technical Manager of Phs. Van Ommeren, devised the basic design for the new ferries. Built by the AG Weser Seebeckwerft at Bremerhaven, the 3,692-ton *Norwind* and *Norwave* were the world's first overnight ferries with two double-height vehicle decks, stacked vertically one atop the other – this at a time when some recent vessels serving British ports had little or no freight capacity whatsoever. Cars and trucks drove on board via bow and stern doors and large hinged internal ramps could be lowered to give access to the upper level, which protruded above the hull, with sloping sections fore and aft denoting where these ramps were located. The lower vehicle deck had three lanes running along the centreline with single lanes between the casings and the shell plating, while the upper deck only had the three centre lanes, the lifeboat promenades being outboard.[53]

In addition, there were cabins and reclining chairs for 249 passengers, spread over two decks above and one deck below the vehicle spaces. The main saloon deck had a forward-facing reclining seat lounge, a large cafeteria amidships (it being part of the North Sea Ferries package that breakfast and dinner were included in the fare) and a galley, located towards the stern. Altogether, the *Norwind* and the *Norwave* were extremely compact ferries and, seemingly, no corner was wasted in what was a very logical configuration. *The Manchester Guardian* described them as:

> 'Simple, slab-sided vessels with only a few frills, but making both the family saloon and the lorry-borne container welcome at a properly organised terminal, they provide a full range of accommodation from cabin with bathroom to aircraft-style sleeperettes, a self-service restaurant and several bars – a long way from the grim masochistic tradition only now beginning to break down on the crowded short-sea Channel routes and the Irish Sea.'[54]

Within only six months of North Sea Ferries commencing operations in 1966, its closest rival, the British Transport Commission-owned Associated Humber Lines gave up trying to compete, abandoning their own Hull-Rotterdam general cargo and passenger service to their upstart rival's ferries.

A third and equally successful ferry venture for P&O was Normandy Ferries which established a route across the Western Channel from Southampton to Le Havre in 1967. Again, this was a joint operation with a continental partner, the French channel shipping company S.A.G.A. (Société Anonyme de Gerance et d'Armement) which was hitherto best known in Britain for having been the operator of Dover-Calais packet steamer services under the French flag between 1920 and 1938 when the national railway SNCF took over.

P&O and S.A.G.A. each ordered a 6,100-ton stern-loading diesel-powered ferry from the Ateliers et Chantiers de Bretagne in Nantes for delivery in 1967. Named the *Dragon* and the *Leopard* respectively, these boasted very superior passenger accommodation for 850, plus garage space for 250 cars. The Normandy Ferries route competed directly with a recently established ferry service owned by a Norwegian entrepreneur called Otto Thoresen, whose Scandinavian-designed and built drive-through vessels had proven popular with the travelling public but, due to their short length and beamy hulls, they tended to give rather a lively ride in all but the calmest of weather. In comparison, Normandy Ferries' vessels possessed more of the characteristics of small liners with fine-lined bows and sufficient length to ride more than one average wave and trough at a time. Indeed, from the outset, they were a great success and they continued to serve on the Channel for over 20 years.

The ***Norwind****, one of two advanced freight and passenger ferries built for the North Sea Ferries consortium's route from Hull to Rotterdam. (Miles Cowsill)*

The 1966 Seamen's Strike was a bitter blow to the British merchant navy and associated industries. Here, the liners ***Arcadia*** *and* ***Canberra*** *are laid up in Southampton. (Mick Lindsay collection)*

So far as international passenger liner traffic was concerned, the 1960s was a period of decline and retraction. The National Union of Seamen's members were disquieted by a growing trend away from traditionally labour-intensive vessels to new specialised tonnage of greater efficiency while, on *terra firma*, the cost of living continued to increase and ever larger wage settlements were negotiated (in 1965, average crew wages on P&O ships had gone up by no less than 14 per cent – but still this was insufficient to placate the NUS). In May 1966, a national strike was called and this immobilised most of the British merchant fleet for a month and a half; its immediate cost to P&O in lost revenue was £1.4 million but far greater was the long-term damage done to Britain's shipping industry as a whole. During the strike, both freight customers and passengers switched to foreign flagged vessels – or took to the air in the new jetliners. Such was the loss of business that it was not until the early summer of 1967 that all of P&O's affected liners finally returned to service.[55]

Shortly thereafter, the advent of wide-bodied, high-capacity long-haul jetliners – most notably Boeing's 747, first unveiled in September 1968 – attracted away the majority of high-value First Class liner passengers for whom time was of the essence. One by one the liner routes were closed down; in 1969 P&O closed its UK/Far East sevice, moving *Cathay* and *Chitral* to the Australia/Japan service of its Eastern & Australia subsidiary. That same year, British India's *Kenya* was withdrawn from service between London and East African ports and sold immediately for scrap, aged only a little over 18, while the *Rangitoto* closed the passenger service to New Zealand in the same year and was sold to C.Y. Tung of Hong Kong for further service. Next, in 1970, the *Chusan* made her final liner voyage to India – but she was already gaining a loyal following as a cruise ship. Indeed, by the latter 1960s, nearly all of P&O's passenger fleet was operating a mix of liner voyages, interspersed by an increasing number of cruises, mainly from Southampton. This trend reflected the growing affluence of Britain's expanding middle classes.

The P&O liners employed in cruise service were, of course, two-class vessels and with a great deal of deck gear to handle general cargo, amongst which Britain's increasingly prosperous holidaymakers staked out places in the sun for their deckchairs. While most foreign-flagged liners employed on cruises operated as one-class ships, P&O rigorously maintained a separation on its larger liners, such as *Canberra* and *Oriana*, and so it tended to be the established upper middle class who enjoyed First Class, while the slightly less affluent went in Tourist, just as they would on liner voyages. Smaller vessels, for example *Chusan* and *Himalaya*, operated one class when cruising, but passengers still tended to gravitate towards the public rooms they felt reflected their social status and so an unspoken class division remained. Of course, the cuisine and entertainment reflected the tastes of each of these clienteles, First Class being rather akin to an upmarket hotel, while Tourist class rather more closely resembled a Butlin's holiday camp. David Trevor Jones recalls the P&O cruise experience in the mid-1960s:

> '*Canberra* was, of course, a two-class ship and we travelled Tourist Class in a 4-berth inside cabin on E-Deck, with a shared public bathroom located along the corridor. Tourist

Formerly a troop transport, the ***Devonia*** *was successfully converted into an educational cruise ship sailing in British India colours. (Mick Lindsay collection)*

Class passengers occupied the aft part of the ship, while a smaller number of First Class passengers had the run of the forward part. So far as we in Tourist were concerned, these spaces were a mystery. My father bought me an Airfix model of *Canberra* to build during sea days and features of this like the First Class lido area [Bonito Pool] ahead of the funnels intrigued me. It was only when it was our turn for an organised visit to the bridge, a formal event which was a greatly anticipated feature of all P&O cruises at that time, that I got a chance to glimpse this pool in passing and to see other fragments of the First Class accommodation, which appeared very empty in comparison with Tourist Class.

All meals were served in the Dining Room at set times – there were no alternatives, except the occasional outdoor buffets, which, like the Bridge visit, were major events. Entertainment was also sparse compared with today. There were quizzes, bingo sessions and horse racing.

Canberra sailed at great speed – 25 or 26 knots – down the Spanish coast. There was no vibration aft and my father was particularly gratified by this; in his view, *Canberra* was a solidly built and soundly operated British ship and she fulfilled all of his expectations for speed and smoothness.'[56]

In 1962, P&O's expanding cruise business received a great boost thanks to the release of a slapstick comedy film called 'Carry On Cruising'. This included footage of the *Orcades* and *Oronsay* and starred the popular character actors Sid James and Kenneth Williams. The film made taking a cruise appear fun, glamorous and with great appeal for people of all ages and backgrounds, rather than just the wealthy and privileged, as was perceived to have been the case in the past. Yet, there was clearly a limit to the extent to which vessels constructed in the late 1940s and early 1950s for liner service could be a success as floating entertainment resorts. Moreover, an outbreak of typhoid on board the *Oronsay* in Vancouver in 1969 showed the inadequate standards of hygiene achieved on obsolescent ships of this kind; the incident cost P&O half a million pounds in compensation payments, extended port fees and lost revenue.

SCHOOLS CRUISING

In 1960, the British Government announced the end of sending troops around the world by sea to imperial outposts and trouble spots and switched instead to air transport. This meant that a number of specially built troopships owned by, amongst others, P&O's British India subsidiary became surplus to requirements. This situation coincided with an era of progressive

Top: The ***Nevasa****, another troopship conversion for schools cruising, proved highly popular throughout the 1960s. Here, she is seen in the Grand Canal at Venice. (Bruce Peter collection)*

Above: School children dine in a dining hall on the ***Nevasa****. (Bruce Peter collection)*

Right: School children play hockey on the ***Nevasa****'s deck while other children and adult passengers spectate from the deck above. (Bruce Peter collection)*

thinking with regard to children's education and so it was decided to convert two of the redundant troop transports into schools cruise ships.

For a privileged few, schools cruises had been popular in the 1930s when older liners struggled to attract fare-paying passengers during the Great Depression. The new initiative would be realised on a far grander scale, reflecting the idealism of 1960s educational policy in a way unimaginable today, and P&O were heavily involved from the outset. At first, British India converted two motor troop ships – the 11,162-ton *Dunera*, built in 1937 and the 12,773-ton *Devonia*, acquired from Bibby Line for whom she had been built in 1939 as the *Devonshire*. As these vessels had mainly dormitory-type accommodation, they were easily altered for their new role. Typically, the vessels sailed from Southampton taking secondary school children and their teachers on latter day 'grand tours' of the Mediterranean's great cities and archaeological sites. Each cruise carried pupils from a particular region of Britain and beforehand the schools encouraged them to earn and save money to pay the nominal fares. In the ships' officers' accommodation, smallish numbers of ordinary cruise passengers were carried and the only time they encountered the school children was during lectures which were open to everyone.

So successful were these cruises that in 1964 a third larger and more modern troopship was added, the 20,527-ton turbine

The famous British India liner ***Uganda*** *is seen in the Dover Strait towards the end of her service from London to East African ports. (FotoFlite)*

steamer *Nevasa*, built in 1956 and latterly laid up as redundant in the River Fal. No less than 60 schools cruises were offered per annum in the mid-1960s – but the ageing *Dunera* and *Devonia* were obviously nearing the ends of their careers. British India therefore made a virtue out of necessity by extensively converting their out-of-use East Africa liner *Uganda* (sister to *Kenya*) into a superior educational cruise ship. The work to add substantial additional superstructure was carried out by the HDW shipyard in Hamburg (where the OCL container ships were constructed). *Uganda*'s elegant First Class accommodation was for cruise passengers, while new dormitories, classrooms and a canteen were added fore and aft; during the rebuild, her tonnage increased from 14,430 to 16,607 tons.

In the latter 1960s and early 1970s the *Uganda* and *Nevasa* enjoyed great success – indeed their cruises had a memorably positive effect on many youthful baby boomers at that time passing through schooling – indeed, many who first experienced sea life on board as teenagers in their spartan dormitories may be among the most enthusiastic patrons of today's large and luxurious P&O Cruises ships.

David Trevor-Jones recalls a cruise with his schoolmates aboard the *Nevasa* in 1971:

> 'We sailed from Southampton to Gibraltar, then continued east towards Venice and the Greek islands. Very quickly, we realised that our boys' dormitory was infested with cockroaches, which came scuttling out at night. Being from rural Hampshire, nearly all of my classmates were very interested in wildlife and so, when ashore in Naples, we examined the foliage in a park to see what kinds of insects we could find. One of my friends spotted a praying mantis on a twig and so we had a good idea. We caught it carefully in an empty cigarette packet and surreptitiously brought it on board the *Nevasa*, where we released it in our dormitory to deal with the cockroach problem. At night, we could hear it munching away. When we put on the light to investigate, we found it with a bloated stomach, holding the chewed remains of yet another cockroach in its arms. Very soon, there were no more cockroaches left. Our praying mantis survived all the way back to England and one of the boys took it home to keep as a pet.'[57]

Schools cruising continued throughout the 1970s and finally came to an end in 1982 when *Uganda* was requisitioned to serve as a hospital ship during the Falklands War. On her return, it was found that found that prospective school customers, used to planning their activities a year in advance, had taken the business elsewhere because they could not be sure if *Uganda* would come back.

P&O survived the great changes experienced by the international shipping industry in the 1960s and adapted successfully to the new post-colonial world order, in which Britain had a reduced role and authority. The first years of the 1970s, however, brought new turmoil and required further radical re-structuring in order that P&O could find renewed prosperity.

A mid-1970s view of the **Uganda** *following extensive rebuilding as a schools cruise ship with extra fore and aft superstructure. (Mick Lindsay collection)*

MARITIME AND OFFSHORE SERVICES

Responding to the emerging interest in North Sea gas exploration and its need for specialised vessels and marine services, P&O Offshore Services was established in 1964, in parallel with similar companies owned by its French, Dutch and Norwegian partners serving the North Sea gas industry. These operations were reconstituted as a single company, International Offshore Services, in 1970, itself taken over by P&O in 1972 and then sold on to American interests in 1974.

On the other side of the world, P&O Maritime Services (POMS) is a company that grew out of the old Beaufort Shipping Agency that had taken care of P&O ship chartering and offshore interests in Australia, and has since specialised in developing shipping solutions for a worldwide clientele, including various government agencies. With the development of offshore oil and gas industries in Australia during the latter 1960s, P&O set up Australian Offshore services in 1970 and, within only a short time, POMS had built and was operating over 20 ships in Australia and South-East Asia. P&O maintained this interest until 2003.

During the 1980s the company was involved in Papua New Guinea carrying copper concentrates along the river system to the coastal ports. Some ten years later they took the long-term contract with the Australian Antarctic Division to manage and build a research supply and expedition icebreaker, the *Aurora Australis*. The company continued to grow in the 1990s establishing business in Europe, the Middle East and in 2009 they expanded operations into South America. Today P&O Maritime Services plays a vital role in Dubai port operations at Jebel Ali.

FERRY EXPANSION

In February 1971, P&O purchased the Coast Line Group for £5.6 million, in so doing gaining ferry routes from Liverpool and Ardrossan to Belfast on the Irish Sea, from Aberdeen to Orkney and Shetland plus a network of short-sea cargo services from Britain to Ireland and the Continent and associated road hauliers. Coast Lines included the Tyne Tees Steam Shipping interest in North Sea Ferries. As with P&O's General Steam Navigation Company subsidiary, some Coast Lines routes had already been converted to ro-ro operation. During the 1970s, P&O invested most successfully in their further modernisation.

In 1975 a new Ro-Ro ferry and related haulage operation between Fleetwood and Larne was given the name 'Pandoro', reminiscent of the 'Pando' names, derived from 'PandO', given to some P&O cargo liners when the Far East service was re-branded in 1967. While Pandoro's freight routes to the Irish Republic prospered, the Ardrossan-Belfast passenger service was negatively affected by a severe outbreak of political and religious violence in Northern Ireland. Operated by a modern 1967-built ferry named the *Lion* and marketed under the historic Burns-Laird brand, the service went into terminal decline. In 1976, P&O redeployed the *Lion* on a new Dover-Boulogne service using the Normandy Ferries brand, already well known on the Western Channel. This bold initiative involved competing directly with the large and powerful British and French state railways' Sealink fleet and with that of the expansive British private sector operator Townsend Thoresen. Notwithstanding tough competition, the *Lion* found a niche on the Dover Strait and P&O subsequently increased its presence on the route by purchasing additional ferries. The Liverpool-Belfast overnight passenger service, operated by the stern-loading *Ulster Queen* and *Ulster Prince*, likewise dating from 1967, survived until 1983. Not only was it too a victim of Ulster's descent into violence, but also of Liverpool's economic decline and the rather old fashioned design of the ferries, which were unable to carry appreciable quantities of freight. In addition, the Ministry of Defence decided to send troops to Northern Ireland by air, rather than using the ferry.

Also in 1971, P&O inaugurated a car ferry service from Southampton to Lisbon and Tangier. Marketed as Southern Ferries, this was operated by the 11,609-ton *Eagle*, a substantial and well-appointed vessel purpose-built at Nantes in France and owned by P&O's General Steam Navigation subsidiary. The following year, P&O added a second route from Southampton to San Sebastian in Spain, operated by the *SF Panther*, formerly the West German-owned TT-Line Baltic ferry *Peter Pan* of 1965.

Within a short time, P&O found its Iberian ferry routes to be only marginally profitable, partly due to the seasonal character of holiday traffic, partly because of the rough conditions so often encountered when traversing the Bay of Biscay but mainly due to the effects of the 1973 Oil Crisis and political irritability in Portugal. Those who endured one stormy passage were frightened from risking any repetition of the experience and so neither the *SF Panther* – which lacked stabiliser fins – nor the *Eagle* ever generated a loyal clientele (on the vessel's deck plan published in *The Motor Ship*, one of the few labelled features is a vomitorium). Once holidaymakers heading for the Algarve switched in increasing numbers to charter flights, there was no longer a sufficient market for a two-ship ferry service to Spain and Portugal and so the *Eagle* was sold to French owners for further use as a Mediterranean cruise ship, a role which she continues to fulfil admirably today as the Israeli-owned *Royal Iris*. The *SF Panther*, meanwhile, was chartered briefly to the Norwegian Da-No Linjen then re-introduced by P&O Ferries from Aberdeen to Orkney and Shetland in 1975 as the *St Clair*.

The ***Ulster Queen****, one of two Liverpool-Belfast overnight ferries sailing in the livery of the Belfast Steamship Company. (Bruce Peter collection)*

Carrying substantial freight volumes all year round, North Sea Ferries' Hull-Rotterdam route was reliably profitable and a second generation of much larger ferries was soon needed. Constructed by AG Weser Seebeckwerft in Bremerhaven, P&O's 12,988-ton *Norland* and her Dutch-operated sister *Norstar* were amongst the largest and most capacious ferries of their era. As North Sea Ferries continued to offer only night crossings, they spent eight daylight hours in port, meaning that large numbers of freight trailers could be loaded throughout the day. Thus, the ferries had no less than three double-height vehicle decks, one stacked above the other. Due to the engine room being located aft, the space forward was used for trailers and, as with the existing *Norwave* and *Norwind*, large hoistable internal ramps accessed the upper vehicle deck. Cabin berths were provided for 1,072 passengers out of a total capacity of 1,243. Otherwise, there was a large buffet restaurant, reflecting North Sea Ferries' 'all inclusive' policy, a lounge, a bar and a shop.[58]

When the *Norland* and *Norstar* entered service in 1974, the existing *Norwave* and *Norwind* were switched to a new Hull-Zeebrugge route – and this too proved highly lucrative. By the

Originally built for Irish Sea service, the ***Lion*** *subsequently found her niche on the Dover Strait, operating between Dover and Boulogne. (Bruce Peter collection)*

Top: Southern Ferries' ***Eagle*** *linked Southampton to Lisbon and Tangier. Here, she is seen at her Southampton berth in the early 1970s. (Bruce Peter collection)*

Above left: The ***Eagle****'s Red Room Lounge. (Bruce Peter collection)*

Above right: The Aquila Restaurant on the ***Eagle****. (Bruce Peter collection)*

Below: P&O Scottish Ferries' ***St Clair****, previously Southern Ferries'* ***SF Panther****. (Bruce Peter collection)*

*One of North Sea Ferries' 'second generation' jumbo ferries, the **Norland**. (Bruce Peter collection)*

mid-1970s, therefore, through far-sighted investment and astute acquisition, P&O had amassed a network of ferry routes radiating all around Britain.

During the late 1970s, P&O Ferries experimented with diversifying its passenger business by adding a high-speed hydrofoil service to the Continent from St Katherine's dock in the centre of London near Tower Bridge. This was primarily aimed at the expense-account business trade with fares that were pegged between those of conventional ferries and the scheduled air carriers then, before the current age of low-fare airlines. The 1976-built Boeing Jetfoil 929-100 craft *Flying Princess* was chartered to inaugurate a 3-hour, 45-minute service to Zeebrugge on a trial basis while two larger Jetfoil 929-115 vessels were built to P&O's own specifications. The *Flying Princess*'s charter was to run until the second of these would be delivered, though the experimental London-Zeebrugge service was only operated between 1st June and 25th September 1977. P&O's first vessel, the *Jetferry One* was delivered in early 1980 and a new

*The Boeing Jetfoil **Flying Princess** at speed in the Dover Strait in the latter 1970s. (FotoFlite)*

service between London and Oostende was inaugurated in late February, with the *Flying Princess* standing in for the *Jetferry Two* until she was delivered in June. The two 43-knot Jetfoils ran as many as three round trips each day through the summer of 1980, though after only seven months the uneconomic service was closed and the two Jetfoils were sold.

THE NEW CRUISE SHIPS

In the latter 1960s, P&O's senior management were casting envious eyes towards North America where a fast expanding cruise industry from Miami to Caribbean ports was proving highly lucrative for a Norwegian shipowner called Knut Kloster. Kloster's activities would have been familiar to P&O as, in 1966, he had attempted to run a luxury cruise ferry service from Southampton to Lisbon and Gibraltar, using a superbly appointed Norwegian-built ferry called the *Sunward*. Kloster's idea was to use these ports to bring British holidaymakers to the Algarve and Costa Del Sol. Alas, because Britain's ongoing dispute with Spain's General Franco over the status of Gibraltar led to the border being closed and, worse still, currency restrictions limited the amount of cash Britons travelling abroad could take out of the country. The result was that Kloster found few passengers to fill his fine vessel, forcing him to withdraw her after only a matter of months in service.

Shortly after being forced to withdraw the *Sunward*, Kloster was contacted by a cruise entrepreneur in Miami called Ted Arison who had the opposite problem – plenty of potential passengers but no ship – and so the two entered a mutually beneficial joint agreement to create Norwegian Caribbean Lines, sailing the *Sunward* twice a week from Miami on three- and four-night itineraries to the Bahamas and Jamaica. So popular was this venture that in 1968 NCL added a second vessel, named the *Starward*, and, in 1969, a third, the *Skyward*, was completed.[59]

By this point, a consortium of three other Norwegian shipowners had been established to finance another rather more upmarket cruise operation from Miami, Royal Caribbean Cruise Line (RCCL). They ordered three purpose-built cruise ships from a Finnish shipbuilder, Oy Wärtsilä Ab in Helsinki. Although this firm was long established, they had only recently begun to build passenger ships at a time when most British yards were giving up on what they erroneously regarded as a declining market segment. Wärtsilä's secret was to use ferry design technology to build relatively shallow-drafted, diesel-engined vessels with light aluminium superstructures and pre-fabricated modular interiors. Whereas cruising in Second Class on P&O's existing liners most likely meant making do without a private bathroom, each of Wärtsilä's modular cabins had its own shower unit and vacuum toilet. Indeed, Wärtsilä's designs embodied a great deal of hidden servicing to make the passengers' experience remarkably comfortable. Apart from powerful air-conditioning, able to cope with the most extreme tropical humidity, there were heated swimming pools, Jacuzzis, sophisticated cold stores for food and well-equipped galleys able to serve food 24 hours a day. As such purpose-built cruise ships did not carry cargo, their decks were uncluttered expanses on which sun worshippers could relax and sports aficionados could play deck games. In short, the new Caribbean cruise ships of the latter 1960s and early 1970s were more floating versions of the latest leisure resorts ashore than they were liners in the traditional sense.

Up the Florida coast in Fort Lauderdale, meanwhile, the Italian Costa Line also had developed a successful Caribbean cruise operation, using mainly ingeniously converted older tonnage. Of much more interest to P&O was a recently built 12,219-ton cruise ship called the *Italia* which Costa operated under a charter arrangement. Her 213 cabins each had private facilities and, much like *Canberra* and *Oriana*, her lifeboats were 'nested' in recesses on each side of her superstructure; this meant that her upper decks were given over almost entirely to sunbathing. Initially, Costa operated the *Italia* in the Mediterranean but, from 1967, they sub-chartered her to a recently formed American firm called Princess Cruises, based in Los Angeles, from which they planned to sail her to the Mexican Riviera.

The nearest that the British merchant fleet came to the *Italia* or to NCL and RCCL's new cruise ships was Cunard's iconic 1969-delivered *Queen Elizabeth 2* which was likewise designed with pleasure in mind. With her crisp exterior profile and fashionable interiors, *QE2*, as she was known, brilliantly captured the youthful spirit of 'Swinging London'. Yet, measuring 65,862 tons, the *QE2* was around four times the size of the newest purpose-built Caribbean vessels and, besides, she was a relatively fuel-hungry turbine steamer. In terms of on-board facilities and décor, however, the *QE2* gave strong clues as to how P&O might proceed to develop a new generation of dedicated cruise ships to tap the lucrative American market.

To progress matters, P&O's Board set up a special committee, led by an ex-Orient Line director, Sandy Stirling, to research and develop a new class of cruise ship. Stirling went with Jim Davis on a fact-finding trip to America, where he sailed from San Francisco on the *Italia* and from Miami on Royal Caribbean's brand new *Song of Norway*. The plan was that P&O would design in-house a cruise ship combining the most successful elements of these vessels. Davis recalls that 'I still smile when I think of Sandy Stirling going round furrow-browed with a tape measure recording cabin sizes, while I felt it more relevant and certainly more enjoyable to experience the entertainment and ambience side of things and succeeded in achieving the vote as the dance champion of the ship.'[60]

P&O reasoned that, as the Caribbean market was already saturated with Norwegian-owned tonnage, it would be better to concentrate its efforts on America's Pacific Seaboard. This made sense also because, thanks to its round-the-world liner service, they had good agency contacts in Los Angeles and San Francisco who could help them quickly establish a presence in the Californian cruise business.

P&O planned to divide its passenger shipping investments into two distinct categories – a 'Tier 1' fleet consisting of steam turbine-powered liner tonnage, also used for cruises from Tilbury and Southampton, and a 'Tier 2' fleet consisting of a new generation of purpose-built diesel-driven cruise ships stationed in America. The intention was that, as the 'Tier 2' fleet expanded, the 'Tier 1' fleet would gradually be run down until only the *Oriana*

*The **Spirit of London** was launched in a completed state at Riva Trigoso on 11th May 1972. (Bruce Peter collection)*

and *Canberra* remained.[61] In 1973 these two ships were adapted for full-time service in the alternative cruising role for which they were originally designed in the first place, with their divergent First and Tourist classes combined for 'open class' operation by merely opening doors on each deck joining the forward and aft parts of either ship, and with a half-a-dozen-or-so lifeboats being replaced with excursion launches carried under the original davits. They became remarkably popular in the British cruise market, where they introduced a whole generation of the travelling public to cruising and even offered ordinary Britons of modest means the opportunity to enjoy world cruises in 'friendly fours' occupying their original emigrant cabins at remarkably low prices. The *Oriana* served until she was retired in 1986, followed by the *Canberra* in 1997.

Between P&O's initial market research and its in-house naval architects actually completing a basic design for a new class of cruise ship, Sandy Stirling made an intriguing discovery. Norwegian Caribbean Line's owner, Knut Kloster, had ordered two additional cruise ships from an Italian builder, the Cantieri Navali e Riuniti at Riva Trigoso, to increase his Caribbean fleet to five. The first of these was delivered to Miami as planned in 1971 as the *Southward* but before the second could be finished the shipyard experienced cash-flow problems and insisted that Kloster re-negotiate the contract for a higher fee. Kloster refused and so the incomplete liner was made available on the open market.[62]

As with Kloster's earlier ferries and cruise ships, his Italian new buildings were largely the work of the Danish naval architect Tage Wandborg, who worked for a Copenhagen-based consultancy called Knud E. Hansen A/S. Wandborg's passenger ship designs were notable for their sleek lines and stylish details – a world away from the rather vertical look of most of the existing P&O passenger liner fleet which, with the exception of the *Canberra*, was a product of an earlier era in design thinking.

P&O directors and technical staff inspected the incomplete ship and offered to purchase her. According to Sandy Stirling, they emphasised to the builders that P&O was a long-established and respectable major British company but, embarrassingly, the following morning when the deal was to be completed, Italian newspapers carried the headline 'Rolls Royce Goes Bust!' Nonetheless, the purchase went through successfully and P&O's naval architect Charles Morris was set to work altering the existing design to meet P&O's requirements. Meanwhile, Colin Anderson, the brother of P&O's Chairman, suggested that Ward Associates be appointed to design the interiors, the idea being to give the vessel a 'Swinging London' aesthetic similar to the highly

*Pearly queens, hussars and a policeman were some of the unusual guests attending the **Spirit of London**'s naming ceremony on 29th April 1972. The ship was actually launched a fortnight later due to construction delays and adverse winds. (Bruce Peter collection)*

The completed ***Spirit of London*** *heads through the English Channel, bound for Southampton. (FotoFlite)*

acclaimed *QE2*. In line with this objective, it was announced that the name chosen for P&O's first dedicated cruise ship would be *Spirit of London*.[63]

According to Jim Davis, when Norwegian Caribbean Line's Ted Arison discovered that P&O had purchased the vessel, 'he accused P&O/me of stealing his ship design. He was so abrupt that I replied with equal asperity that he should remember that I represented the world's greatest shipping company and accordingly he should temper his language (which he did). In view of more recent events in P&O [Cruises'] history, that conversation has almost legendary significance.'[64]

Designed and operated with the requirements of American passengers in mind, the *Spirit of London* was very different in layout, appearance and atmosphere from any passenger liner P&O had ever previously operated. Publicity material for her maiden voyage described her as 'a sparkling new cruise ship more like a luxury yacht than an ocean liner. She is 17,000 tons, superbly modern, designed for fun cruising and is all one class.' Inboard, she was bright and spacious with open-plan public rooms decorated in vivid hues – the Union Jack Bar being finished in red, white and blue stripes, the Thameside Restaurant with striking black and white murals of London's skyline by David Gentleman, while the Beehive Disco had hexagonal furniture and bulkheads laminated with images from pop album covers. Informality was the key and a wide choice of organised shipboard activities was advertised.

Spirit of London's maiden voyage left Southampton on 11th November 1972, bound for the Caribbean with calls at Madeira, Barbados, Grenada, Martinique, Antigua, St Thomas and, finally, San Juan, from which British passengers were flown home. Fares for this fortnight-long trip ranged from £338 to £523 – meaning that she was in the same price bracket as First Class on Cunard's *Queen Elizabeth 2* for a similar itinerary.

From the outset, *Spirit of London* was a great success – but P&O as a whole continued to struggle to come to terms with rapid changes in the wider business, finance and shipping worlds. The Company retained an overly complex and bureaucratic managerial and reporting structure – 127 subsidiaries, each with varying degrees of answerability to the main board and 23 senior managers reporting directly to the chairman. Ford Geddes (1913-2002), a P&O director who was Sir Donald Anderson's second cousin, argued that the McKinsey management consultancy should be employed to help streamline P&O's corporate hierarchy and many subsidiary businesses. McKinsey had recently overseen the implementation of a similar process at Cunard. Its plan for P&O was to reduce the Company to only five divisions: general cargo shipping, passenger shipping, bulk shipping, European and air transport and 'general holdings' to combine all other activities.[65] A consequence of this very necessary initiative was that numerous famous names and liveries disappeared, amongst these being Hain-Nourse, the New Zealand Shipping Company and the General Steam Navigation Company. British India survived – but only as a marketing name for educational cruises. The entire cargo liner fleet received a new blue funnel colour with 'P&O' in bold white letters on either side and the majority of vessels were given 'Strath…' names in place of the various types of nomenclature favoured by their former operators.

Ford Geddes succeeded Sir Donald Anderson as P&O Chairman in August 1971. Geddes, while remembered as being personally kind and gentlemanly, unfortunately proved to be a weak Chairman at the very point when P&O more than ever

Top left: The ***Spirit of London****'s Union Jack Bar. (Bruce Peter collection).*

Top right: The Thames-side Restaurant on the ***Spirit of London****, featuring a mural by David Gentleman. (Bruce Peter collection)*

Above: The main lounge on the ***Spirit of London*** *was located directly beneath the lido area, with raised sections on either side above the recessed lifeboats. (Bruce Peter collection)*

required strong corporate governance. As he evidently could not himself foresee in which direction the Company should chart its future course, he relied on McKinsey's young management consultants to make decisions on his behalf. Jim Davis recalls that:

> 'The McKinsey boys were making their bruising way through all departments of the company. It was somewhat mesmeric to be faced with one of these young investigators in one's office and to be asked "And what do you do?" just like that.'

Unfortunately for him, Davis' position of Global Marketing Director of P&O Lines was one of those scrapped by McKinsey and so, notwithstanding his intense loyalty and long service to P&O, like many others, he found himself suddenly redundant to the Company's needs.

*The new order and the old order together at Southampton where **Spirit of London**'s streamlined superstructure provides a marked contrast with the rather vertical styling of **Oronsay** and **Orcades**. (Mick Lindsay collection)*

While the reorganisation instigated with McKinsey doubtless improved the P&O Group's managerial and operational efficiency, the early 1970s remained troublesome for operators of cargo liners as freight rates were low while labour costs were rising exponentially. Furthermore, as the Suez Canal remained closed, liners heading east were required to make long and expensive detours via Southern Africa. In contrast with P&O's shipping problems, the value of their growing property portfolio now accounted for no less than a quarter of the Group's assets.

In 1971, Cunard was the victim of an aggressive takeover by a recently established property development company called Trafalgar House. This had been founded in 1958 by Nigel Broackes and Victor Matthews, the former an ex-Guards officer and the latter a building contractor. Their speciality was taking over under-performing businesses and cutting costs to yield greater short-term profits. Ford Geddes believed that even after P&O's major reorganisation, it too might easily become a takeover target for like-minded entrepreneurs.

In May 1972, Lord Poole, the Chairman of Lazard's merchant bank, joined P&O's board. As the construction company Bovis had its account with Lazard's, Poole believed that a union between Bovis and P&O would be mutually beneficial as it would strengthen both firms and enable P&O to increase its interests beyond the presently unstable world of shipping. Investment analysts believed that, in the proposed merged business, the value ascribed to P&O, £100 million, was far too low and that given to Bovis, £130 million, ridiculously high. Three executive directors made their opposition public and one of P&O's non-executive directors, Kenneth Mackay (1917-94), the third Earl of Inchcape, grandson of the first Earl of Inchcape, who had served as chairman between 1914 and 1932, became the figurehead for P&O's increasingly sceptical stockholders. In an earlier era, P&O's Chairman and directors could have made deals behind closed doors with little opposition – but now there was open mutiny from within. Inchcape subsequently tendered a rival bid for P&O, valuing the Group at £230 million – nearly two and a half times its worth should the Bovis deal have gone ahead. Meanwhile, P&O's voting structure was changed from one allowing only a maximum of 20 votes per stockholder to a one share, one vote system. This enabled P&O's stockholders to reject the Bovis merger on 17th November 1972. As a result, Ford Geddes resigned after only 18 turbulent months as Chairman. The post of Managing Director was reinstated and this was taken by Alexander (Sandy) Marshall, previously an executive director of P&O's British India subsidiary and one of the three executive directors opposed to the Bovis merger.[66] Lord Inchcape was appointed Chairman – but in a non-executive capacity, his role being to offer impartial advice to the Managing Director, whose duty it was to run the Group. Thus P&O emerged from the Bovis debacle with a much more modern and accountable corporate structure.

In the following year, shipping grew in profitability while property values slumped. As P&O had accumulated a substantial shareholding in Bovis, when the builder fell on hard times, other investors asked P&O to help and so in 1974 they bought the remaining shares for a fifth of the value ascribed to them in the 1972 merger proposal. Consequently, real estate development became a very significant aspect of the enlarged P&O Group which, within a decade, had been transformed from an operator of liners into a diversified shipping and property conglomerate.

The former British India cargo liner ***Mulbera*** *repainted in P&O General Cargo division's livery and renamed* ***Strathmuir****. (Mick Lindsay collection)*

In 1973, the shipping world received a severe shock when Arab oil producing countries constituting the bulk of the OPEC alliance decided greatly to increase the price per barrel of Gulf crude in protest against American support for Israel in the Yom Kippur war. The ensuing Oil Crisis profoundly changed the economics of the entire industry as the cost of marine bunker fuel immediately more than quadrupled. In particular, steam turbine liners became less affordable to operate than relatively economic motor ships – and so the bulk of P&O's 'Tier 1' passenger liner fleet was consigned for scrap. Even the *Canberra* was threatened with premature withdrawal in 1974 after an ill-judged programme of cruises out of New York the previous summer; this had demonstrated how unsuitable she was for a non-British clientele. She survived, however, but, by the mid 1970s, she was one of only three remaining traditional P&O passenger liners, the others being *Oriana* and *Arcadia*. Indeed, from 1974 to 1980, half of P&O's overall fleet was sold off, reducing the number of ships from 178 to only 89. Most of the disposals were of general cargo liners. Yet, with a consequently denuded passenger fleet, the only sailings resembling line voyages now offered were occasional repositioning cruises when the three passenger vessels were moved from one cruising region to another. P&O's Passenger Division was now exclusively a cruise operator. In 1977, the title P&O Cruises was adopted for its management company.

Previously operated by P&O's Federal Line subsidiary, the ***Piako*** *also was re-liveried in the standard P&O General Cargo Division colours. (Mick Lindsay collection)*

*In the 1970s, British India's passenger and cargo routes from India and Pakistan to the Persian Gulf and to East Africa still provided inexpensive transport links by sea. Here, the **Karanja** is seen at Durban in October 1973. (Trevor Jones)*

Yet, remarkably, one very traditional passenger liner route remained – from India and Pakistan to the Persian Gulf operated by the late 1940s vintage British India motor ships *Dwarka* and *Dumra*. In P&O's early 1970s reorganisation, the Gulf route and other ex-BI services between Bombay and East Africa, and between Madras and Singapore had come under the aegis of the Group's General Cargo Division. The other two services were closed but the Gulf route, whose 'cargo' consisted mainly of Pakistani migrant workers seeking employment in the newly oil-rich Gulf states and wishing to travel there as cheaply as possible, continued until 1982 when the *Dwarka* was finally withdrawn. She was the last of a once great fleet of British India liners to operate from the sub-continent. Towards the end of the *Dwarka*'s long career, she was the subject of a 1979 BBC documentary entitled '*Dwarka* London: An Arabian Voyage'. Viewers of this film caught a final glimpse of an era otherwise ended – the British officers in tropical whites, the few First Class passengers sweltering in the shade of the promenade decks, the clutter of cargo-handling gear on deck and the hundreds of Indian and Pakistani men travelling in the 'tween decks below, being served curry on tin trays. Around the base of the funnel, the Chief Engineer grew tomatoes in old oil drums. Truly, the *Dwarka* was a world away from the modern ferries and cruise ships by that time constituting the remainder of the P&O passenger fleet.[67]

*The **Pacific Princess**, one of two modern sisters acquired by P&O in 1974-75 for Princess Cruises' American-based operations represented the future of the passenger fleet. (Andrew Kilk)*

P&O's success with *Spirit of London* convinced them to make further investments in the American cruise industry. Rather than developing its own purpose-built 'Tier 2' cruise fleet as had originally been its intention, instead it purchased an up-and-coming American cruise line, Princess Cruises, headquartered in Los Angeles. Founded by a cruise entrepreneur called Stanley McDonald, Princess had begun operations only in 1965, initially using a chartered Canadian Pacific coastal steamer called the *Princess Patricia* to offer coastal trips on the Western Seaboard of North America to ports in Canada, Alaska and Mexico. After the *Princess Patricia*, the fleet comprised two chartered Italian-owned liners – the *Carla C.* of Costa Line, which was marketed as *Princess Carla*, and the *Italia*, which was sub-chartered from Costa. The former had been rebuilt in Italy in the latter 1960s from the 1952-vintage French transatlantic liner *Flandre*, while the latter had been purpose-built for cruising in 1967. While the *Carla C.* had

*Top: The **Island Princess**, also purchased in 1974, departs from San Francisco. The **Pacific Princess** and **Island Princess** had formidable reputations and a high profile due to their featuring in 'The Love Boat' on television. (Andrew Kilk)*

*Left: Tiffany's Bar on P&O's **Sea Princess**, formerly the Swedish **Kungsholm**. (Bruce Peter collection)*

*Above: The aft-facing Carousel Room on **Sea Princess** was a new addition to the ship by P&O. (Bruce Peter collection)*

*The newly converted **Sea Princess**, ex **Kungsholm**, was fitted with a tall funnel while the aft section of her Promenade Deck was converted to cabins with small portholes - an unthinkable decision nowadays as balconies are highly sought after on cruise ships. (Bruce Peter collection)*

generous space for 748 passengers, the *Italia* could carry only 452 – equivalent to the load of a wide-bodied jet aircraft – making her useful for fly-cruises.

In 1972, Princess Cruises chartered the younger of two handsome Norwegian-owned sister ships, the 19,300-ton *Island Venture* in order to expand its fleet; this almost brand new vessel became the *Island Princess*. She was built in West Germany by the Rheinstahl Nordseewerke shipyard at Emden in 1972, for a joint venture into cruising by the shipowners Oivind Lorentzen and Fearnley & Eger, she and her 1971-built sister, the *Sea Venture*, had operated hitherto in summer mainly from New York to Bermuda under the Flagship Cruises brand. As with the *Spirit of London*, the two ships' basic design was by Knud E. Hansen A/S while Robert Tillberg, a Swedish interior designer, who worked jointly with the Norwegian Finn Nilsson and the American Mildred Masters, devised their notably elegant interiors.[68]

After P&O bought Princess Cruises, it purchased the *Island Princess* from Oivind Lorentzen and, in 1975, also the *Sea Venture*, which was renamed *Pacific Princess*. In a stroke of marketing genius, Princess permitted the television series 'The Love Boat', which had been conceived aboard their chartered liner *Princess Carla*, to use the *Island Princess*, and later the *Pacific Princess*, as a setting. The resulting extensive positive publicity for cruising in general, and for the Princess fleet in particular, was enormous. The series, which reached tens of millions of Americans, promoted a fashionable, youthful and glamorous image – cruising was now perceived as fun and available to everyone, not just older and richer holidaymakers. Within five years, 'The Love Boat' was being cited as one of the prime factors influencing the growth of the cruise industry in North America. With P&O/Princess, the *Pacific Princess* and the *Island Princess* gained a formidable reputation and usually sailed filled to capacity with delighted passengers. Simultaneously, the *Spirit of London* was re-branded as a Princess ship and renamed the *Sun Princess*.

By the latter 1970s, P&O's one remaining 1950s passenger liner to escape the early 1970s cull of the fleet, the *Arcadia*, was operating as an Australian-based cruise ship. Obviously approaching the end of her useful life, P&O sought a suitable replacement as it valued their leading position in the Australian cruise market. Scouring the second-hand market, its choice was a surprising one – the luxurious and exclusive 1966-built former Swedish-American flagship transatlantic liner *Kungsholm* – which, like the *Arcadia*, had been built by John Brown & Co. of Clydebank. Measuring 26,677 tons and powered by twin Götaverken Diesel engines, which at the time of their construction formed the most powerful twin-screw plant ever built by the Gothenburg-based company, her maximum speed was 23 knots. Widely regarded as being among the world's most beautiful ships, her profile featured two tapering funnels with fins, although the forward of these was a dummy containing generators and water tanks. In Atlantic service, she could carry 750 passengers in two classes but in her more regular cruising role she usually carried only 450 with 438 officers and crew. Inboard, the *Kungsholm* was superbly appointed, reflecting the very best of Swedish interior and furniture design of her era. Amidships, between the funnels, was a sheltered lido area with a sun deck cantilevered over the ship's sides, one deck above.

While the *Kungsholm* was highly acclaimed, especially by the wealthy Americans who formed the bulk of her clientele, rising labour and fuel costs caused Swedish-American to close down its passenger business entirely in 1975 and so the *Kungsholm* was sold to Oivind Lorentzen. He used her to re-open his Flagship Cruises business which had been dormant since the *Island Princess* and then *Sea Venture* had been sold to P&O the previous year. Placed under the Panamanian flag, the *Kungsholm* offered cruises mainly out of New York with neither a change of name nor livery (except for the emblem on her funnels). Yet, Lorentzen struggled to turn a profit as the overheads associated with running a single cruise ship were considerable. He must have been very pleased therefore when P&O bought the vessel to add to its existing ex-Flagship cruise vessels.

P&O sent the *Kungsholm* to the Bremer Vulkan shipyard at Bremen for a £3.5 million refit which lasted almost four months. When she emerged as the *Sea Princess* in January 1979, her appearance had been radically altered – many thought for the worse – by the removal of the forward funnel and by the heightening of the aft funnel. As well as modernising the ship's appearance and bringing her profile into line with that of other recent P&O vessels, the taller funnel had the advantage of stopping soot falling onto the after sun decks and so was also practical. Inboard, public rooms at the aft end of the veranda deck were replaced with new cabins to increase capacity and profitability.

The *Sea Princess* was probably too ostentatious a vessel to succeed in the Australian cruise market, a sector in which informality was key. Her main competitor was the Sitmar liner *Fairstar*, a solid but unpretentious liner, ingeniously converted by Sitmar from the old Bibby Line troop transport *Oxfordshire*, which was a near sister to British India's *Nevasa*. After only three years, the *Sea Princess* was pulled from Australia and re-located to Southampton, her place 'Down Under' being taken by the *Oriana*. The latter was better suited to Australian cruising and gained a loyal following. Unfortunately, by the mid 1980s, her aluminium superstructure had become seriously fatigued and, as repairs to the 26-year-old ship would have been too costly to have been worthwhile, she was abruptly withdrawn in March 1986. At that time, P&O cited lower cost competition from Soviet cruise liners and from Sitmar Line's *Fairstar* as the reasons for withdrawing her. Thereafter, she was sold for conversion to a floating attraction in Beppu Bay, Japan.

Although P&O's sparkling cruise ships were the Company's most glamorous operation, its share in the OCL container business and its ferry services were likewise profitable. By 1980, P&O had increased its shareholding in OCL to over 44 per cent. Notwithstanding these successes, the 1973 Oil Crisis cast a long shadow over the business world and, in Britain, its knock-on effects took the form of runaway inflation, which hit 26 per cent at one point in 1976, and industrial unrest. In such an environment, profits in one division were offset by worries and frustration in others as strikes plus a sterling crisis in the autumn of 1976 undermined efforts to grow P&O's businesses. The Company's management therefore had little option but to reconsider planned investments and to hope that better trading conditions lay ahead.

THE FALKLANDS WAR

The election of a new Conservative government, led by Margaret Thatcher, in May 1979 effectively ended the post-war consensus in British politics and brought into practice a new economic ideology. Since the mid 1930s, macro economic policy in the Western industrialised world had been dominated by theories propounded by John Maynard Keynes, who believed that a mixture of private entrepreneurship and state intervention was the best way to secure stability and steady growth. The idea was that, during downturns, government intervention would create jobs and thus stimulate the economy, enabling debt to be recouped during the ensuing upswing.

With the post-war growth of industries in South East Asia, coupled with the ongoing negative effects of the Oil Crisis, during the 1970s, Keynes' ideas were challenged by Western problems of increasing debt, inflation and unemployment, especially in Britain and the USA. Rather than being short-term interventions to maintain stability, many now saw government intervention and protectionism as fundamental reasons for Western decline. Sceptics of intervention found their hero in Milton Friedman, Professor of Economics at Harvard Business School, who believed in small government and in regulating growth only through the adjustment of interest rates to regulate the supply of money. Margaret Thatcher was a Friedman disciple, as was her political soul mate, the new American president, Ronald Reagan. Thus, 'monetarism', as Friedman's theories were known, came to define the 1980s business world in which P&O now found itself operating.

As Britain's new government inherited high inflation, it was necessary greatly to increase interest rates to bring it under control. Inevitably, this caused the value of the pound to grow relative to other leading currencies, reducing British industry's ability to export as products and services were suddenly more expensive for foreign customers to purchase. Thanks to P&O's 1970s reorganisation, as well as the disposal of most of its ship repairing activities, the closure of an ill-advised Energy Division, and the growing international success of Bovis, the Group was lean, fit and therefore better able to prosper in the new political and economic order. P&O's dividend for 1981 was a healthy 10 per cent and pre-tax profit was £41 million.

The government's requirement to slash public expenditure to rebalance the British economy led to drastic cuts in the Royal Navy and the withdrawal of South Atlantic patrols. The Argentinean dictator General Galtieri interpreted this as a sign that Britain was no longer particularly interested in retaining the Falkland Islands, which Argentina claimed as its own territory. Therefore, on 2nd April 1982, Argentine forces invaded the Falklands. That same afternoon, the British Government contacted P&O to advise them that members of its fleet would be requisitioned to support a military task force to liberate the Falklands from Argentine occupation. On Monday 5th April, the *Canberra* was ordered to Southampton for conversion to a troop transport to join the North Sea freight ferry *Elk*, which normally operated between Middlesbrough and Gothenburg and had already been requisitioned to carry munitions and general supplies.

On Wednesday, *Canberra* arrived in Southampton at the end of a world cruise and, as soon as her passengers had disembarked, she was hastily converted, her midships lido area

Top: Following distinguished Falklands service as a hospital ship, the ***Uganda*** *returns to Southampton. Her officers, crew and medical staff received heroes' welcomes. (Mick Lindsay collection)*

Above: Weather-beaten but otherwise intact, ***Norland*** *is seen at her berth in Hull in the condition in which she returned from the Falklands and badly in need of a refit. (Ferry Publications Library)*

Right: North Sea Ferries' ***Norland*** *in the thick of the action in San Carlos Water on 24th May 1982. It is clear from this image how close the ferry came to taking a direct missile hit from Argentine aircraft. (M.O.D/Ferry Publications Library)*

being partially dismantled to enable a helicopter landing platform to be constructed while another landing pad was built atop her forward superstructure, above the Crow's Nest Bar (which also needed partial dismantling so that extra strengthening could be fitted). This work was achieved in less than 48 hours and on Friday, only a week after the Falklands invasion, *Canberra* and *Elk* left Southampton, the former carrying 3,000 Royal Marines and members of the Parachute Regiment.[69]

Shortly thereafter, two further P&O vessels were requisitioned – the educational cruise vessel *Uganda*, which was converted into a hospital ship, the North Sea Ferries vessel *Norland*, to carry troops and supplies, while the cargo liner *Strathewe* and the part-owned tanker *Anco Charger* were chartered later in the campaign. The great contrasts between these various vessels served to demonstrate how diverse P&O's shipping interests had become; two decades previously, practically the entire P&O fleet consisted of ships such as *Uganda* and *Strathewe* but, by the 1980s, in terms of P&O's total tonnage, passenger and cargo liners such as these were very much in the minority.

Uganda was converted for medical duty in Gibraltar, the work taking a mere 65 hours, thereafter she steamed for Ascension Island, where she joined *Canberra* and *Elk*. Meanwhile, *Norland* had departed from Portsmouth carrying the 2nd Parachute Regiment. Almost simultaneously, at the United Nations, intense diplomacy was underway to resolve the Falklands crisis – but apparently Britain would accept nothing less than Argentine capitulation.

At the start of May, Britain sank the Argentine cruiser *General Belgrano* and the Argentine Air Force bombed the British destroyer HMS *Sheffield*. When *Uganda* arrived the following week, she embarked the war's first casualties – injured navy personnel from HMS *Sheffield*. Meanwhile, it was decided that British forces would be landed by sea in San Carlos Water, an area chosen because of its hilly surroundings which theoretically made it less vulnerable to aerial attack by the Argentine Air Force. On 19th May, the process of transferring troops from *Canberra* to naval landing craft began. Mounting such a large-scale seaborne military landing by sea had not been necessary since the liberation of Europe in the Second World War. It would be a relatively slow process, fraught with risk. British vessels anchored in San Carlos Water were, after all, sitting targets for the Argentineans. Such had been the speed of the requisition and conversion process that nearly all remained in their bright civilian liveries, making them all too easy to target from the air. The great white mass of *Canberra*'s hull and superstructure made her particularly vulnerable, as was the orange, black and white-painted ferry *Norland* (whose crew had tried to tone down her funnel with daubs of camouflage).

The San Carlos landings began during the night of 20th-21st May and, shortly after dawn, Argentine fighter jets were overhead – and both *Norland* and *Canberra* were in the thick of the action to follow, *Norland* putting the first assault troops ashore and *Canberra* following her with the reserves. In contrast, Cunard's

*The **Canberra** inward bound to Southampton at the end of the Falklands War. Note all the army lorries on her top deck. (FotoFlite)*

*On 11th July 1982, the **Canberra** returned from the Falklands to Southampton. The rust-streaked liner was welcomed home by a large flotilla of small craft. (Mick Lindsay collection)*

*A dramatic view of the P&O Dover-Boulogne ferry **n.f. Tiger** crossing the Dover Strait. (FotoFlite)*

Queen Elizabeth 2, which had also been requisitioned as a troop transport, was kept well out with the Falklands military exclusion zone. It was suggested, for the Argentineans, damaging or sinking a ship carrying the name of the British monarch would have been a great propaganda coup. *Canberra*, in contrast, seemingly was regarded as being expendable. Fortunately, the Argentine Air Force's pilots evidently had orders primarily to target naval vessels and so, while *Norland* was landing troops on 24th May, less than a kilometre astern, the frigate HMS *Antelope* was sunk. The only merchant ship casualty of the Falklands campaign was the Cunard-owned container ship *Atlantic Conveyor*, the radar profile of which was apparently rather like that of an aircraft carrier.

Canberra and *Norland*'s officers and crews accomplished their duties with great bravery and professionalism. Indeed, 860 P&O employees served aboard the six Group ships involved in the campaign. As well as landing troops, leading to the Falklands' liberation on 14th June, P&O staff and ships were involved in replenishing stores and munitions and treating the wounded. In her hospital ship role, *Uganda*'s staff, consisting of the Royal Army Medical Corps and 16 Field Ambulance, had treated 730 British and Argentine wounded and carried out 504 operations. Finally, following the Argentine surrender, *Canberra* and *Norland* had repatriated over 6,000 prisoners of war back to Argentina, after which the *Canberra, Elk* and *Uganda* returned to Britain in triumph.[70]

The rust-streaked and work-weary *Canberra* arrived in Southampton on 11th July – a memorable day in the port's history as over 30,000 spectators and a vast flotilla of small craft turned out to welcome her home. Among other messages festooned over the *Canberra*'s deck railings, such as "Allo mum,' 'Lock up your women, the boys are back' and 'Call off rail strike or we call an air strike,' one particularly large banner read '*Canberra* cruises where *QE2* refuses' (*Queen Elizabeth 2* was already berthed in Southampton, undergoing a post-Falklands refit). Similarly large and enthusiastic crowds feted P&O's other 'Falklands veterans' when they too returned. The passenger ships all received government-sponsored renovations before returning to civilian service.

Norland remained in the South Atlantic until the following February, carrying supplies between Ascension and the Falklands, and her ultimate return to the UK was much more low-key as the weather in her homeport of Hull was very poor. When, after a refit, she re-entered ferry service between Hull and Rotterdam, a new feature was the 'Antelope Bar', decorated with war memorabilia commemorating the sinking of HMS *Antelope* in San Carlos Water.

Canberra was restored to cruising service – but she never fully recovered her pristine pre-Falklands appearance. For example, the rubber composition decking of her lifeboat promenade had been chewed up by thousands of troops jogging in their army boots and this was only patched up. *Uganda* too was restored as an educational cruise ship – but only for two months. The idea of educational cruising belonged with the progressive social democracy of the 1960s, not with the market-led monetarism of the Thatcher era. After only a brief spell, *Uganda* was chartered

The ***Royal Princess*** *makes progress towards completion at Wärtsilä's Helsinki shipyard in the early summer of 1984. (Mick Lindsay collection)*

once again to the Ministry of Defence to replace *Norland* on South Atlantic supply duties between Ascension and the Falklands until a new airport was completed.

Of the various P&O ships requisitioned for Falklands service, only one still survives in commercial service – the ro-ro freighter *Elk*. She is now the DFDS-owned *Tor Baltica* and continues to earn a living carrying trailers across the Baltic Sea between Kiel and Kapleida.

SWAN HELLENIC CRUISES

In 1983 P&O acquired Swan Hellenic Cruises, a specialist niche operator first established in the 1950s by the family-owned Swan travel agency to replace the cabin passenger 'Discovery Cruises' formerly offered by *Uganda*. Swan Hellenic offered specialist cruises to a small but loyal and discerning clientele who wished to undertake modern equivalents of the 'Grand Tour' by visiting archaeological sites and classical ruins, mainly around the Eastern Mediterranean. Swan Hellenic was very much a 'no frills' operation in those days and the vessel chartered for cruises was actually the former British & Irish Line overnight ferry *Munster*, built in 1948 for the Liverpool-Dublin service, which had since been renovated by Greece's Epirotiki Lines as a small and rather basic cruise ship named the *Orpheus*.

Able to anchor in secluded Aegean harbours, the Orpheus was chartered by Swan Hellenic season after season. Distinguished British academics, members of the House of Lords and senior Anglican clergymen were represented in her passenger lists and often were engaged as specialist on-board lecturers as, rather than conventional cruise ship entertainment, as Swan Hellenic cruises were characterised by its focus on 'high culture'.

A ROYAL PRINCESS

Growing consumer confidence in the early 1980s, coupled with the first of the 'baby boomers' reaching an age at which they were now sufficiently wealthy and leisured, led to the development of a new generation of large, purpose-built cruise ships. The first of these were built mainly to serve the American market; Norwegian Caribbean Line's bold conversion of the laid-up transatlantic liner *Norway* in 1980 arguably kicked off the cruise

Top: The ***Royal Princess*** *catches morning sunlight as she arrives in Southampton for the first time in November 1984. (Mick Lindsay)*

Above: The two-deck-high atrium on the ***Royal Princess****, featuring a sculpture of herring gulls by David Norris, entitled 'Spindrift'. (Bruce Peter)*

Right: 'Californian modern' imagined through the eyes of a Norwegian designer, Njål Eide, on a British-owned ship, the Riviera Bar on ***Royal Princess*** *typifies the internationalism of cruise ship interiors in recent decades. (Bruce Peter)*

Bottom right: The Horizon Lounge at the base of the funnel on the ***Royal Princess****. (Bruce Peter)*

boom. Where the ex-*France* differed greatly from, say, P&O's contemporary 1960s flagship liners *Canberra* and *Oriana* was in her cabins all having private facilities – one of the reasons why *Canberra's* 1973 New York cruise programme was such a conspicuous failure – and in her being equipped with a large theatre space in which Broadway musicals could be presented. These features became vital ingredients in the American cruise experience and the industry as a whole grew exponentially during ensuing decades.

Various established cruise operators had different approaches to the development of new tonnage. Some – such as Holland America and Sitmar – were essentially conservative, the former operator's *Nieuw Amsterdam* and *Noordam* having an obvious affinity with its 1959 flagship *Rotterdam*, while the new Sitmar-owned *Fairsky* was, like her rather elderly fleet mates, a steam turbine vessel. Of the new generation, the most innovative vessel was arguably Royal Caribbean's *Song of America* of 1982. A mass-market liner, dedicated to the Caribbean cruise trade from Miami, she was built by the Wärtsilä shipyard in Helsinki. This builder had only become involved in passenger ship design and construction during the 1960s but, thanks to its use of innovative design and construction ideas, it had quickly established itself as one of the leading producers of large ferries and cruise ships. In several respects, *Song of America* was rather ferry-like; her hull was straight lined and with a rather fulsome bow profile, while her superstructure featured the same 'cabins forward, public rooms aft' layout favoured on many of the latest Scandinavian overnight vessels. She was, however, a very efficient and economical ship – and of impressive appearance.[71]

Wärtsilä's Project Manager Kai Levander was a highly perceptive and imaginative naval architect who successfully gained new contracts for the yard by wowing potential clients with futuristic concept ship designs. He devised these 'ships of tomorrow' by examining and addressing changing lifestyle and economic trends through his design innovations.

One such potential client for a new cruise ship for the American market was P&O's Princess Cruises. Its existing three-strong fleet, comprising *Pacific Princess*, *Island Princess* and *Sun Princess*, was already highly regarded and very profitable and so a new liner, more than twice their size, would be a lucrative investment. Levander's plan was that this ship should only have outside cabins and that an unprecedented proportion of these would have private balconies. Although in the past a small number of medium-sized liners had featured L-shaped 'Bibby' cabins to ensure everyone a porthole, Levander's proposal was altogether more radical. Using a *Song of America*-type hull as a platform, he proposed a narrower 'hotel block' superstructure containing only cabins with the lifeboats recessed on either side and public rooms in the upper decks of the hull. A 'service core' would run the length of the centre line, containing the bulk of the liner's vertical circulation, pipework and crew-only areas. So intrigued were P&O's directors by Levander's economic arguments in favour of this design – outside cabins would sell for around 25 per cent more than insides – that a contract was signed for a 1,200-passenger approximately 45,000-ton vessel with delivery scheduled for October 1984.[72] Wärtsilä agreed not to reveal any details of what would be the most innovative and significant of the new generation of cruise ships – indeed renderings of an inaccurate 'decoy' design were released to the press, revealing none of the new ship's innovative design features.

Design development was carried out jointly by Wärtsilä's drawing office, the Copenhagen-based consulting naval architects Knud E. Hansen A/S, who were the designers of Princess Cruises' existing vessels as well as numerous other highly rated cruise ships, and Three Quays, P&O's 'in-house' naval architecture firm. A great deal of intensive detailed work was carried out to optimise the cabin and public room arrangements while tank tests in Copenhagen and Trondheim helped to refine the hull lines for maximum efficiency at the liner's required 18-knot service speed (her maximum was 22 knots). As with *Song of America*, four 8-cylinder medium-speed diesel engines were installed, coupled in pairs via gearboxes to each propeller shaft. Under normal operational conditions, only two engines, one on each shaft, would be in operation, giving excellent fuel economy. Pielstick machinery was chosen over the Sulzer type hitherto usually favoured by Wärtsilä for its newbuildings.

The new liner would be among the first of many large cruise ships to feature an internal atrium as the focus for her internal circulation. Otherwise, the public rooms were accessed by means of peripheral arcades. As with *Song of America*, a cocktail lounge was built around the funnel, overlooking the extensive outdoor lido area. Decoratively, the interiors would, in the words of P&O Cruises' Chairman Dr Rodney Leach, 'create the ambience of a well-to-do California home.' Thus, P&O employed the Californian architects and interior designers Hirsch-Bedner, who were to work in close collaboration with the Norwegian cruise ship specialist Njål R. Eide, whose previous recent work included spaces on the *Song of America*. Throughout the ship, pastel shades, polished metalwork, glass and mirrors were enhanced by abstract artworks to create a light and spacious ambience. The designs were highly reflective of the aspirations of their era – a period of growing wealth (at least for some) and conspicuous consumption.[73]

By the time building work commenced, P&O had settled on the name *Royal Princess* for its new liner. The 'royal' connection honoured HRH Diana, Princess of Wales, who named the ship in Southampton in November 1984. Thanks to the glamorous young royal who was becoming a global media superstar, the naming ceremony brought worldwide attention. The maiden voyage of the *Royal Princess* was transatlantic to the Panama Canal and this sold out in only three hours.

Although she encountered severe storms and suffered superficial damage on her maiden voyage, once in American waters, *Royal Princess* became a sensation. Every cruise was booked solid and she won almost universal acclaim from her many delighted passengers. Indeed, aspects of her design influenced that of nearly every major cruise ship built thereafter. P&O held options to build two sister vessels – but these were not taken up. One reason was that, while *Royal Princess* was under construction, P&O was cutting costs to stave off hostile attempts at a takeover.

Chapter 5

The Sterling Era

In 1980, Lord Inchcape appointed new members to the P&O Board, one of whom, Jeffrey Sterling (b. 1934), was quickly to prove a vital force in the Company's subsequent development. Sterling's background was in finance and property; he had established his own financial group, Sterling Guarantee Trust, in 1969. He first came to P&O's attention when, in the early 1970s, he arranged a 99-year lease on Beagle House, an office block in London's Aldgate, for use as the OCL container consortium's new headquarters. Subsequently, he attracted positive recognition in the City when his hard work salvaged a severely troubled developer, Town & City Properties, which he restructured as part of Sterling Guarantee Trust.

Meanwhile, in the shipping world, the purchase of the Furness Withy group – one of P&O's fellow members of the OCL consortium – by C.Y. Tung of Hong Kong in April 1980 reflected the growing clout of Hong Kong shipowners. Shortly thereafter, in the autumn of 1981, another rapidly expanding Hong Kong owner, Carrian Investments, increased its stake in P&O – suggesting that it might be planning a takeover. That this did not happen was partly due to the fact that P&O's Royal Charter contained a paragraph forbidding non-British owners from holding more than 25 per cent of the Company's stock. Moreover, Carrian was neither sufficiently well known nor established to impress P&O's major institutional investors. Subsequently, in the summer of 1983, Trafalgar House, the owners of Cunard, made a hostile bid for P&O. The imminent retirement of P&O's Chairman, Lord Inchcape, perhaps signalled to Trafalgar's Nigel Broackes that there was a window of opportunity to pounce while P&O's corporate governance was weakened.

In making its bid for P&O, Trafalgar House emphasised the synergies to be achieved by merging the two companies' shipping and property divisions – but, beyond that possibility, each business had a very different *modus operandi*. P&O was a long-term investor, whereas Trafalgar had a reputation for being asset strippers. As David and Stephen Howarth observe in *The Story of P&O*, 'Broackes launched his campaign with a lordly tone of co-operation… but his purpose was deadly.'[74]

Lord Inchcape rejected Broackes' bid as unacceptable, withdrew his retirement and vowed to fight off Trafalgar House. Inchcape probably feared that P&O's institutional investors might all too easily be persuaded that Trafalgar House could sweat P&O's assets for a higher short-term yield than its own management would find acceptable. Fortunately, as Trafalgar's portfolio so closely matched that of P&O, its bid was referred to the Monopolies and Mergers Commission. This gave P&O ten months' breathing space to mount a strong defence.

Lord Inchcape was persuaded to appoint Jeffrey Sterling as Deputy Chairman as from July 1983. His earlier salvation of Town & City Properties had made him a highly respected figure in the City and it was hoped that P&O's institutional investors would be confident that, with Sterling in a position of influence, the Group would henceforth be run to maximise revenues as best possible. Succeeding Inchcape as P&O Chairman in November 1983, Sterling disposed of risky assets – such as investments in the

*The former Normandy Ferries-operated **Dragon** in P&O Ferries livery in the English Channel during the early 1980s. (FotoFlite)*

American oil industry – and insisted on the production of P&O's 1983 accounts two months ahead of schedule. Thus, although the Monopolies and Mergers Commission finally approved Trafalgar House's takeover, P&O regained its major investors' confidence and Trafalgar withdrew its bid. In 1985, Sterling merged P&O with his own Sterling Guarantee Trust, which included the now-profitable Town & City Properties. This meant that the combined P&O property development business now was substantial – and, as London's financial services industry boomed, there was a property boom in the City and along the banks of the Thames. Through Sterling Guarantee Trust, P&O also controlled major regional shopping centres, the largest of which was the Arndale in Manchester, as well as the Earl's Court and Olympia exhibition centres in London, catering and warehousing businesses. All were profitable and gave P&O a substantial presence in the booming service sector on *terra firma*.

As a financier hitherto involved in the property development and service sectors, rather than having a background in shipping, Sterling was very much a man of his time. During the 1980s, British business became more closely involved than ever in the City's increasingly aggressive speculative culture. In such a context, it was considered desirable that a large blue chip company such as P&O should be run by senior managers with mastery over the financial world, rather than by shipping specialists, as had been the situation in the past. Yet, Sterling quickly gained a deep understanding of – and a great liking for – the shipping sector.

In 1984, Sterling sold the P&O building in Leadenhall Street and relocated the current P&O headquarters from Beaufort House, to which Inchcape had moved in 1979, to appropriately smaller premises at 79 Pall Mall in the West End. Conveniently for him, this new location was closer to Westminster, where he was in demand as an unpaid government advisor on trade and industry matters. In 1985, he installed his long-serving right-hand man, Bruce MacPhail from Sterling Guarantee Trust, a P&O director ever since Sterling's appointment in 1983, as P&O's new Managing Director. P&O's headquarters bureaucracy was slashed from the approximately 600 who had worked in its Leadenhall Street offices in the 1970s to only around 60 in Pall Mall a decade later. Greater responsibility for the day-to-day operation of each P&O subsidiary was vested with local managements, who were offered the incentive of bonus pay to improve their operating results.[75]

As P&O was the biggest shareholder in OCL, holding 47 per cent of the consortium, Sterling also was installed as Chairman of its holding company, Overseas Containers Holdings, replacing Lord Inchcape as he had done at P&O. Sterling had a particular interest in the possibilities offered by container shipping. Back in the early 1970s when he had leased Beagle House to OCL, he had impressed OCL's then Chairman Sir Andrew Crichton with his observations about container shipping's possible future development. As Overseas Containers Holdings Chairman, Sterling sought to enable P&O to gain control of the remaining 53 per cent of the business from the remaining fellow consortium members Ocean Transport & Trading (Alfred Holt) and British & Commonwealth. Furness Withy had already surrendered its stake

Townsend Thoresen's ***Viking Venturer*** *one of four near-sisters built for the Felixstowe and Portsmouth routes in the early seventies for the company. The Danish-built ships were later acquired by P&O in 1987. (FotoFlite)*

A busy mid-1980s scene in Dover's Eastern Docks with various Townsend Thoresen ferries at their berths. From left to right, they are the ***European Clearway, Free Enterprise V*** *and* ***Herald of Free Enterprise****. (Miles Cowsill)*

to the remaining three partners at the time of its acquisition by C.Y. Tung. While British & Commonwealth's owners, the Cayzer family, were happy to sell in exchange for P&O stock, Ocean proved more of a challenge. Prior to joining the OCL consortium, they had been P&O's long-standing rivals in the Far East trade and so they might be unlikely to sell their remaining sake in this to P&O. Sterling therefore bought Ocean stock in order to signal that, if they were unwilling to sell their stake in OCL, P&O might bid for the entire company. Through this tactic, P&O succeeded in achieving full control of OCL. In agreeing to sell its interest to P&O, however, Ocean insisted that P&O should sell its Ocean shares on the market and transfer its 50 per cent stake in the Panocean short sea tanker shipping and storage concern to Ocean. In May 1986 therefore, P&O became the sole owner of OCL and just before Christmas that year the business was renamed P&O Containers Ltd. Having reclaimed the routes it had surrendered to OCL between 1969 and the early 1980s, P&O was now once again Britain's premier operator of freight-carrying vessels in international liner service.

Sterling was knighted in 1985 and, as a result of the OCL takeover, was named 'City Personality of the Year' in 1986. In the previous financial year, P&O produced a record profit of £125 million. Commenting on the OCL takeover, Ivan Fallon wrote in the *Sunday Times*: 'If Britain has any serious future in shipping, it now lies with P&O.'[76]

P&O next sought to become Britain's leading ferry operator through taking over the struggling European Ferries group, the parent company of the leading Channel and Irish Sea operator Townsend Thoresen. Since the untimely death of its enterprising Managing Director Keith Wickenden in 1983, European Ferries had lost momentum. As with P&O, it had invested heavily in property during the 1980s – mainly in the United States, but its management apparently lacked the know-how to profit from such speculative investments. P&O had first purchased some shares in European Ferries as long ago as 1965 and, two decades later when Townsend Thoresen had become the dominant Channel ferry business, European Ferries purchased P&O's Normandy Ferries routes linking Southampton, Le Havre, Dover and

The a la carte restaurant on the ***Pride of Dover*** *was in marked contrast to the dreary Channel Tunnel Shuttle experience. (Bruce Peter collection)*

Top: The Nedlloyd-owned ***Norstar****, sister of P&O's* ***Norland****, is seen in Hull following lengthening and repainting in North Sea Ferries' new livery in 1987. At this point, she was switched from the Hull-Rotterdam to the Hull-Zeebrugge route. (Miles Cowsill)*

Above: The ***Pride of Bruges*** *(ex* ***Pride of Free Enterprise****) following repainting in P&O European Ferries' livery. (Miles Cowsill)*

Above right: The ***European Endeavour*** *maintained the freight service between Dover and Zeebrugge. (FotoFlite)*

Bottom right: A new addition to the Aberdeen to Orkney and Shetland routes in 1988 was the ***St Sunniva****, ex* ***n.f. Panther****. (Bruce Peter collection)*

*The **Pride of Dover** with her funnel painted in P&O European Ferries' dark blue but her hull still in Townsend Thoresen orange, albeit with the company name painted out. (Miles Cowsill)*

Boulogne. By this point, P&O's Dover Strait operation consisted of three ferries – the *Lion*, *n.f. Tiger* and *n.f. Panther*, the latter two being former Danish domestic route vessels. None was big enough to compete effectively with the latest generation of Sealink and Townsend Thoresen vessels.[77] The Southampton-Le Havre route continued to be operated by the 1967-vintage stern-loaders *Dragon* and *Leopard*. Unfortunately for P&O, the growth of Portsmouth as the main British Western Channel ferry port, coupled with the increasing dominance of Brittany Ferries, had marginalised Normandy Ferries service. P&O's failure to re-invest in its Channel ferry routes was unfortunate – but the sale of Normandy Ferries to European Ferries was tactical.

As European Ferries' under-exploited American property interests would enjoy greater yields through P&O's expertise and its ferry business, with routes across the Dover Strait, Western Channel and Irish Sea, this would complement P&O's existing operations, and the City expected P&O to mount a takeover. The deal was finalised in January 1987, with P&O paying £345 million. With their purchase of European Ferries, P&O became Britain's leading ferry operator, gaining routes from Cairnryan to Larne, from Portsmouth to Cherbourg and Le Havre, from Dover to Calais, Zeebrugge and Boulogne (plus a marketing agreement with Belgian ferry operator RMT to promote its Dover-Ostend route) and from Felixstowe to Zeebrugge and Rotterdam.[78]

DISASTER STRIKES

The year of 1987 was P&O's 150th anniversary year and its purchase of European Ferries was to have been an early highlight in a year of celebrations. Not two months thereafter, on the evening of 6th March, disaster struck when Townsend Thoresen's

*The **Europic Ferry,** another former Townsend Thoresen vessel, in P&O European Ferries' dark blue livery. (Miles Cowsill)*

Ordered by Townsend Thoresen, the **Pride of Calais** *was delivered new to P&O European Ferries in December 1987 wearing their blue livery. Here, she is seen approaching Calais. (Miles Cowsill)*

Dover Strait ferry *Herald of Free Enterprise* left Zeebrugge bound for Dover with her bow doors open. As her speed increased, her vehicle deck scooped increasing amounts of water and she became unstable, rolling onto her side and ending up half-submerged on a sand bank. Out of her 454 passengers and crew of 80, a total of 193 lives were lost in what was Britain's worst peacetime maritime tragedy since the Liverpool-registered *Empress of Ireland* sank after a collision in the St. Lawrence on 30th May 1914 with the loss of 1,012 lives. Had she not come to rest on a sand bank, the number of lives lost undoubtedly would have been far higher.

The ensuing public enquiry revealed a deeply ingrained culture of sloppiness permeating Townsend Thoresen's operations. The Company's management apparently valued making money above all other considerations and it was insufficiently rigorous in imposing a uniform safety culture across its entire ferry operation. Thereafter, P&O's recently installed management from the former Townsend Thoresen operation, led by Peter Ford, reformed the business and the ferry fleet was re-branded as P&O European Ferries, using a new dark blue hull and funnel livery. This was also applied to P&O's container ships and bulk carriers, giving the fleet a more uniform identity than at any time in the recent past.[79]

In July 1985 it had been announced that a rail tunnel would be built beneath the Dover Strait, a decision ratified by the signing of the Anglo-French Treaty of Canterbury in February 1986. From the moment that the tunnel was announced, the major ferry operators, Townsend Thoresen and its recently privatised rivals, Sealink British Ferries, began planning their responses. Townsend Thoresen's solution was to develop a pair of 26,443-ton 'Chunnel Beaters' – large, double-deck triple-screw ferries, each with space for 2,260 passengers and 650 cars – to a design evolved from the successfully established 'Spirit' class. The first of these, named the *Pride of Dover*, was delivered from the Schichau Unterweser shipyard in Bremerhaven only three months after the sinking of the *Herald of Free Enterprise*. In the wake of the tragedy, her entry into service was low-key – but it was a most significant event in the development of P&O's Dover-Calais service. Her sister, the *Pride of Calais*, made her debut that December and, thereafter, the two ferries enjoyed very successful 24-year careers on the Dover Strait – a remarkable achievement, given that this is one of the most competitive continental ferry routes.

P&O's other major new ferry of 1987 was a large overnight vessel representing a third generation for its successful North Sea Ferries route from Hull to Rotterdam. The vessel was ordered from Govan Shipbuilders on the River Clyde, making her the final large passenger ship to be built in a British shipyard. It was hoped that her Nedlloyd-owned, Dutch-flagged sister ship would be built by the Van Der Giessen shipyard at Krimpen in the Netherlands, which was at that point constructing the *Koningin Beatrix*, a large ferry for the rival SMZ/Sealink service from the Hook of Holland to Harwich. In the end, when the Dutch government refused to subsidise the project, the Nedlloyd ship, named the *Norsun*, was ordered from Nippon Kokan in Japan to a design similar, but not identical, to that of the *Norsea*.

As the *Norsea* and her sister had to navigate through a tidal lock at the mouth of the harbour in Hull, the width of the ship was severely restricted to only 25.4 metres, meaning that her hull was long and narrow. Above were three luxuriously appointed

The impressive North Sea Ferries-operated Hull-Rotterdam jumbo ferry ***Norsea*** *was the last large passenger ship to be built on the Upper Clyde in Govan. Here, the 1987-delivered vessel is seen passing through the tight confines of the lock at Hull. (Miles Cowsill)*

passenger decks, with cabins located forward and public rooms aft. These were colour coded in green, red and blue, to enhance passenger orientation. The *Norsea* and the *Norsun* each had 2,250 lane metres for 180 trailers or 250 cars – twice the capacity of the existing *Norland* and *Norstar*, which were lengthened, refurbished and transferred to North Sea Ferries' Hull-Zeebrugge route. All four vessels were given a smart new blue-based livery and an extensive marketing campaign was instituted to heighten North Sea Ferries' profile amongst motorists travelling to the continent.[80]

P&O's desire to restructure its European Ferries business to improve productivity and profit yield led to a protracted and fractious dispute with the National Union of Seamen between January and May 1988. The NUS was understandably outraged by the possibility of substantial job losses. The fact that Sir Jeffrey Sterling was an unpaid advisor to the Conservative government – indeed, he was one of Margaret Thatcher's favourite industrialists – led the union to claim a political dimension for the dispute – as well as raising safety concerns if fewer crew were to operate the ferries on a more intensive schedule (although a substantial crew had failed to prevent sloppiness leading to the sinking of the *Herald of Free Enterprise*).

As P&O employed around 3,500 at Dover, for both sides in the dispute, a great deal was at stake. P&O needed to make its ferries more competitive while the union was mandated to fight for its members' jobs. After months of picketing of P&O's premises and the laying-up of its entire ferry fleet, the strike ended and P&O's reforms were implemented. Following the miners' strike and a print workers' dispute, it was one of the last major labour disputes of the 1980s – yet it seemed to emphasise the continuation of a wide gulf in terms of politics and purpose between British senior managers and their employees.

THE GLOBAL ECONOMY

During the 1990s, 'globalisation' became a media buzz-word for the increasingly apparent internationalisation of business and commerce. Shipping always has been an international business; the difference between the past and present being that power was gradually slipping from traditional owning nations in Northern Europe, where hitherto it was centralised, to multiple nodes around the world. In particular, the Far East was buoyant (the Carrian interest in P&O in the 1980s though it came to nothing evidenced that fact).

During the 1987-88 period, P&O stock was quoted for the first time on exchanges in Sydney, Tokyo, Amsterdam, Frankfurt and Paris. In 1991, it was listed in Hong Kong and, the following year, the clause forbidding foreign investors from owning more than 25 per cent of P&O was struck from the Company's Royal Charter. P&O was setting itself up for a more obviously globalised era in which operations and investment would be diffuse and multi-centric, rather than having a predominantly British focus. The collapse of the Communist Bloc in Eastern Europe and the Soviet Union and the commencement of economic reforms in China meant that, during the 1990s, Milton Friedman's monetarist ideology became orthodoxy nearly everywhere and this situation led to a considerable expansion of international sea trade.

P&O, for so long involved in the Far East trade, set about expanding its container and bulk shipping divisions to reap new rewards in the expansive Pacific Rim economies. Thanks to containerisation, it was possible to transport items of relatively high value more quickly, cheaply and securely than ever before. In 1991, P&O purchased the Cunard-Ellerman container business from Trafalgar House, thereby becoming the major British operator on routes from Europe to Australia and New Zealand and also enlarging its presence in the Southern African market. Already the dominant user of Hong Kong's container port in which for some years it had a minority shareholding, P&O ordered no less than nine 58,000-ton container ships from Japan to enhance its Europe-Far East service. Once these entered service, the passage time from Southampton to Hong Kong went down to only 23 days.

In America, increasing wealth and leisure time saw the cruise industry's continued expansion. In December 1987, the *Sovereign of the Seas*, a new Miami-based liner for Royal Caribbean, became the world's largest passenger ship, knocking *Norway* and *Queen Elizabeth 2* into second and third place respectively. Within little over a decade, P&O would own cruise ships that were larger still.

The cruise industry was beginning to consolidate as larger operators with access to substantial financial resources – such as P&O – took over smaller players, thereby increasing its market share. In 1988, P&O bought Sitmar Cruises, operating a fleet of four rather traditional steam turbine cruise liners. Three of these were American-based and the fourth, the *Fairstar*, operated from Sydney. Sitmar had been founded in Genoa in 1938 by a Russian émigré, Alexandre Vlasov, who, after the Second World War, entered the emigrant trade from Europe to Australia and New Zealand. In the latter 1960s, Vlasov began instead to operate the better of his liners as cruise ships. He bought Cunard's mid-1950s-vintage Liverpool-Montreal vessels *Sylvania* and *Carinthia* and, some years later, had these extensively converted in Trieste as upmarket cruise ships named the *Fairsea* and *Fairwind* (these, P&O renamed *Dawn Princess* and *Fair Princess*; fortunately they avoided Wind Princess!). The Australian-based *Fairstar* was a much more basic former troopship, but had a loyal following of repeat passengers who appreciated her unpretentious atmosphere and low bar tariffs. Only the *Fairsky* (subsequently known as *Sky Princess*) was of recent construction, having been delivered by Chantiers de l'Atlantique in 1983. She was a handsome vessel, but anachronistic in terms of layout and propulsion in comparison with P&O's Princess Cruises contemporary, *Royal Princess*. Sitmar's patriarch, Boris Vlasov, Alexandre's son, was a traditionalist so far as ship design was concerned. Only eight months after his death in November 1987, Sitmar's cruise operation was acquired by P&O for £125 million. (The successful and expansive Monaco-based ship management company V-Ships continued as the surviving portion of the Vlasov family business.)[81]

For P&O, the two great attractions of Sitmar were firstly, its strong position in the American cruise market as, once integrated with Princess Cruises, the number of berths in P&O's US-based cruise operations more than doubled. (Already, P&O had increased capacity by switching *Sea Princess* from the British market to America in 1986.) Secondly, Sitmar had commenced a new building programme, ordering no less than three very large new cruise ships for delivery during the 1989-91 period. The first of these, a 63,524-ton vessel which they had intended to name *Sitmar FairMajesty*, was under construction at Chantiers de l'Atlantique at St Nazaire. The others, being built at Fincantieri's Monfalcone shipyard near Trieste, were larger still and would be of very innovative design and appearance. Upon completion, these three new buildings would add 5,200 berths to Princess Cruises' capacity. When Sitmar ordered these vessels, shipyard prices were considerably lower than when P&O took over and so the latter were getting a remarkable bargain – a total of seven ships plus infrastructure and personnel for not much more than

When P&O purchased Sitmar Cruises, they acquired two steam turbine-powered former transatlantic liners, the ***Fairsea*** *and the* ***Fairwind****. Here, the latter is seen in Princess Cruises' livery at San Francisco as* ***Fair Princess****. (Andrew Kilk)*

The newly completed ***Fairsky*** *(later* ***Sky Princess****) in San Francisco bay in May 1984. (Andrew Kilk)*

the cost of a single new cruise ship at 1988 prices. The delivery of Sitmar's new buildings to Princess meant that, when Margaret Thatcher named the *Regal Princess* in New York in 1991, P&O was briefly the world's largest cruise ship operator, although the rapid expansion of Carnival and Royal Caribbean soon eclipsed them.[82]

The vessel to have been *Sitmar FairMajesty* was instead completed as *Star Princess*. Large and bulky, her overall design perhaps reflected the fact that she was an engineers' solution, rather than one in which precedence had been given to aesthetic considerations. While Boris Vlasov initially had considered steam turbine propulsion for the ship, instead she was diesel electric, with four 8-cyliner MAN-B&W diesels powering Alsthom generators. This followed the successful 1987 conversion of Cunard's *Queen Elizabeth 2* from a turbine to a diesel electric ship. The significant advantage of electric drive for cruise ships was that power could be varied more precisely depending upon the required cruising speed to get overnight from one port to the next and this resulted in enhanced fuel economy. A further benefit was that the main engines and drive units could be dissociated, removing bulky propeller shafts while reducing low frequency noise vibration in the aft body. Indeed, *Star Princess* was a successful early example of the design solution subsequently applied to the majority of large cruise ships.

The two new buildings from Fincantieri – named *Crown Princess* and *Regal Princess* – were similar in layout to *Star Princess*, but of far superior external appearance. To give them a memorable silhouette, the distinguished Italian architect Renzo Piano was employed. Piano took inspiration from dolphins and so a beak-like bow profile was combined with a highly raked forward superstructure with a streamlined dome, fabricated from lightweight aluminium alloy, containing an observation lounge. Otherwise, the upper works were flush sided, apart from the lifeboat recesses making for a bold and harmonious composition. Like *Star Princess*, these too were diesel-electric powered.

On all three ships, the interiors were designed by the California-based Welton Becket Associates, already well known for its hotel work for Hyatt and Disney. The centrepiece was a three-storey atrium, connecting the main run of public rooms on Promenade Deck with the embarkation lobby below.

Built in France and Italy with interiors designed by Americans, flying the Italian flag and with international crews, the three new ships reflected how internationalised P&O's cruise business had become – although, from the outset, P&O always had a global reach and employed different nationalities. The Princess fleet comprised 11 vessels, ranging from the 1950s-vintage steamers *Dawn Princess* and *Fair Princess* to the sleek, state-of-the art *Crown* and *Regal Princess*. The ageing *Canberra* continued alone to serve the British market while the elderly *Fairstar* remained in Australia.

Understandably, P&O were anxious to be rid of its four oldest turbine liners which were fuel-hungry and mechanically less reliable than motor ships. *Fairstar* was the first to go, her cruise programme from Sydney being taken over by *Fair Princess* in 1996. Princess Cruises therefore chartered the *Birka Queen* from Finland's Birka Line. Originally this 1973-vintage vessel had been the luxurious Norwegian-owned *Royal Viking Sky*, in her day one of the world's top-rated cruise ships. She appeared on the US West Coast in 1993 as *Golden Princess* – but this was only a stop-gap measure pending the construction of further new ships for the Princess fleet.

Top: The dolphin-shaped ***Regal Princess****, the superstructure of which was styled by the distinguished Italian architect Renzo Piano. (Andrew Kilk)*

Above: The ageing ***Fairstar*** *was a basic but popular cruise ship operating from Sydney. Upon acquiring Sitmar, she was obviously an early candidate for P&O to replace. (Andrew Kilk)*

Left: Upon delivery to Princess Cruises in 1989, the ***Star Princess*** *was the biggest passenger ship in the P&O Group's history. Here, she is seen in Vancouver. (Andrew Kilk)*

Uniquely for a cruise ship built during the 1980s, Sitmar's modern ***Fairsky*** *was also steam turbine-powered. For P&O Princess Cruises, she operated as the* ***Sky Princess****, as shown here. (Andrew Kilk)*

BRITAIN'S NEW CRUISE SHIPS

The *Canberra*'s replacement would require an altogether more sophisticated solution. By the early 1990s, three decades of punishing service had taken their toll on the liner. Her ageing turbo-electric machinery required careful nursing by her engineers while her fuel consumption of up to 400 tons a day was a source of anxiety to P&O's money men. Over the years, P&O had superficially upgraded *Canberra*'s passenger accommodation, some of her interiors being given a *Royal Princess*-like treatment in Californian-style pastel shades during a major 1987 renovation at Lloyd Werft. At the same time, many of her former-Tourist Class cabins were upgraded with private lavatories and shower units. Shortly thereafter, P&O made its first tentative investigations to draw up the criteria for a suitable *Canberra* replacement.

Whereas Princess's vessels typically sailed sedately in the main cruising regions, spending their summers in Alaska or the Mediterranean and their winters in the Caribbean and Mexican Riviera with one port of call per day and with a strong emphasis on on-board entertainment and shore excursions, P&O's British cruise operation involved lengthy itineraries, including world cruises when numerous days were spent traversing the open

Laying the ***Oriana****'s keel at the Jos. L. Meyer shipyard at Papenburg in the Spring of 1993. (Ferry Publications Library)*

ocean, sometimes at considerable speed. Being a thoroughbred ocean liner, *Canberra* was well suited to this kind of operation. Many of P&O's British passengers were repeaters who sailed primarily because they enjoyed being on board *Canberra* in the convivial company of like-minded admirers of the ship. Indeed, some rarely went ashore; for them, the liner was a kind of island representing a particularly intensified form of Britishness.

While most cruise ships offered contemporary hotelier service in their staterooms *Canberra*'s passengers did their own laundry in the public laundrette. Ironing rooms were located at intervals throughout her cabin decks and, there, much shipboard gossip was exchanged. Rather than the typical 'international cuisine' served in most cruise ships' restaurants, *Canberra*'s passengers dined on traditional British fayre and, instead of courses being completed in the galley, silver service was retained. Menus usually featured a curry option and the waiters and galley staff were Indian, their families often having served for generations aboard P&O liners.

As *Canberra* aged, what had once been standard practices across the entirety of P&O's once vast liner fleet now were charming peculiarities unique only to her. Indeed, for many passengers, *Canberra* now had a distinctly nostalgic appeal – something P&O would surely seek to perpetuate in any forthcoming replacement aiming to retain her loyal clientele. Besides, in 'nineties Britain, the first of the post-war 'baby boomers' would be retiring – an affluent generation who might be persuaded to spend some of their leisure time cruising with P&O, thereby expanding the existing clientele.

Already, P&O's British cruise operation was experiencing solid bookings – so much so that in 1991 P&O switched its *Sea Princess* from America back to the UK as a consort for *Canberra*. (In 1995, *Sea Princess* was renamed *Victoria* in order more clearly to distinguish her as a British cruise ship, rather than as a former member of the Princess fleet.) Initial negotiations took place with Lloyd Werft, which produced a design concept known as 'Project Gemini'; this was unveiled by the yard's parent company, Bremer Vulkan at the 1991 Cruise and Ferry Conference in London. P&O decided, however, that the cost of proceeding to build this would have been prohibitive.

In January 1992, however, another West German shipbuilder, Meyer Werft at Papenburg on the River Ems, emerged as P&O's favoured builder for its new flagship liner. Although the family-owned yard was long established (it was founded in 1795), it only launched its first cruise ship, Home Lines' *Homeric*, in 1985. Until 1987, when a covered building dock was completed, ships were launched sideways into the River Ems – including the *Homeric*. The new dock was state of the art and enabled Meyer to become one of four leading builders of cruise ships in Europe (its main rivals were Wärtsilä in Finland, Fincantieri in Italy, Chantiers de l'Atlantique in France). The first vessel built in the dock was the *Crown Odyssey* – nowadays Fred. Olsen's *Balmoral* – a vessel rather similar in design and layout to P&O's own *Royal Princess*.

Very quickly, Meyer Werft became expert builders of cruise ships. The yard's high level of workmanship, extremely efficient processes and constant investment in the latest technology are reflected in the outstanding fit and finish of every vessel built

Dressed overall in the Hudson River, the ***Sea Princess*** *is seen during her second phase as a British-based P&O cruise ship after a spell in the Princess fleet. She ended her P&O career as the Victoria. (Andrew Kilk)*

***Canberra** and **Oriana** are lined up for comparison in Southampton on the day of the latter's maiden arrival, 8th April 1995. (Mick Lindsay)*

there. P&O's new flagship would benefit greatly from this proficiency.

Early on, P&O announced that its new cruise ship would be named *Oriana*. The general dimensions and layout of the abortive 'Project Gemini' were retained to form the basis for the new vessel, which would measure 69,153 tons. While Lloyd Werft's original 'Project Gemini' rendering had been rather blandly streamlined, somewhat resembling the contemporary Norwegian Cruise Line vessels *Dreamward* and *Windward* in elongated form, as the *Oriana*'s design developed, a much more distinctive ship emerged. This was thanks to the early employment of the Swedish cruise ship design specialist Robert Tillberg, whose office re-styled the liner's silhouette. Taking inspiration from *Canberra*'s highly successful design, which had stood the test of time remarkably well during her 30-year career to date, Tillberg suggested forward-slanted lifeboat recesses and a single tall funnel, the casing of which was styled to hint at *Canberra*'s characteristic twin stacks. Of course, *Oriana* would have flat decks with none of *Canberra*'s sheer or camber but Tillberg made a virtue out of this necessity, giving the liner a rigorous and very contemporary appearance with neatly resolved and harmonious details.[83]

Being intended to undertake lengthy cruises with long trans-oceanic segments, *Oriana*'s hull form was finer at the bow than was typical for vessels of her size and type. She was also rather more robustly constructed with thicker plates better to withstand the rigours of the open ocean. Thus, from a structural viewpoint, she was in essence a hybrid ocean liner and cruise ship. *Oriana*'s sharp bow profile, slender forward lines and transom stern enhanced her good looks. To maintain the high service speed necessary to carry out long voyages from Southampton with reserves of power to make up for storm delays, *Oriana* was fitted with four 9-cyliner MAN-B&W diesels, generating 47,750 kW, enabling a speed of 24 knots to be maintained when necessary. (This output may be compared with the 24,000 kW generated by *Star Princess*' four 8-cylinder main engines, but her speed was a mere 21 knots.)

In order to appeal to a diverse British clientele, a wide array of cabin types and sizes were specified – as well as an unusually large number and variety of public rooms (*Oriana* would have no less than 26 different rooms, as opposed to the mere 15 on P&O's American-based *Star Princess*). As with the majority of new cruise ships, most public rooms were spread across two decks in the upper hull and lower superstructure with the dining rooms and galley aft and the theatre forward. (The theory of entertaining passengers at the bow, feeding them at the stern and extracting revenue from them amidships is widely employed throughout the cruise industry.) A further subtle refinement on *Oriana* was the positioning of the more elegant and exclusive public rooms aft of the midships atrium with the more populist and fun-orientated, such as the disco and casino, forward. In some respects, this layout reflects the two-class structure of P&O liners of the past, albeit in a one-class ship.

Oriana's public rooms would be required to serve rather different purposes from those of her America-based contemporaries. Rather than the Las Vegas-style show lounge (or copa room) found on most recent cruise ships, she would instead boast a theatre, staging plays and London West End musicals. Ballroom dancing, classical recitals, a cinema auditorium, a pub plus

ORIANA

*The **Oriana** inward bound to Southampton. (FotoFlite)*

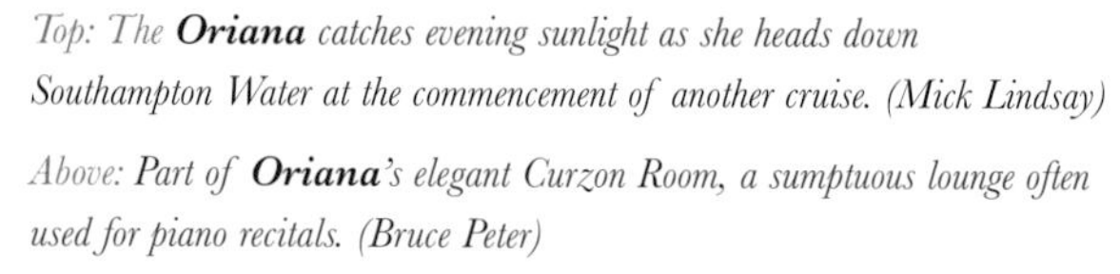

Top: The ***Oriana*** *catches evening sunlight as she heads down Southampton Water at the commencement of another cruise. (Mick Lindsay)*

Above: Part of ***Oriana****'s elegant Curzon Room, a sumptuous lounge often used for piano recitals. (Bruce Peter)*

Right: ***Oriana****'s Lord's Tavern – a wittily designed pub by John McNeece featuring 'cricket stump' bar stools. (Bruce Peter)*

Bottom right: The ***Oriana*** *has an unusually large and varied selection of public rooms, reflecting her diverse and discerning clientele. This is her Pacific Lounge. (Bruce Peter)*

an elegant lounge suitable for hosting afternoon tea were all distinctly 'British' requirements, already well catered for on the *Canberra*.

Oriana's interiors were largely the work of a London-based Scot, John McNeece, who was a mid-1960s graduate of the Glasgow School of Art's Interior Design department. McNeece had since established himself as a successful designer of cruise ship interiors. He worked alongside Robert Tillberg to realise *Oriana*'s extensive and lavish interiors. Particularly outstanding are The Anderson Room, named after P&O's co-founder, Arthur Anderson and the adjacent library space, both of which are furnished by the cabinetmaker David Lindley, nephew of H.M. The Queen. The Curzon Room, named after the controversial Governor of India, Lord Curzon, was sumptuously furnished and specially designed acoustically for piano recitals. All of these spaces were essentially conservative in their decorative approaches, seeking to reflect the traditionalism of English country houses and Pall Mall gentlemen's clubs, as well as evoking something of the shipboard style of the grandest P&O liners of the inter-war era.

McNeece took a more light-hearted approach when designing the Lord's Tavern pub, Harlequin's – which, by night, serves as the ship's disco – and the Pacific Lounge. The former was intended to replicate the role of *Canberra*'s popular Cricketers' Tavern. Therefore, McNeece, produced a witty post-modern take on the Marylebone Cricket Club's headquarters, featuring a green carpet in broad two-tone stripes, bar stools resembling cricket stumps and window blinds bordered in MCC 'ham and eggs' colours. As the name suggested, Harlequin's was decorated in bright hues and featured a sophisticated lighting installation.[84] Elsewhere – notably the restaurants and atrium – *Oriana* tended towards Tillberg's favoured pastel tones. Throughout, the standard of finish was exceptionally high, however. Further public rooms – and extensive lido areas – were located on *Oriana*'s topmost decks, but these were rather more shaded than on the majority of cruise ships, it being expected that a greater proportion of her passengers would prefer to take the sea air than to sunbathe.

At Meyer Werft, *Oriana*'s construction proceeded a-pace as, with incredible accuracy, prefabricated steel sections were assembled in the building dock. In June 1994, *Oriana* was floated out. Then began the lengthy journey down the River Ems to reach the North Sea. On trials, *Oriana* performed well – but one unfortunate problem was pronounced vibration in her aft body at certain speeds. Modifications were carried out, but *Oriana* remained troubled by vibration at certain speeds for the first couple of years of her otherwise outstandingly successful career.

Oriana was named by H.M. The Queen in Southampton in April 1995. There, she berthed astern of the *Canberra*, enabling a fascinating comparison to be made between the 1960s liner and the brand new cruise ship. Thanks to the impressive massing and ingenious styling of her hull and superstructure, *Canberra* had always seemed so much bigger than her actual 44,807-ton size but, now, beside *Oriana*, she suddenly looked small and obsolescent. Yet, rather than being withdrawn immediately, she was kept on in the P&O fleet for another two years. On the day of *Oriana*'s naming, Lord Sterling was interviewed by BBC Radio Solent, whose presenter questioned him on whether P&O had not made a terrible mistake in building the ship. Sterling's memorable response was 'our only mistake was not ordering two of her.' Within only a few years, P&O would remedy this matter.

The *Canberra* finally bowed out in 1997. On the morning of 30th September, she emerged from a bank of mist off the Isle of Wight into bright sunshine. A flotilla of small craft came out to greet her and to escort her to her berth – just like the famous day when she returned from the Falklands War. Although from a

With her clean lines and striking details, the ***Oriana*** *makes a fine sight at speed – the epitome of a modern world cruise liner. (Mick Lindsay collection)*

Top: The ***Dawn Princess*** *leaving Vancouver. (Andrew Kilk)*

Above: The ***Sun Princess*** *in azure Caribbean waters. (Andrew Kilk)*

Right: The ***Ocean Princess*** *at sea. (Andrew Kilk)*

distance, she appeared pristine, upon closer inspection, the pitted layers of paint on her hull testified to her long and eventful career. There was a rumour that she might be on the verge of being sold for further service – and the American company Premier Cruises did consider making a bid for her. In view of her worn condition, P&O sold her instead to Pakistani ship breakers. After de-storing and the removal of selected artworks from her extensive on-board collection, she sailed for Karachi, where she was scrapped at Gadani Beach, a graveyard for so many life-expired ships. Her memory lived on, however, in the fond recollections of the many thousands of passengers – and British soldiers – who had known her in her heyday.

When ordering *Oriana* from Meyer Werft, P&O simultaneously contracted from the Fincantieri shipyard at Monfalcone, Italy, the first two of what would eventually become a series of four 77,449-ton cruise ships for its Princess Cruises division. The *Sun Princess* entered service in 1995 being followed less than two years later by the *Dawn Princess*. These vessels could each carry 2,250 passengers, many in outside staterooms with balconies. There were, however, fewer public rooms than on *Oriana* and the shipboard design style reflected American tastes. The interiors were designed by Teresa Anderson, an American of Peruvian birth who had studied interior design in Maryland in the 1970s, thereafter working with a local practice called H. Chambers & Company. In the early 1990s, she was involved in designing parts of the *Crown Princess* and *Regal Princess* and, consequently, she came to be employed full-time by Princess Cruises from 1994 as its 'in house' designer, producing interiors for all of its subsequent new-buildings, commencing with *Sun Princess*. As the new Princess ships were Italian-built, Anderson was assisted in these projects by the Italian Giacomo Mortola. In comparison with the glamorous light-toned Californian styling of previous Princess vessels, Anderson's oeuvre was conservative, her penchant being ornate mouldings and brown imitation wood panelling. Thus, the disjunction between the new Princess ships' very streamlined exterior profiles, topped off with futuristic parabolic funnels, and their traditionalist interiors, was extreme. This notwithstanding, Princess passengers evidently appreciated Anderson's approach as she has since designed numerous other cruise ship interiors continuing with the same design formula.

P&O'S CRUISE FERRIES

P&O inherited from Townsend Thoresen a fairly modern fleet of ferries, dating mainly from the mid-1970s. Several of these had been radically rebuilt during the mid-1980s to increase their capacities. This was achieved by raising their superstructures and inserting an extra upper vehicle deck. While effective as a stop-gap measure, this procedure had resulted in ships that appeared most eccentric and rather top-heavy.

Simultaneously, in Scandinavia, a generation of very large and luxuriously appointed cruise ferries had been built, mainly for operation across the mid-Baltic between Sweden and Finland. The big attraction was the tax-free sale of alcoholic drinks (in both countries, liquor stores are state-owned).

Most British ferry routes hitherto had primarily a transport function, rather than being leisure-orientated, but that situation changed quickly during the early 1990s. On the Western Channel, Brittany Ferries were in the vanguard of bringing Scandinavian-style, comfort and diversity of facilities to the British market. Its 1989-delivered *Bretagne* quickly became an outstanding success operating from Plymouth across the Bay of Biscay to Santander in Spain – so much so that P&O decided to follow suit with its own Spanish route from Portsmouth to Bilbao. The latter had a reputation as a declining industrial city but very quickly massive civic expenditure transformed its reputation into one of Spain's leading cultural destinations. In particular, a striking new Guggenheim contemporary art gallery, designed by Frank Gehry, became one of Europe's leading tourist attractions.

To serve Bilbao, P&O chartered the 37,799-ton Swedish ferry *Olympia* from Rederi AB Slite in 1993, renaming her the *Pride of Bilbao*. At that time, Rederi AB Slite formed one half of the well-known Viking Line consortium and, during the latter 1980s, they had built a succession of new ferries, each one larger and more glamorous than the last. With a severe economic downturn in the early 1990s, which badly affected Sweden, Rederi AB Slite got into financial difficulties and its mortgage lender foreclosed, forcing the company into bankruptcy on the very day when P&O took over the *Pride of Bilbao*. The charter nonetheless proceeded as planned and the magnificent ferry made her Channel debut to great acclaim. Slotted in between her Bilbao sailings, every Friday evening, *Pride of Bilbao* made an overnight 'party cruise' to Cherbourg, which apart from being popular and profitable for P&O, added much-needed capacity supporting the existing much smaller and less well appointed *Pride of Cherbourg* and *Pride of Winchester*.

Next, P&O European Ferries sought to acquire two further, even bigger and more modern vessels from Rederi AB Slite's liquidators – the *Athena* and the *Kalypso*, which suddenly became available on the open market. P&O hoped to use these to upgrade its Portsmouth-Le Havre route but while their managers and technical staff were tallying up the ships' inventory to work out the price they were willing to pay, another unknown buyer from Malaysia was signing a purchase deal. Most unfortunately for P&O, the two ferries escaped its grasp and instead headed for the Far East as the casino cruise ships *Star Aquarius* and *Star Pisces*. Their new owner, the Genting group, was primarily a casino operator. Genting's founder, Tan Sri Lim Goh Tong, was however a cruise enthusiast who wished to commence his own line, Star Cruises. For Genting, the two former Baltic ferries were a great success, but P&O still badly needed new ships to serve Le Havre, better to compete with Brittany Ferries' increasingly glamorous fleet.

Some months later, P&O European Ferries instead struck a deal to charter from Germany's TT-Line the modern Sheerness-Vlissingen Olau Line sisters, the 33,336-ton *Olau Britannia* and *Olau Hollandia*. These ferries were too large for their existing route and, as it was widely believed that the end of tax-free shopping between European Union countries was imminent, TT-Line decided that they would best be disposed of for use elsewhere. TT-Line, however, were tough negotiators and, to

The ***Pride of Portsmouth****, one of two jumbo ferries chartered by P&O at considerable expense from Germany's TT-Line for service between Portsmouth and Le Havre. (Miles Cowsill)*

operate the ships, P&O were required to pay a relatively high charter fee of £15,000 per day per ship. They were introduced in June 1994 as the *Pride of Portsmouth* and *Pride of Le Havre*.[85] The charters benefited the owners of these ships more than they did P&O's shareholders at a time when profit margins were already thin against stiff competition from the ever more glamorous ships of rapidly expanding Brittany Ferries.

DOVER STRAIT DEVELOPMENTS

The latter 1990s proved challenging for the ferry industry as a whole. The tragic sinking in 1993 of the Baltic cruise ferry *Estonia* greatly reduced public confidence and the abandonment of tax-free shopping between European Union member states in 1999 further compounded the sector's difficulties. Meanwhile, the Channel Tunnel challenged the ferries' dominance on the Dover

To boost capacity on the Dover Strait and to offer drivers a 'turn up and board' service, P&O needed five ferries in constant circulation and so they had a new freighter modified while under construction in Germany to enter service as the passenger carrying ***Pride of Burgundy****. (Miles Cowsill)*

Strait and newly established 'low cost' airlines began to emerge to attract away increasing numbers of foot passengers.

On the other hand, a growing economy and the opening up of Eastern Europe saw an increased consumerism in Britain and this was reflected in an exponential increase in lorry and trailer traffic across the Dover Strait. In 1991-92 P&O European Ferries commissioned a series of new 'European' class freighters from Schichau Unterweser of Bremerhaven for the Dover-Zeebrugge route to handle this; these were the *European Seaway*, *European Pathway* and *European Highway*. A fourth example, the *Pride of Burgundy*, was built with an enlarged superstructure to carry private passengers as well as truck drivers. In 1993, P&O introduced a five-ship Dover-Calais service, the idea being to counter the Channel Tunnel's forthcoming 'Le Shuttle' car and freight operation by guaranteeing that a ship was constantly loading in each port with check-in times streamlined to as little as 20 minutes. P&O European Ferries' intensive operation on the route was an outstanding success. The ferries were fitted with 'Club Class' lounges and therefore could offer those willing to pay a small supplement a service standard far better than Le Shuttle, which P&O's Brian Langford scathingly observed would offer customers nothing more than 'a light bulb and a loo'.[86] Ferries offered the luxuries of space, fresh air and retail therapy. Indeed, during the 1990s, Dover Strait ferries increasingly became filled with shoppers seeking to buy bargain drink and cigarettes in the various hypermarkets located near Calais and on board the ferries. For foot passengers, day returns cost as little as £1 and so the ferries often seemed as though they were filled with day-trippers, smoking and drinking their way to France and back.

The era of the Dover Strait booze cruise was not to last, however, as it was widely predicted that the European Union would call time on tax-free sales on routes between EU member states – an anomaly which hitherto had greatly benefited the ferry industry. Forestalling this eventuality, in 1998 P&O European

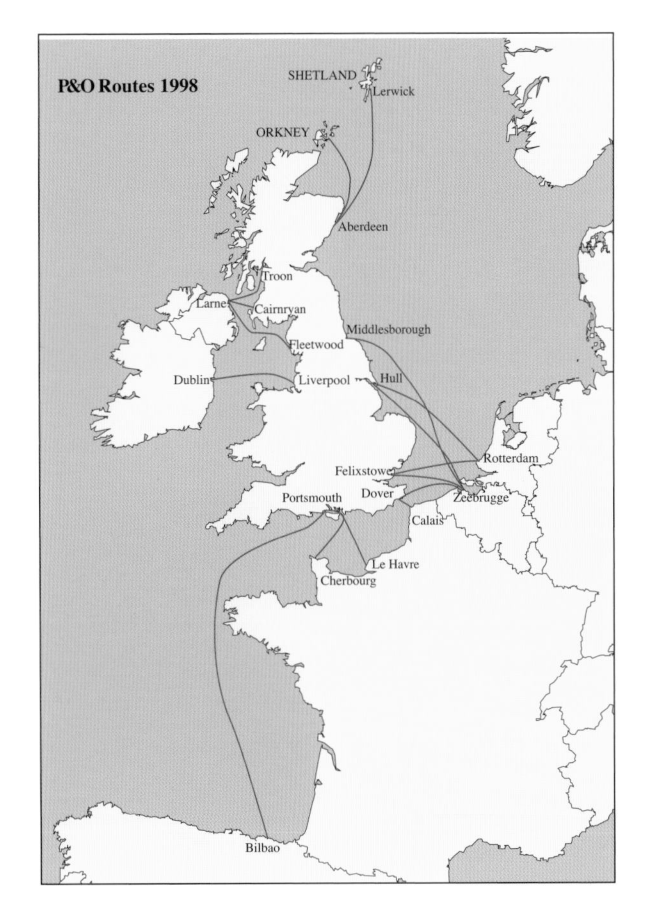

The ***Pride of Bilbao****, ex* ***Olympia****, the former Baltic cruise ferry operated under charter by P&O from Portsmouth to Bilbao and Cherbourg. (Miles Cowsill)*

The freight ferry ***European Highway*** *had the same hull design as Pride of Burgundy and operated mainly from Dover to Zeebrugge. (Ferry Publications Library)*

Ferries and its Dover Strait rival Stena Line (formerly Sealink British Ferries) decided to join forces to create a streamlined ferry service better to compete with Le Shuttle in the forthcoming post tax-free shopping era.

Stena had acquired Sealink British Ferries from Sea Containers through a hostile 1990 takeover. Stena somewhat insensitively believed that the type of leisure and retail-orientated ferry service it offered in Scandinavia would also work in British waters and, furthermore, that it would be possible successfully to use ferries designed for usage elsewhere on the Dover Strait. On both

The ***Pride of Bilbao****'s hallway was typical of 1980s Baltic ferries, somewhat resembling an American hotel of the same era with marble, mirrors, glass sculptures and red carpets. (Bruce Peter)*

counts, they were wrong and so Stena's additions to the Dover-Calais fleet proved less than successful, primarily because they were too slow and with tortuous loading arrangements in comparison with P&O's entirely purpose-built fleet.

Seven vessels were involved in the P&O Stena Line joint venture, five from P&O and two from Stena's fleet. All lost their 'Pride of...' and 'Stena...' names in favour of the prefix 'P&OSL...' and all vessels were refitted with the same branded eateries and public rooms, although these continued to be operated separately by P&O European Ferries. Despite some belated lobbying from the ferry industry, tax free shopping ended in 1999, as had been predicted. Later, in 2002, P&O bought out Stena's 40 per cent share in the Dover Strait joint venture for £150 million and consequently the fleet reverted to the P&O identity.[87]

P&O NORTH SEA FERRIES

In 1996, P&O bought out its Dutch partner Nedlloyd's share of North Sea Ferries and thereafter the ferry fleet from Hull too was painted in P&O Ferries' standard dark blue livery. Subsequently, in 1999 two new 'fourth generation' vessels, each measuring 59,925 tons and thus the world's largest ferries, were ordered from Fincantieri's Venice shipyard to replace *Norsea* and *Norsun* on the Hull-Rotterdam route. P&O's Italian new-buildings were delivered as the *Pride of Rotterdam* and the *Pride of Hull* in 2001 and 2002 respectively. Striking-looking vessels with massive towering superstructures, each boasted 3,300 lane metres for freight as well as superbly appointed accommodation for 1,360

In P&O Stena livery, the much rebuilt ***POSL Kent****, ex* ***Pride of Kent****, ex* ***Spirit of Free Enterprise*** *is seen in Calais. (Miles Cowsill)*

passengers. P&O's North Sea Ferries operation remained far more relaxed than its Dover Strait and Western Channel ferry services; as the ships lay over during the day, passengers and freight hauliers could board almost at their leisure and enjoy several hours' respite in the ferries' comfortable and spacious accommodation before each vessel actually put to sea. As the new ferries were far too big to fit through the tidal lock into Hull's King George V Dock, a new berth was constructed in the River Humber to accommodate them. (At the same time, the *Norsea* and *Norsun* were renamed *Pride of York* and *Pride of Bruges* and switched to the Hull-Zeebrugge service.)

At the same time as the *Pride of Rotterdam* and *Pride of Hull* entered service, P&O North Sea Ferries' two modern freight vessels, the 1994-built *Norbay* and *Norbank*, which in recent years

North Sea Ferries' ***Norbay*** *boosted freight capacity on the busy Hull-Rotterdam route from 1994 onwards. (Miles Cowsill)*

P&OSL
DOVER
DOVER

***POSL Dover**, ex **Pride of Dover**, crossing the Dover Strait in her P&O Stena colours. (FotoFlite)*

Top: The vast Italian-built ***Pride of Rotterdam*** *greatly increased capacity on the Hull-Rotterdam route. (Bruce Peter)*

Centre left, centre right and lower left:: Inboard, the ***Pride of Rotterdam*** *and* ***Pride of Hull*** *have well-appointed passenger accommodation. Their relaxed scheduling means that a trip is rather more like a short hotel stay than is typical of ferries trading on more southerly routes. (Bruce Peter and Ferry Publications Library)*

Right: The ***Pride of Rotterdam*** *in drydock during overhaul. (Ferry Publications Library)*

P&O's Japanese-built Irish Sea ro-pax ferry ***European Causeway****. (Ferry Publications Library)*

duplicated the *Norsea* and *Norsun*'s rosters between Hull and Rotterdam providing much needed extra capacity, were transferred to P&O's Irish Sea freight routes.

P&O IRISH SEA

In 1998, at the same time as P&O Stena was established to operate Dover Strait services, P&O re-organised the management and promotion of its Irish Sea routes. Hitherto, its Scotland-Northern Ireland passenger link from Cairnryan to Larne, purchased as part of European Ferries in 1987, was managed from Felixstowe, whereas its freight services from Liverpool, Heysham, Fleetwood and Ardrossan to Ireland were managed and marketed as Pandoro. To address this anomaly and to create a unified identity, all of these routes came under the aegis of P&O Irish Sea. The following year, P&O announced that three new combined freight and passenger ferries would be built by Mitsubishi in Japan, two for the well-established Cairnryan-Larne service and the third for use on a new route from a purpose-built ferry port at Mostyn in North Wales to Dublin. Delivered in 2000-2001, these vessels were named the *European Causeway*, *European Highlander* and *European Ambassador* respectively. In the same period, P&O Irish Sea's introduction of the modern former P&O North Sea Ferries freighters *Norbay* and *Norbank* provided a necessary boost to the successful Liverpool-Dublin route.

P&O SCOTTISH FERRIES

Since taking over Coast Lines in 1971, P&O had operated ferry services to Orkney and Shetland under Government contract. As the main routes to Lerwick and Kirkwall departed from Aberdeen's rather constricted harbour, second-hand Scandinavian ferries dating from the 1970s proved optimal in terms of size. Since 1987, the *St Sunniva*, a 1972-built vessel originally intended for a sheltered Danish domestic route and subsequently used by P&O Normandy Ferries on the Dover Strait as the *n.f. Panther*, had been one of the vessels used. Another was the former *Travemünde* of 1971, first operated between Denmark and West Germany and deployed by subsequent owners in the Adriatic and across the Western Channel. P&O bought her in 1992 and, after renovation, she became its *St Clair*. A third, smaller ferry was needed for the short

Following the P&O Stena joint venture, the entire P&O Ferries fleet was gradually refitted. Their a la carte restaurants became 'Langan's Brasseries' through a tie-in with the famous London restaurant of that name. This is the example on ***Pride of Bilbao****. (Bruce Peter)*

The Aberdeen to Orkney and Shetland ferry ***St Sunniva*** *leaves Aberdeen in 2001 towards the end of P&O Scottish Ferries' operation of the route. (Bruce Peter)*

daytime crossing from Scrabster in the very north of Scotland to Stromness on Orkney and P&O found a suitable ship in Sweden, where the 1971-built *Eckerö* (ex *Svea Scarlett*) brought Swedes on short shopping trips to and from the Aland Islands. P&O introduced her as its *St Ola* in 1992. During the ensuing decade, these three ferries performed remarkably well on the treacherous Northern Isles routes, often coping with sea conditions they were never intended to encounter. Short five-year franchises to operate the subsidised passenger service, coupled with competition for the more lucrative freight market from other shipping entrepreneurs dissuaded P&O from investing in more modern tonnage – or even building anew.

In the latter 1990s, the Labour-controlled Scottish Government began a new tendering round which the state-owned West Coast ferry operator Caledonian MacBrayne appeared determined to win – so much so that in November 1998 they sent its flagship *Isle of Lewis* to Orkney where she was opened to the public. At first, P&O Scottish Ferries suggested continuing with second-hand tonnage but, with Caledonian MacBrayne and its partners proposing new vessels, P&O too produced plans for purpose-built ferries at an estimated cost of £100 million. In the end, a consortium led by Caledonian MacBrayne won the Northern Isles contract and so P&O Scottish Ferries' ageing fleet made their final sailings in September 2002.

PORTS AND LOGISTICS

P&O had been a port and logistics operator in Australia since 1968 when P&O Australia was established to consolidate the Group's business interests there and to spread into emerging markets around the Pacific Rim; this coincided with the initial development of the OCL container consortium, which subsequently became P&O Containers. On *terra firma*, P&O's specialities were container port operation (P&O Ports) and cold storage for refrigerated cargo vessels (P&O Cold Logistics). The first P&O overseas port development contract with Australia was gained in 1986; this was to build and manage a new Kelang Container Terminal in Malaysia. Thereafter, P&O Ports underwent steady international growth through a mix of new development and the absorption of existing facilities. By the millennium, P&O operated 25 container ports in 16 countries and additionally had cargo handling interests in a further 30 ports.

P&O Cold Logistics also originated in late-1960s Australia, expanding into New Zealand in 1989. Next, in 1994, the American market was entered with the acquisition of cold stores and associated logistics in California, Nevada, Texas and New England, making the USA its largest business area. Investment in Argentina followed in 1996, giving P&O a profile in the country very different from the Falklands War only 15 years previously, in which its liners and ferries serving as troop transports had been prominent and legitimate military targets for the Argentine Air Force.

In the late 1990s, P&O was one of the world's leading shipping companies and property developers. Its ship-operating subsidiaries included P&O Ferries, P&O Cruises, P&O Princess Cruises, P&O Containers, P&O Bulk Carriers, P&O Tankships, while ship-related businesses included P&O Ports, the P&O Ferrymasters European road haulage business and Australian Offshore Services. Yet, within only a decade, the majority of subsidiaries had been sold and only the ferry, ports, UK property and Australian Maritime Services businesses remained.

Top: The ***Norsun*** *manoeuvres off her Rotterdam berth. Subsequently, she was cascaded to the Hull-Zeebrugge route and renamed* ***Pride of Bruges****. (Miles Cowsill)*

Above: The former Dover-Zeebrugge vessel ***European Clearway*** *was transferred to the Irish Sea routes in 1998 and renamed* ***European Pathfinder****. (Miles Cowsill)*

Left: The ***POSL Canterbury****, ex* ***Stena Fantasia****, at Calais. (Miles Cowsill)*

Chapter 6

Dismantling the Empire

For half a century – from the time of Franklin Roosevelt's 'New Deal' in the USA of the 1930s until the latter 1980s – the 'conglomerate model' was widely reckoned to be the best way for large businesses to achieve stability and growth. The idea was that poor results in one sector might be offset by large profits in another. So long as a conglomerate's individual subsidiaries were efficiently managed, the fact that they might have little commonality was not widely thought to be problematic. With its diverse property, construction, shipping and logistics subsidiaries, P&O was a very successful example of how a conglomerate was supposed to work as its main business areas operated according to different cycles.

Come the 1990s, a new generation of fund manager in the city observed that conglomerates often were bureaucratic and therefore relatively slow to act when new opportunities to make quick profits presented themselves, as approval first was required at various board levels, possibly taking many days or even weeks to achieve. In the bulk cargo shipping sector, smaller private owners (frequently Greeks) could buy and sell ships as they saw fit, often acquiring tonnage second hand from large operators such as P&O, then selling it on for a profit when the market for a particular ship type reached its peak, whereas large conglomerates might take weeks to achieve board approval by which time the opportunity could have passed.

As the shipping world had become more specialised since the 1960s (and the property and construction worlds likewise), P&O's senior management came under intense pressure from City investment fund managers to concentrate only on the most profitable parts of the Group and to sell the remainder. For City analysts, the most obvious disjunction in the P&O Group's activities was between its shipping businesses (including port facilities) and its construction and property assets. If P&O sold these latter activities and reverted solely to being a shipping and ports management company, that would placate the city – at least for a while. In 1998, P&O made a £398 million profit on a £5.91 billion turnover, construction and property accounting for 46 per cent of this result, shipping and port operation generating the remainder.

By selling off its construction and international property interests, P&O intended to generate £2 billion, just over half of which they would use to purchase several very large new cruise ships, four for its successful American Princess Cruises division and one for the UK cruise market. It was expected that, in the new millennium, P&O's cruise division would account for three quarters of operating profits and more than half of its net assets. Bovis Homes was floated at the end of 1997 and the sale of Bovis Construction, along with the P&O Group's property interests, was announced in March 1999. Lord Sterling observed that 'by streamlining the Group so as to focus on core expertise and strong position in the maritime sector, we will be able to exploit opportunities to the full as well as provide shareholders… with a clearer picture of the Group's potential.' It is evident,

*The **Aurora** berthed at Sydney during a world cruise. (Mick Lindsay collection)*

however, that, to a significant extent, Sterling was acting under duress as both his own background in property development and his business instinct suggested that the better course of action might be to keep charge of both of P&O's major divisions. While certain institutional investors even went so far as to call for Sterling's resignation, his position was supported by the credit rating agency Standard & Poor's, which argued that P&O's construction and property portfolio was a 'significant element in the Group's business strength.'[88] This notwithstanding, the split went ahead anyway.

Even before re-investing part of the capital generated through the sale of Bovis, P&O was preparing to capitalise on increasing demand in the British and American cruise markets. P&O's Southampton-based flagship *Oriana* was proving so popular that in 1998 a second cruise ship was ordered as her consort – the *Aurora*. Again, the contract was awarded to Meyer Werft but, rather than merely producing an *Oriana* clone, a new design was prepared. While this retained most of *Oriana*'s successful features and, wherever possible, improved upon them, the new *Aurora* would emerge as a ship with a distinctive personality of her own. Since *Oriana* was completed, cruise ships had come to have increasing numbers of staterooms with balconies and so *Aurora* too reflected this trend. Externally, her profile was somewhat more severe than that of *Oriana*, mainly due to her lifeboat recesses being vertical, rather than slanted forward (they were in fact very similar to those on *Sun Princess* and *Dawn Princess*). A dramatic design feature was the curvature of her after superstructure, starting at her lido and arcing upwards to form the deck island containing her air-conditioning plant, from which her tapering funnel protruded at a jaunty angle, then curving downward through tiers of aft-facing sun decks towards her stern. This made *Aurora* a very beautiful and distinctive ship, particularly when viewed from stern-quarter angles.

Inboard, *Aurora* was largely the work of a different team of designers from *Oriana*. She was generally darker and richer with detailing evoking the 1930s, rather than *Oriana*'s tendency towards pastel-shaded Edwardiana. SMC, a London interior design firm, designed her Art Deco atrium and adjacent shops, her library, card room and theatre, while her restaurants (also Art Deco), nightclub and cabins were by the Norwegian Yran and Storbraaten.[89]

The *Aurora* was named in Southampton on 27th April 2000 by HRH The Princess Royal after which she set sail on what was supposedly her maiden voyage. Most unfortunately, after only a few hours' sailing, the new liner became so beset with mechanical difficulties that her cruise was terminated and she returned to Southampton to disembark her very disappointed passengers. Following several weeks' rectification work, *Aurora* re-entered service and has since performed superbly.

The **Grand Princess** *– the first of a highly successful and innovative series of very large cruise ships for P&O Princess Cruises and P&O Cruises – approaches Malaga. (Bruce Peter)*

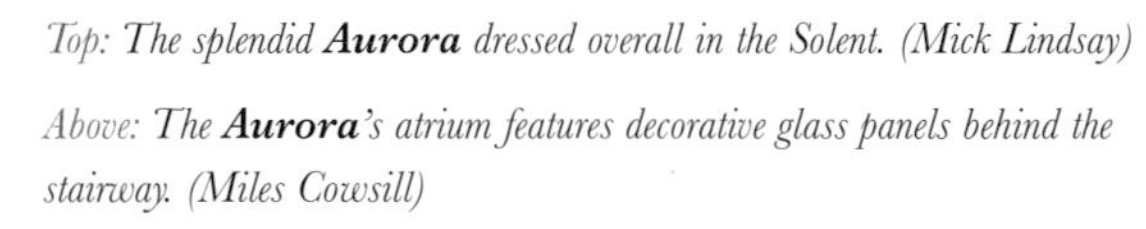

Top: The splendid ***Aurora*** *dressed overall in the Solent. (Mick Lindsay)*

Above: The ***Aurora****'s atrium features decorative glass panels behind the stairway. (Miles Cowsill)*

Top right: The Sports Bar on the ***Aurora****. (Miles Cowsill)*

Right: The ***Medina Restaurant****, the Aurora's midships dining room. (Bruce Peter)*

*The atrium on **Grand Princess**, designed by Teresa Anderson in a surprisingly traditionalist manner for such an otherwise futuristic-looking vessel. (Bruce Peter)*

***Grand Princess'** interiors feature displays of P&O memorabilia, as a corner of her Explorers' Lounge shows. (Bruce Peter)*

RECORD-BREAKING PRINCESSES

Four new Princess Cruises ships were ordered from Fincantieri at Monfalcone, the *Sea Princess* (1998) and *Ocean Princess* (1999) being near sisters of the recent *Sun Princess* and *Dawn Princess*. The *Grand Princess* and *Golden Princess* were however altogether more spectacular. Measuring 108,806 gross tons, upon delivery in 1998, *Grand Princess* was the world's biggest ever passenger ship. Not only was *Grand Princess* a giant in terms of volume and capacity (she could carry up to 3,209 passengers), but she was also of striking and revolutionary external design. Indeed, she was among the first cruise ships with an external superstructure that was composed entirely of stateroom balconies. Rather than cutting openings in continuous shell plating, as on previous vessels, the balconies took the form of horizontally expressed external decks with slim retractable vertical partitions. This meant that the sides of *Grand Princess*'s superstructure looked more like a tropical resort hotel than a conventional passenger ship. To lend her a memorably stylish 'design signature', the Italian architect Gianfranco Bertaglia designed a convex-shaped bow profile with a swan-neck and a whale-back form above the mooring deck. A passenger promenade continued round the forepeak, enabling guests to enact a famous romantic scene from the motion picture 'Titanic'.

Grand Princess's aft profile was even more remarkable. Her superstructure was continued all the way to her transom stern, with aft-facing staterooms above, rather than the tiered public decks found on previous P&O cruise ships. High above, a large aluminium 'pod' was held aloft by broad aluminium box-sections and this gave *Grand Princess*'s stern the appearance of a shopping trolley. The pod contained a large state-of-the-art discotheque, accessed from abaft the funnel by a 'travelator' in a blue tinted glass tube. Copious additional use of the same blue glazing for cabin balcony balustrades and deck screens gave *Grand Princess* a cool, futuristic aura, which was further enhanced by her dramatic parabola-shaped funnel casing. While traditionalists found *Grand Princess*'s appearance hard to accept, she was certainly memorably distinctive.[90]

*Inside the disco on the **Grand Princess**. (Bruce Peter)*

The **Golden Princess** *in the Hudson River with New York's impressive skyline forming a backdrop. (Andrew Kilk)*

Inboard, the situation was different. Princess Cruises' newly appointed 'in house' designer Teresa Anderson worked with the Italian interior designer Giacomo Mortola, who had been involved in designing the interiors of previous Princess new-buildings. True to form, Anderson's approach was traditionalist and with a ready reliance on ornate mouldings and brown panelling. Considering her great size, *Grand Princess* had only a relatively small atrium and her dining rooms were blandly nondescript. Yet, Princess clearly knew its market as the vessel was an immediate success. Indeed, she was the first of numerous similar cruise ships to be built for Princess Cruises. *Golden Princess* arrived in 1999 and was followed during the next decade by seven further slightly varied examples of the type for Princess Cruises plus two for P&O Cruises. Existing Princess ships displaced by this new armada mainly were shifted either to P&O Cruises Australia, or to other newly established P&O cruise brands.

RED LIPS AND ROSES

In 1999, P&O made an inspired investment in a recently established German cruise operator, Aida Cruises. This firm was a subsidiary of the Deutsche Seereederei Rostock (DSR) which, until the fall of the Berlin Wall in 1996, had been the main Communist East German shipping line. DSR had long operated passenger ships under charter in the Western market – most famously the *Volkerfreundschaft* and, latterly, the *Arkona*. DSR's Chairman Horst Rahne's visionary proposal was that, in future years, the cruise market in a prospering united Germany would have an exponential growth potential. After all, Germans have a strong maritime tradition and affinity with the sea and, just as in Britain and America, there was a relatively well off post-war 'baby boom' generation approaching retirement age en masse and also a younger generation looking for value-for-money all-inclusive holidays in German-speaking environments. Aida would serve these markets with what were described as 'club ships' – which were essentially floating informal holiday resorts. DSR ordered its first new cruise ship – which was named *Aida* – from the Kvaerner-Masa shipyard in Turku, Finland for delivery in 1996.

Painted in a distinctive livery, featuring red lips painted on her bow and eyes with a trailing shadow on her hull's topsides, she was instantly recognisable. Inboard, her bright décor, featuring parasols and awnings to create a festive atmosphere, was by a German interior designer, Kai Bunge of Partnership Design. From the outset, Aida's 'Club Ship' concept was a great success.

What Rahne and his DSR colleagues badly needed was substantial investment quickly to expand its fleet. To his credit, Sir Jeffrey, now Lord Sterling, was convinced that Aida's business plan was a good one and so in 1999 P&O purchased the brand from DSR and immediately placed orders for two further ships, the *Aida cara* and *Aida aura* (the original Aida became *Aida vita*).[91]

Only one year later, P&O de-merged its growing portfolio of cruise businesses from the on-going P&O Group. The cruise business, comprising 22 ships operating under four brands – P&O Cruises, P&O Cruises Australia, Princess Cruises and Aida Cruises – gained a separate stock market listing as P&O Princess Cruises PLC, of which Lord Sterling was Chairman in addition to his Chairmanship of the P&O Group.

In 2001, P&O Princess Cruises PLC experimentally launched two new cruise brands – A'Rosa Cruises and Ocean Village. The former was an additional German subsidiary to Aida, offering both sea and river cruises. Positioned slightly upmarket of Aida, this received the *Crown Princess*, which was renovated internally and re-liveried with a red rose funnel logo as the *A'Rosa Blu*.

Top: The ***Star Princess****, a further addition to Princess Cruises' successful 'Grand' class. In this stern-quarter view, her discotheque can clearly be seen – a feature which caused vessels of the class to be nicknamed 'shopping trolleys'. (Andrew Kilk)*

Above: The ***Sapphire Princess*** *amid a Caribbean setting. (Andrew Kilk)*

Left: A bow view of the ***Star Princess*** *showing the distinctive bow form and silhouette of the 'Grand' class. (Andrew Kilk)*

Ocean Village, in contrast, sought to do for the British market what Aida had so successfully achieved in a German context. The long-established British P&O cruise brand, P&O Cruises, was perceived by the travel trade as rather conservative and attractive to an older, solidly middle class clientele. Ocean Village, by contrast, was launched with the rather contradictory and self-defeating slogan 'The cruise line for people who don't do cruises'. The idea was to offer an Aida-style Mediterranean holiday resort atmosphere, attracting 'first time' cruisers and those not keen on the more traditional and formal aspects of a conventional P&O Cruise. Ocean Village received the *Arcadia* as its initial ship and she was brightly painted in a pink, red and orange colour scheme, featuring coloured hoops along her hull and stripes around the superstructure and given the name *Ocean Village*. As with Aida's vessels, the emphasis was on entertainment, buffet dining and, at ports of call, cycles were provided by the gangway for passengers to use at will.

While the Aida brand was from the outset a great success, in the longer term, neither A'Rosa nor Ocean Village lived up to expectations. The former was hard to distinguish from Aida and

The ***A'Rosa Blu****, ex* ***Crown Princess****, one of a number of P&O Princess Cruises-owned vessels in the German market. (Bruce Peter)*

so, after only a year, *A'Rosa Blu* became *Aida Blu*. Ocean Village lasted a while longer and at one point it ran two ships (the *Aida Blu* briefly became *Ocean Village II* in 2007-2009). In the end, however, too few 'people who don't do cruises' could be persuaded to change their non-cruising habits and so the two Ocean Village ships were redeployed to P&O Cruises Australia becoming the *Pacific Pearl* and *Pacific Dawn* respectively.

To expand its British-based fleet, in 2002, P&O Princess Cruises switched the *Sea Princess* and *Ocean Princess* to P&O Cruises, for whom they became the *Adonia* and *Oceana*, in a stroke doubling the size of P&O Cruises' operation from Southampton. *Adonia* was an unusual name for a P&O Cruises ship, it having been invented to signify that this was an 'adults only' vessel. As Saga Holidays for the over-50s had expanded successfully into the cruise business, P&O Cruises probably felt compelled to respond. Apparently, a fairly substantial segment of the British cruise market considers British children to be sufficiently unpleasant that one dare not risk the presence of any being on board when planning a cruise. Evidently, P&O Cruises' 'adults only' concept has been successful and expanded to include

The P&O bulk carrier ***Ullswater****, a ship in a trade which P&O was shortly to exit at what, with hindsight, proved an inopportune moment. (Mick Lindsay collection)*

Top: The ***Oceana*** *and* ***Adonia*** *berthed bow-to-bow at Southampton for their joint naming ceremony in the Spring of 2003. (Bruce Peter)*

Above left: The ***Oceana*** *gliding through perfectly still water. (Mick Lindsay)*

Above right: The ***Ocean Village****, ex* ***Arcadia****, ex* ***Star Princess****, in Genoa. (Bruce Peter)*

Below: The ***Ocean Village Two****, originally* ***Crown Princess****, during a Mediterranean cruise. (Bruce Peter)*

P&O Containers' ***Shenzhen Bay****, one of a large fleet engaged in worldwide trading. (Mick Lindsay)*

subsequent additions to its fleet. Taken together with Saga's vessels, a significant proportion of British-based cruise ships exclude children – an unfortunate phenomenon unique to the UK.

EXITING THE BULK TRADES

In 1998, P&O expanded its P&O Bulk Carriers subsidiary when it entered into a joint venture with the Chinese Shougang steel group which also owned a substantial fleet of Cape-size vessels using the revived name Associated Bulk Carriers (ABC). In April 2000, P&O bought out its Asian partner, briefly becoming ABC's sole owner, but later the same year. After failing to float the company on the Norwegian stock exchange, it sold half of ABC to Eurotower Shipping, owned by the Monaco-based Israeli shipowner Sammy Ofer.

Bulk shipping is a sector whose profitability fluctuates markedly depending upon the state of the global economy and the numbers of particular size categories of bulk carriers available at any moment. (South East Asian shipyards can build such vessels very quickly and in quantity, meaning that the market can fast overheat, then suddenly collapse due to overcapacity.) Although many established liner companies invested in bulk shipping during the 1960s-70s period, it was individual entrepreneurs who generally were most successful in the sector as, when the market changed suddenly, they could buy and sell spontaneously without first seeking board approval. Ofer was one such successful independent bulk carrier operator and, by the 1990s, he was reckoned to be by far the wealthiest Israeli. Initially, he purchased half of Associated Bulk Carriers for £68 million.[92] The 22-strong ABC fleet of Cape-size bulk carriers had lost £20.2 million in 1999 but, during the first six months of 2000, it made a £3.5 million profit. A P&O spokesperson commented that P&O had received 'a good cash offer' and that, as ABC's operation would be taken over by an independent ship manager, Zodiac Marine Agencies, 'ABC will no longer be a management distraction for us.' In 2002, ABC lost £800,000, but again made a profit of £5.8 million in the first six months of 2003. At this point, P&O sold its remaining interest in ABC to Ofer for what was believed to be a generous sum: £38 million. Thereafter, the market for Cape-size bulk carriers experienced a very strong and sustained upswing –

P&O Nedlloyd Kobe *in the joint P&O Nedlloyd livery. (Mick Lindsay)*

The ***Maersk Madrid****, originally P&O Containers'* ***Peninsular Bay****, off Singapore. (Bruce Peter)*

*P&O Ferries' chartered catamaran **Caen Express** ran services from Portsmouth to Caen and Cherbourg in 2004. Owned by Denmark's Mols-Linien, she otherwise traded as the **Max Mols**. (Miles Cowsill)*

one of the biggest booms in maritime history – but it was Sammy Ofer who profited from this and not P&O.[93]

Some years later, Sammy Ofer generously financed the construction of a substantial new exhibition wing at the National Maritime Museum in Greenwich, of which Lord Sterling is Chairman of the Board of Trustees. Ofer's philanthropy is good example of how wealth generated by international shipping and associated business connections in the shipping industry can benefit the nation.

P&O NEDLLOYD NEXT TO GO

In 2002, Lord Sterling was approached by Jess Soderberg, the managing director of the A.P. Moller Group – the parent company of Maersk Line, one of the world's larger operators of container ships. Soderberg wanted to investigate the possibility of Maersk Line acquiring P&O's container shipping operations. In December 1996, P&O had agreed a merger of their container division with the Dutch container operator Royal Nedlloyd as a 50/50 joint venture. The merged P&O Nedlloyd marketed itself as 'a worldwide port-to-port, or door-to-door, service using an extensive global network.' With over 70 routes connecting 250 main ports in 120 different nations, P&O Nedlloyd was the largest partner in the Grand Alliance, which also included Orient Overseas Container Lines, Nippon Yusen Kaisha and Hapag Lloyd. In 1998, P&O Nedlloyd had purchased Blue Star Line's container business from the Vestey Group plus the Harrison Line's services. Two years thereafter, they added those of Farrell Lines. By 2002, P&O Nedlloyd had expanded to become the world's third largest container shipper, operating 160 vessels and 400,000 containers.

Sterling, under pressure from the City to dismantle P&O, welcomed Soderberg's initiative as P&O had been considering how to remove itself from the deal with Nedlloyd. Unfortunately, at that time, Soderberg's hands were tied, as A.P. Moller's Chairman and majority shareholder Maersk Mc-Kinney Moller quickly vetoed any possibility of concluding a deal at that time. Apparently, Moller was strongly of the opinion that Maersk Line would best grow organically, rather than through the acquisition of P&O Nedlloyd.

Once Maersk Mc-Kinney Moller had retired as A.P. Moller's Chairman, however, the idea of a deal was revived. In the end, it was struck in three parts. Firstly, in April 2004, P&O sold to Royal Nedlloyd its 50 per cent stake in P&O Nedlloyd in return for 25 per cent of the listed company, renamed Royal P&O Nedlloyd plus cash. Next, in June 2005, P&O sold its 25 per cent stake in Royal P&O Nedlloyd to A.P. Moller. Finally, in August the same year, A.P. Moller bought the remainder of Royal P&O Nedlloyd. The integration of the two companies' operations did not begin until February 2006, however, so as to enable P&O Nedlloyd to honour its existing conference agreements. (Until being taken over by Maersk Line, they were members of Grand Alliance, a group of container shippers also including Hapag-Lloyd and Nippon Yusen Kaisha.)[94]

TROUBLE AT PORTSMOUTH

By the millennium, P&O possessed Britain's biggest and best ferry fleet – but all was not well on the Western Channel. There was too much capacity and the market for foot passengers and private cars was shrinking, partly due to the ending of tax-free shopping and also as a consequence of the rise of the so-called 'budget' airlines which appeared to promise better value, greater speed and more convenience than taking a ferry. The situation was compounded by the high charter rates P&O was paying for its cruise ferry fleet operating there.

Worse still, the passenger experience on P&O's Portsmouth fleet was inferior to that provided by its French rival, Brittany Ferries. Following P&OSL's demise and a subsequent reintegration of the Portsmouth operation into its Dover counterpart, P&O had re-branded the catering and retail facilities on the ferries to

The ***Pride of Cherbourg*** *(ex* ***Isle of Innisfree****) was chartered by P&O Portsmouth to replace their ageing 'Super Vikings' on their Portsmouth-Cherbourg link in 2002. (Miles Cowsill)*

match the short, high-throughput Dover Strait fleet and redecorated the interiors to match. The truckers' canteen style of a P&O 'International Food Court', as the ferries' cafeterias were now known, was no match for the considerably more swish shipboard environments offered by Brittany Ferries.

In September 2004, P&O Ferries announced that its Western Channel routes from Portsmouth to Le Havre, Caen and Cherbourg, and from Cherbourg to Rosslare would be closing and that 350 jobs would be lost. The decision was expected to save £55 million. Before announcing the routes' closure, P&O had sought to acquire alternative vessels to the expensive *Pride of Portsmouth* and *Pride of Le Havre*. When that failed, they next considered a joint venture with Brittany Ferries – but the French company was unwilling to co-operate. After that rebuff, they again approached Brittany Ferries, this time with a view to them entirely taking over the Portsmouth-Le Havre route and the two chartered cruise ferries. Brittany Ferries were enthusiastic and it was announced that the *Pride of Portsmouth* and *Pride of Le Havre* would be renamed *Honfleur* and *Etretat*. Unfortunately, the British Monopolies and Mergers Commission vetoed the deal and so the sisters were instead withdrawn and returned to their owner, TT-Line, before being sold to Italian interests. Subsequently, in the late

The former freight vessels ***European Pathway*** *and* ***European Highway*** *were converted to passenger ships for the Dover-Calais link in 2003. The* ***Pride of Kent*** *(ex* ***European Highway****) is seen here arriving at Calais in June 2011. (Miles Cowsill)*

*The **European Seaway** leaves Calais on another freight run to Dover. (Miles Cowsill)*

*The **Pride of Bruges** heads away from Hull on her early evening sailing to Zeebrugge. (Miles Cowsill)*

summer of 2010, P&O Ferries' last remaining Western Channel route from Portsmouth to Bilbao was also closed and the *Pride of Bilbao* too became surplus to requirements. As a result of withdrawing from the Western Channel, P&O Ferries' route network was reduced from a peak of 14 routes to 10.

With hindsight, it is clear that these closures were as much a result of poor management as they were caused by changing market trends. Unlike Brittany Ferries, P&O Ferries failed to invest in its own purpose-built Western Channel tonnage and, equally, they did not focus on the customers' needs and aspirations, leaving their French competitor to conquer the market by offering better – rather than cheaper – ships and a considerably more attractive shipboard milieu.

In the 2002-2004 period P&O Ferries disposed of its Felixstowe-Rotterdam and Fleetwood-Larne freight routes to Stena Line, thus also reducing their presence on the North and Irish Seas. Initially, P&O had also wanted to sell its freight ferry services from Liverpool but the competition authorities would not accept this proposal. A Mostyn-Dublin route, opened late in 2001, failed to live up to P&O's expectations and was closed down in 2004. The modern *European Ambassador* was sold to Stena Line, becoming their *Stena Nordica* and operating thereafter across the Baltic. She later returned to the Irish Sea on Stena's Holyhead-Dublin service.

P&O PRINCESS CRUISES AND CARNIVAL

If the expansion of P&O's cruise divisions during the 1980s and 90s had been impressive, it was as nothing compared with that of its US and Norwegian counterparts, Carnival and Royal Caribbean. By the millennium, Carnival in particular, had grown rapidly into the world's leading cruise line and, having absorbed into its corporate fold Holland America in 1989, Seabourn in 1992, Costa Crociere in 1997 and Cunard in 1998, the Corporation was well placed to make further acquisitions and the de-merged P&O Princess Cruises PLC, no longer encumbered with the rest of the P&O Group but not really large enough to defend itself from large predators, was a potential candidate.

Carnival's origins go back only to the mid-1960s when Ted Arison, an Israeli businessman who had retired to Florida but could not resist a business opportunity, set up a ro-ro ferry service from Miami to Nassau in the Bahamas and to Montego Bay in Jamaica. Arison chartered the modern Israeli ferry *Nili* from Somerfin Lines of Haifa, and marketed its services to American holidaymakers as the *Jamaica Queen*. The idea was to transport freight trailers to and from these Caribbean ports while, simultaneously, carrying tourists on short cruises. This was short lived, as the *Nili*'s Israeli owners went into receivership and the vessel was seized. Arison then teamed up in 1966 with the Norwegian shipowner Knut Ulstein Kloster to offer a similar cruise service aboard his then newly built ferry the *Sunward*, then

*The Meridien Restaurant on P&O Cruises' **Arcadia**. (David Trevor-Jones)*

With a dramatic sky behind, P&O Cruises' ***Arcadia*** *heads to sea from Southampton. The vessel's funnel and mast clearly show her owner's original intention that she should have joined the Cunard fleet as* ***Queen Victoria****. (Mick Lindsay)*

displaced from her original intended service between Southampton, Lisbon and Gibraltar. The two men later parted ways over various difficulties, leaving Kloster to develop his Norwegian Caribbean Line and Arison to found Carnival Cruises.

With the help of his friend, shipbroker Elie Schalit, Arison bought the laid-up Canadian Pacific flagship liner, *Empress of Canada*, and with but a bit of paint and general touch-up, introduced her on short cruises from Miami in 1972 as the *Mardi Gras*. After a somewhat rocky start – the ship grounded outside Miami on the maiden voyage – Carnival became well established as a provider of inexpensive, down-to-earth, fun party cruises under the Carnival Fun Ship brand. By the latter 1970s, the line had three ships – the others being the *Carnivale* (ex *Empress of Britain*) and the *Festivale* (ex *S.A.Vaal*). Moving into the 1980s, Carnival began building its first new cruise ships and each was carefully designed to maximise revenue. With such a fleet, Carnival successfully rode the 1980s leisure and entertainment boom, and so lucrative was its Caribbean operation that it paid for new buildings out of profits earned by the existing fleet. By the 1990s, they had a substantial war chest to invest by purchasing existing cruise lines and, moreover, by that stage, the industry was also beginning to consolidate.

P&O Princess Cruises PLC were already in negotiations with the other cruise industry giant Royal Caribbean when Carnival's CEO, Micky Arison (Ted's son) approached Lord Sterling in his capacity as Chairman of P&O Princess Cruises in December 2001. In January 2002, Arison wrote again, making an improved offer, valuing P&O Princess Cruises PLC at £3.5 billion (or £5 per share). Arison also pointed out that Royal Caribbean's rival offer had underplayed the American tax implications should a deal have come to fruition.

When Carnival concluded its acquisition of P&O Princess Cruises PLC in April 2003, the latter had no less than nine new cruise ships on order – five from Fincantieri at Monfalcone and two from Mitsubishi in Japan for Princess Cruises plus two for Aida from the Aker-MTU shipyard at Wismar in Eastern Germany.

P&O Princess Cruises PLC was reorganised by Carnival and the new owner's British-based cruise operations were re-named Carnival UK PLC, retaining the existing P&O Cruises management team. Cruise activities based in the UK consisted of P&O Cruises, Ocean Village and, quite remarkably, Cunard. As Princess Cruises predominantly attracted an American clientele, logically it henceforth was managed as part of Carnival's American portfolio while the German Aida brand was shifted to come under the aegis of Costa Cruises, controlled from Genoa. Micky Arison, who admired Lord Sterling's business acumen, made him Carnival UK's Life President.

Carnival had considerable expertise when it came to designing the most efficient, enjoyable – and profitable – cruise ships. As successive vessels grew in scale and ambition, the complexity of their hidden technical servicing likewise increased. Nowadays, cruise passengers experience a highly thought through 'design spectacle', consisting of captivating décor, food and beverage service, entertainment facilities, health and beauty treatments, retail therapy, swimming and sunbathing. To ensure that all the advertised services and attractions happen with absolutely perfect precision, there is a whole hidden world of servicing and supply – involving the movement of luggage, food, drink, laundry, retail supplies and even conditioned air, fresh water, stale air, grey water and sewage for treatment. All of these circulate 'behind the scenes' in a series of very efficient flows.

Whereas in the past, liners spent several days in port loading and unloading, today's much larger cruise ships can be turned around in a matter of hours and, upon embarkation, passengers rightly expect their vessel to appear absolutely pristine and as though it has been prepared especially for them. Once the cruise is under way, it is important that the sequence of public rooms and on-board activities are appropriate to allow the maximum number quickly and easily to find the facilities they desire – and for the cruise line to generate the optimum on-board revenues. The appropriate location of complementary facilities and attractions is known as 'adjacency' and, bearing in mind the relationship between what passengers experience and the hidden servicing making it all possible, coupled with the need to make the most efficient use of space, it is not surprising that, over time, modern cruise ships have evolved into fairly standardised designs. Additionally, it is easier for travel agents and shipping line booking departments to cope with the layouts of standard ships as one vessel's cabin plan will be similar to another – and so staff will more readily become familiar with where best to book their customers. Moreover, standard ships reduce costs because spare parts – and even officers and crew – are interchangeable, thereby bringing the price of cruises down and making cruising an affordable holiday option of wider cross-sections of society. Indeed, thanks largely to Carnival, it is now the world's fastest-growing leisure industry. Carnival's naval architects, interior designers and technical staff, led by their then Chief Naval Architect, Stephen Payne, were among the leading thinkers in developing such strategies which effectively applied Fordist theories of mass manufacture to the design and operation of passenger ships.

On a typical modern cruise ship of the type favoured by Carnival, usually, there will be an atrium amidships, cutting through most of the passenger decks and providing the ship's public focal point. Two main saloon decks will be located in the top of hull and lower superstructure, with restaurants aft and the casino, theatre, nightclub and associated bars forward. The majority of the superstructure will be given over to cabins with all servicing located along the centreline between the cabin corridors. Above will be another deck of public rooms, with the fitness centre and an observation lounge forward and the lido buffet restaurant aft with open-air swimming pools between. From ship to ship, the décor will vary wildly, but the overall layout will stay more or less the same. The reason is that it has been refined carefully over the years and experience has proven that it works best.

In the early 1990s, Carnival took delivery from the Kvaerner-Masa shipyard in Helsinki, Finland, of eight liners, specially tailored for the Caribbean market, known as the 'Fantasy' class. Next, they ordered a further series of six, referred to as the 'Spirit' class. These were among the first cruise ships to have a very substantial number of outside cabins with balconies. Simultaneously, Carnival developed a strong relationship with the Italian Fincantieri shipbuilding group, whose yards at Monfalcone, Venice Marghera and Genoa Sestri went on to build nearly all of their subsequent

The ***Ventura****, shown here during a cruise to the Norwegian fjords, and her near-sister* ***Azura*** *are the two largest ever P&O Cruises vessels. Their design is derived from Princess Cruises' 'Grand' class. (John Peter).*

*The atrium on P&O Cruises' newest vessel, the **Azura**. (Bruce Peter)*

*The Jade Restaurant on the **Azura**. (Bruce Peter)*

standard cruise ship designs – namely, the 'Destiny' class, operated by the Carnival and Costa brands, and the 'Vista' class, used by Holland America, Cunard and P&O Cruises under Carnival ownership. (Fincantieri already had built several of the 'Grand' class for Princess Cruises which also had developed a strong relationship with the shipbuilder.)

On the technical side, as with most modern generation cruise ships, diesel electric propulsion was installed, six Wärtsilä engines supplying power to electric generators which, in turn, drive electric motors in pods located outside the hull, onto which the propellers are directly attached. The advantages of this system are that an optimal power supply can be generated to provide the ideal speed to sail most economically between ports, simply by firing up only the number of engines actually needed. Secondly, podded propulsion eliminates the need for rudders to change the ship's course as instead moving joysticks on the navigation bridge can change the direction of the pods. As the thrust remains constant, rather than varying according to the position of the rudder, this makes such vessels highly manoeuvrable. Generally, a service speed of around 20 knots is maintained.

In 2005, P&O Cruises acquired its first Carnival-era newbuilding, the 'Vista' class *Arcadia*, almost by accident. The ship had been ordered from Fincantieri by Carnival for its Cunard brand for which she was to have been named *Queen Victoria*.

*The **Azura**'s Glasshouse Bar. (Bruce Peter)*

*The deck area adjoining the **Azura**'s Oasis Spa features tubs of lavender and comfortable settees. (Bruce Peter)*

A recent addition to P&O Cruises' fleet is the ***Adonia****, originally Renaissance Cruises' strangely named* ***R Eight****. The vessel's more intimate scale and adults-only designation enable her to serve a niche market somewhat different from P&O Cruises' larger fleet members. (Mick Lindsay)*

With that intention, she was given a funnel and mast somewhat resembling Cunard's famous 1969 liner *Queen Elizabeth 2* and recent Carnival-era flagship *Queen Mary 2*.

Between the commencement of construction and delivery, Carnival decided instead to order a further new cruise ship for allocation to Cunard and to switch the existing Cunard hull to P&O Cruises. The subsequent new Cunarder, actually delivered as *Queen Victoria*, is also a 'Vista' class, but with a hull 60 metres longer than her P&O Cruises half-sister *Arcadia*. Inboard, *Arcadia* is largely the work of the London-based cruise ship specialists SMC Design. She is bright, fresh and spacious but being of a 'mass produced' standard design, she lacks the finesse and fine detailing of *Oriana* and *Aurora*, which are unique in terms of quality and ambience and with a loyal clientele reflective of their special status.[95]

Historically, P&O passenger liners had served a broad cross-section of the British middle class, a very wide, diverse and complex social grouping which, by the latter-twentieth century, had expanded considerably to take in a growing post-working class who, for the first time, were sufficiently affluent to take cruises in large numbers. The former Princess Cruises vessel *Oceana* (ex *Ocean Princess*) was P&O Cruises' first ship aimed at this market, with lower fares and a less opulent style than *Oriana* and *Aurora*. Subsequently, P&O Cruises added further Princess-type vessels to its fleet, the 116,017-ton *Ventura* arriving from Fincantieri in 2008, followed by the slightly larger *Azura* in 2010. These mighty vessels are derived from Princess's successful decade-old 'Grand class' design and are in fact the biggest passenger ships ever to fly the P&O house flag; each can accommodate over 3,500 passengers.

These vessels are more akin to vast floating leisure resorts than previous Southampton-based P&O Cruises ships with impressively bewildering arrays of entertainments and dining options. Clearly, their design and layout is greatly influenced both by Princess Cruises' successful formula and by P&O Cruises' brief experiment with Ocean Village to attract a younger demographic on board. Reflective of our present highly mediated and celebrity-conscious age, there are branded extra-tariff dining options. At first, the spiky-haired celebrity chef Gary Rhodes lent his name to these facilities (thus emulating the Todd English restaurants on recent Cunard vessels). Later, P&O Cruises entered an agreement with Marco Pierre White and, on *Azura*, Atul Kochhar.

With *Oriana* and *Aurora* attracting mainly loyal P&O Cruises' traditionalists and *Oceana*, *Ventura* and *Azura* fulfilling the aspirations of the mainstream of British holidaymakers, Carnival UK successfully expanded P&O Cruises' fleet to reflect modern-day British society and leisure habits. A third area in which P&O Cruises traditionally had excelled but which they had neglected in recent years was cruisers who wanted a more intimate shipboard experience than even the smallest of P&O Cruises' present fleet was capable of providing. In the past, P&O's liner *Chusan* had a unique following which, a generation later, passed to the *Sea Princess* (ex *Kungsholm* and latterly *Victoria*). When that vessel was sold in 2002, P&O Cruises effectively abandoned its 'small ship' clientele to rival operators. Three years thereafter, in an inspired move, the 1984-built *Royal Princess* was moved from the Princess brand to P&O Cruises. She was re-christened the *Artemis*, Greek for Diana and thus recalling the late Princess of Wales, who was the liner's lady sponsor. When new some 21 years previously, the *Royal Princess* had been among the world's largest cruise ships – and certainly the most sophisticated. Now, her 44,588-ton measure and capacity for only 1,318 made her, as *Artemis*, the baby of the P&O Cruises fleet.[96]

LORD STERLING'S EXIT FROM P&O

In 2005, Lord Sterling retired as Chairman of P&O, his 22-year reign having brought the Group some of its greatest successes. While his first decade was unequivocally a triumph of corporate acumen, which built the Group into a powerful force in numerous shipping and property sectors, his latter years were marked by a continuing struggle to please rapacious city interests by selling subsidiaries to realise their short-term value. By the end of his second decade at the helm, P&O was refocused into a ferry, ports, logistics, estates and maritime services business, many of its other operations having been sold. Alas, P&O's fate mirrored that of numerous once-proud British blue chip companies and, in dismantling P&O, Sterling was merely responding as best he could to circumstances largely beyond his immediate control. During his Chairmanship, the businesses constituting the P&O Group in 1983 came to be worth £20 billion.

P&O's new – and final – Chairman as a listed company was Sir John Parker. Born in County Down, Northern Ireland in 1942, Parker trained as a naval architect and marine engineer. Beginning his career as a Harland & Wolff apprentice naval architect in 1958, by 1974 he was Managing Director of the Austin & Pickersgill shipyard in Sunderland. In 1983, he returned to Harland & Wolff as Chairman with a mandate to prepare the yard for privatisation. Subsequently, he held numerous directorships and chairmanships, one of which was P&O.

His predecessor, Lord Sterling, was not the type of man to enjoy a quiet life in retirement. When he left P&O, he took the Sterling Guarantee Trust name with him with the intention of finding new investment opportunities. Having started out as a property developer, he had however become a shipping man and so, only two years after retiring as P&O Chairman, he resurfaced again having acquired from Carnival UK the dormant Swan Hellenic cruise brand (originally owned by P&O since 1983). As Swan Hellenic was popular with wealthy and discerning British passengers, Sterling's aim was to re-launch the brand as a niche cruise operator. To bring his plan to fruition, he struck a deal with the cruise entrepreneur Roger Allard to work with his All Leisure Group, operator of the cruise company Voyages of Discovery. This ran a single vessel, the *Discovery*, once Princess Cruises' *Island Princess*. Sterling sold the Swan Hellenic brand to All Leisure, thereafter becoming Swan Hellenic Chairman and overseeing the re-introduction of the small luxury cruise ship *Minerva*. Later, he also became chairman of another All Leisure subsidiary, Hebridean Island Cruises. Needless to say, his involvement with All Leisure Group reputedly caused some consternation at Carnival UK as its management regarded the *Discovery* as a rival to P&O Cruises' British-based fleet (of which he remained as Life President). Such had been the growth of cruise ships since *Discovery* was first built in the early 1970s, however, that P&O Cruises' smallest vessel measured more than twice her tonnage.

*The **Oriana** in Southampton dressed overall at the start of another cruise to the Mediterranean. (Miles Cowsill)*

Epilogue

In the 1979 BBC television documentary '*Dwarka* London: An Arabian Voyage', the vintage British India passenger-cargo liner called at Dubai in the United Arab Emirates en route from Bombay and Karachi to Gulf ports, loaded with migrant workers and their belongings relocating from Pakistan to the newly oil-rich Gulf states. The narrator, John MacKenzie, described Dubai thus:

'The Creek is Dubai's Grand Canal. Here, hundreds of dhows load cargoes, transhipped from the modern harbour. The same sacks of spices and chests of tea which Dubai has bought from India will be transported by traditional vessels all along the coast of the United Arab Emirates… Dubai is an emporium where everything can be bought tax-free from carpets to washing machines and refrigerators. Everything from mopeds to stuffed Bengal tigers… In Dubai, the numbers of migrants are more striking than elsewhere in the Gulf, accounting for two out of three of the population… They create Dubai, whose future they can not share…'[97]

Strategically located at the south end of the Persian Gulf on the Arabian Peninsula, Dubai was a British protectorate from 1892 until 1971. The discovery of oil in the mid-1960s caused its population quickly to triple in size as migrant workers flooded in. The modern port referred to by MacKenzie was a free trade zone and this became the lynchpin of Dubai's second wave of expansion. Realising that oil reserves would not last forever, the Dubai government decided to emulate Hong Kong and Singapore, transforming the emirate into an international hub for business and commerce, tourism, real estate and financial services.

During the sustained economic boom of the latter 1990s and early 2000s, Dubai's rate of growth increased exponentially, thanks largely to large-scale inward investment. Within not much more than a decade, Dubai was transformed by massive property and infrastructure development into a Middle Eastern hub for finance, business and leisure, comprising American-style skyscrapers and freeways, interspersed with shopping malls and grand hotels, surrounded by villas, sometimes developed on artificial islands constructed in the Gulf itself. Nearly all of this glittering real estate was actually built by migrant workers from Pakistan and elsewhere in Southern Asia – the very people first brought there by the *Dwarka*.

By the first decade of the new millennium, the State-owned port operator DP World was in a position to buy up major overseas ports and logistics businesses with P&O an obvious target. DP World was created in 2005 through a merger of the Dubai Ports Authority (DPA) and Dubai Ports International (DPI), established only in 1999. Upon its creation, DP World began a major global expansion programme, firstly buying CSX World Terminals (CSX WT), an American-headquartered ports operator previously associated with the Sea-Land container shipping business. Next, DP World submitted a £3.3 billion bid for P&O.

In November 2005, P&O's Chairman Sir John Parker announced that DP World's bid had been accepted. While DP World wanted control of P&O's ports and stevedoring businesses, they promised also to retain the P&O Ferries business, notwithstanding its recent £15 million loss on £1 billion of turnover. For a Dubai-based business to acquire the surviving 'core' of the once-mighty P&O was a remarkable turn of events – particularly as, when *Dwarka* was withdrawn from service in 1982,

The ***European Highlander*** *on passage to Cairnryan from Larne in April 2011. (Miles Cowsill)*

*The **Spirit of Britain** in her construction dock in Finland on 6th June 2010 pending her moving out to her fitting-out berth. (Miles Cowsill)*

there remained the clause in P&O's charter preventing foreigners from possessing more than a quarter of the Group's shares. Only as recently as 1992 had this clause been revoked but DP World's acquisition of P&O clearly symbolised that, in the new globalising world order, the ruled had become the rulers.

Before purchasing P&O, DP World operated 22 container terminals in 15 countries. Although its focus was on the Arabian Peninsula, where it ran seven ports from Port Rashid to Jeddah, it also managed facilities in Australia and South-East Asia. P&O Ports operated 29 ports in 18 countries. The combined firm would become the world's third largest ports operator, behind the Hong Kong-based Hutchison Whampoa and the Singaporean Temasek Holdings, which had also been a bidder for P&O.

Neither DP World nor P&O foresaw the firestorm of negative American reaction to their deal. P&O Ports managed container port facilities in New York, New Jersey, Philadelphia, Baltimore, New Orleans and Miami, as well as providing stevedoring services at 16 other US ports. America's febrile political climate in the wake of the September 11th terrorist attacks meant that any acquisition of American infrastructure by interests in the Arab world – even relatively progressive and peaceful Dubai – would be likely to cause controversy. DP World was aware of the potential concern and sought – and received – approval for the transfer of the terminal leases from the Committee on Foreign Investments in the United States (CFIUS) before the deal was finalised. Once the finalised deal was reported in the business press, one of P&O's American partners, Eller & Company, already in litigation with P&O to try to take control of the Miami operation, began lobbying against becoming an involuntary business partner of DP World as part of that effort. With congressional elections around the corner, what began as a business matter became a heated political issue. Press reports and the attention of a Democratic New York Senator put the deal in the national media spotlight and there was cross-party scepticism as the deal was spun by politicians and media pundits to appear a threat to American national security. Indeed, the Republican Bill Frist, a close ally of President George W. Bush, threatened to introduce legislation to block DP World from taking over the management of American container terminals.[98]

To his credit, President Bush intervened, stating that 'it would send a terrible signal to friends and allies not to let this transaction go through.' At that time, the United Arab Emirates was a strategic American partner, allowing military access to its land, ports and airspace as a base for US operations in Iraq and Afghanistan. Notwithstanding this co-operation, DP World volunteered to postpone its takeover of P&O's American port operations to give US lawmakers time to convince themselves that, just because the Company was headquartered in an Arab country, its management of terminals within American ports would not pose any threat whatsoever. Even though DP World

Pride of Kent (Miles Cowsill)

The ***Spirit of Britain*** *outward bound from Calais in June 2011. (Miles Cowsill)*

hired the former Republican presidential candidate Bob Dole to lobby in favour of the deal, in March 2006, the House Panel voted 62-2 against. Just ahead of that vote, DP World announced it would part with the US assets to an American company, in the end selling them to Global Investment Group, the asset management division of American International Group (AIG).

GIANTS OF THE DOVER STRAIT

While DP World's primary interest in P&O was its port infrastructure and services, rather than the ferry operations, the latter have not been neglected. Far from it – Dubai World quickly

The Club Class Lounge on the ***Spirit of Britain*** *attempts to recapture the style of P&O's great liners of the past. (SMC)*

gave P&O Ferries permission to build two very large new vessels for its flagship Dover-Calais service to replace the ageing mid-1980s vessels *Pride of Dover* and *Pride of Calais*. The Dover Strait requires highly efficient bespoke tonnage as the shortest sea route to France is operated intensively in almost all weathers and has vast throughputs of trucks, cars and passengers. Essentially, a Dover Strait ferry is a vast lorry park and motorway service station – and P&O Ferries decided early on that its new vessels should be very upmarket examples of this genre.

Following an intensive design process, P&O Ferries placed an order with the Finnish STX Shipyard in Rauma for the building of the new *Spirit of Britain* and *Spirit of France*. Measuring 47,592 tons and with accommodation for 2,000 passengers, 170 trucks and additionally 195 cars on a separate upper car deck, these sisters are amongst the world's largest and most sophisticated short-sea ferries. Driven by four MAN diesels, they have a 22-knot service speed – but their hull forms, propellers and rudders are optimised to enable fast sailing even over the notorious shallows off Calais.

From their passengers' viewpoint, they are also superbly appointed. Their deck heads are lofty and all around the superstructure large windows mean that light floods inside, making them bright and airy – the very opposite of the claustrophobia experienced in the Channel Tunnel, or on a budget airline's Boeing 737. All the lounge, retail and dining facilities are connected by an 'orbital motorway' round which passengers can quickly find the space they most like. Staircases are colour-

The Family Lounge on the ***Spirit of Britain*** *offers outstanding views forward for passengers on the Dover Strait. (SMC)*

coordinated with the yellow, red and blue colours of the P&O flag. Altogether, the *Spirit of Britain* and *Spirit of France* are outstanding ferries and offer comfort, hospitality and safety in the best P&O tradition.[99]

Throughout, their passenger accommodation is adorned with old P&O travel posters from the P&O Heritage Collection while a summary of P&O's lengthy and distinguished history is displayed on panels in one of the hallways.[100] This is a popular feature with passengers, many of whom spend quite a while reading and examining the illustrations. Looking back at this material, however, one might conclude nostalgically that P&O's rapid dismemberment for the short-term gratification of some of its shareholders was unnecessary and regrettable. The history of modern shipping – and of the parallel narratives of the nations served by modern ships – is, however, one of constant flux and change, reflecting the dynamic characteristics of modernity itself. Great business empires are created through mercantile and military expansion and, when conditions change, they are broken up or reconfigured to suit new and emerging conditions.

Yet, as former P&O Lines Director Jim Davis, observes, 'Carnival and even the mighty Maersk were comparatively small companies a little while ago. Why have they prospered and grown while P&O has melted away? The answer may lie in the fact that P&O was indeed apprehensive of the City and its analysts. Maybe shipping is not very well suited to be a quoted Stock.' While Davis is correct that many successful shipping businesses are privately owned, both A.P Moller-Maersk and Carnival are in fact publicly quoted companies, though the former is constituted in such a way that shares with voting rights are kept largely 'in house', meaning that external investors have very little influence upon business strategy. While this has doubtless enabled Maersk to enjoy a stability that eluded P&O in its latter years, the City of London would surely have found such an undemocratic corporate structure hard to accept.

From being intimately involved in the imperial project in the nineteenth century, through the turbulent decades of the twentieth to survival in today's global economy as a brand name inextricably associated with British identity, yet owned abroad, P&O's development has closely reflected that of Britain itself. P&O ships have always been among the best of their type in each era. Those liners operated in the Age of Empire were representative of Britain's projection of power and influence abroad. During the post-colonial era of the last half-century, P&O changed more quickly and radically than at any time in its previous history and its new areas of activity – such as property development, leisure and logistics – were reflective of changing life and work patterns on *terra firma*. For a decade or more, the most likely place one would have seen the P&O initials and its flag would have been on its thousands of trucks on the roads of Europe, or on its tens of thousands of containers on the oceans of the world. These are now gone and today the P&O name no longer represents the whole of the mighty shipping enterprise it once did. But in the ongoing businesses of P&O Maritime and P&O Ferries and on the separately owned P&O Cruises fleet, the P&O flag still flutters.[101]

The following presentation of P&O's fleets through the past 175 years is but a partial fleet list that serves to detail the key ships discussed in this book. These are listed here chronologically, for the most part in the order of their building, but also functionally in the sequence of their appearance in the text. Only the lead or best-known ship of class- or series-buildings are listed, with for instance the *Moldavia* representing the M Class and the *Strathnaver* standing for the 'Straths,' and for instance, the *Ventura* being the lead ship in the *Azura*'s class. For further reference, a more complete fleet resource can be found on the P&O Heritage web site.

In the following list, ships' hulls are assumed to be made of steel unless otherwise noted as in the cases of early wood and iron constructions. Tonnage is generally given as 'gross register tonnage' (grt) though deadweight figures (dwt) are also given for tankers, and for more recent ships current 'gross tonnage' (gt) figures are quoted. There may be some minor discrepancies against other sources for tonnage, passenger and crew figures, and cargo capacities as to the way these are measured over the years, owing to changes made during a ship's service career. For the most part, the information presented here is taken from P&O Heritage.

William Fawcett • liner • 1835, 1837-8, 1840 • 44.42m x 6.76m (145.8ft x 22.2ft) • 206grt • Hull wood • Pass. n/a • Crew n/a • Cargo n/a • Mach. 140hp, 2 paddle wheels, n/a knots • Built Caleb and James Smith, Queen's Dock, Liverpool, UK & Son, Port Glasgow, UK • Employment London Spain and Portugal

Liverpool • liner • 1835-36, 1837-45 • 41.76m x 6.71m (137.0ft x 22.0ft) • 330grt • Hull wood • Pass. n/a • Crew n/a • Cargo n/a • Mach. direct-acting steam engine, 2 paddle wheels, 7.0knots • Built John Wood & Son, Port Glasgow, UK • Employment London or Liverpool/Spain and Portugal

Don Juan • liner • 1837 • 45.22m x 7.31m (148.4ft x 24.0ft) • 923grt • Hull wood • Pass. 24 • Crew n/a • Cargo n/a • Mach. two-cylinder direct-acting steam engines, 360hp, 2 paddle wheels, 7.0knots • Built Fletcher, Son and Fearnall, Poplar, London, UK • Employment London and Falmouth/Spain and Portugal

Tagus • liner • 1837-64 • 55.45m x 7.92m (182.0ft x 26.0ft) • 909grt • Hull wood • Pass. 86 • Crew 36 • Cargo 305tonnes (300tons) • Mach. two-cylinder side-lever steam engines, 286ihp, 2 paddle wheels, 9.5knots • Built John Scott & Sons, Greenock, UK • Employment UK/Spain and Portugal and UK/Eastern Mediterranean

Great Liverpool • liner • 1840-46 • 65.11m x 7.77m (213.7ft x 25.5ft) • 1,382grt • Hull wood • Pass. n/a • Crew n/a • Cargo n/a • Mach. direct-acting side-lever steam engines, 468ihp, 2 paddle wheels, 9.0knots • Built Humble & Milcrest, Liverpool, UK • Employment Southampton/Alexandria

Oriental • liner • 1840-61 • 61.55m x 10.21m (202.0ft x 33.5ft) • 1,673grt • Hull wood • Pass. 98 • Crew 55 • Cargo 355tonnes • Mach. side-lever steam engines, 450hp, 2 paddle wheels, 11.0knots • Built Thomas Wilson & Co., Liverpool, UK • Employment Southampton/Alexandria

Lady Mary Wood • liner • 1842-58 • 48.99m x 7.77m (160.8ft x 25.5ft) • 650grt • Hull wood • Pass. 60 first class, 50 second class • Crew 89 east of Suez, 40 west of Suez • Cargo 200tons • Mach. side-lever steam engine, 259ihp, 2 paddle wheels, 12.0knots • Built Thomas Wilson & Co., Liverpool, UK • Employment Peninsular service and later the Far East

Hindostan • liner • 1842-64 • 66.3m x 10.91m (217.6ft x 35.8ft) • 1,800grt • Hull wood • Pass. 102 first class, 50 second class • Crew 53 • Cargo 300tons • Mach. direct-acting steam engine, 520ihp, 2 paddle wheels, 10.0knots • Built Thomas Wilson & Co., Liverpool, UK • Employment India/Suez and seasonal trooping

Bentinck • liner • 1843-60 • 66.27m x 10.97m (217.5ft x 36.0ft) • 1,800grt • Hull wood • Pass. 102 first class, 50 second class • Crew 173 • Cargo n/a • Mach. side-lever steam engine, 520ihp, 2 paddle wheels, 10.0knots • Built Thomas Wilson & Co., Liverpool, UK • Employment Suez/Calcutta mail service

Pottinger • 1846-67 • 68.25m x 10.36m (224.0ft x 34.0ft) • 1,300grt • Hull iron • Pass. 90 first class • Crew 82 (1852) • Cargo 325cubic metres (1,493cubic feet) • Mach. direct-acting oscillating steam engine, 450ihp, 2 paddle wheels, 10.0knots • Built William Fairbairn & Sons, Millwall, UK • Employment India/Hong Kong

Haddington • liner • 1846-70 • 66.21m x 10.18m (217.3ft x 33.4ft) • 1,500grt • Hull iron • Pass. n/a • Crew 177 • Cargo n/a • Mach. two-cylinder direct-acting oscillating steam engine, 450ihp, 2 paddle wheels, 10.5knots • Built Thomas Vernon & Sons, Liverpool, UK • Employment Suez/Calcutta and other Eastern services later modified as a sailing stores ship

Chusan • liner • 1852-61 • 57.89m x 8.99m (190.0ft x 29.5ft) • 750grt • Hull iron • Pass. n/a • Crew 45 • Cargo n/a • Mach. direct-acting oscillating steam engine, 800ihp, 1 propeller, 9.5knots • Built Miller Ravenhill & Co. Ltd, Walker-on-Tyne, UK • Employment Australia/Singapore and other Eastern services

Madras • liner • 1852-74 • 71.27 x 9.63m (233.9ft x 31.6ft) • 1,200grt • Hull iron • Pass. 80 first class • Crew n/a • Cargo 600 tons • Mach. beam-geared steam engine, 754ihp, 1 propeller, 9.5knots • Built Tod & MacGregor, Glasgow, UK • Employment Suez/Calcutta and other Eastern services

Bombay • liner • 1852-78 • 71.3 x 9.57m (234.0ft x 31.4ft) • 1,200grt • Hull iron • Pass. n/a • Crew n/a • Cargo n/a • Mach. geared beam steam engine, 750ihp, 1 propeller, 10.0knots • Built Tod & MacGregor, Patrick, Glasgow, UK • Employment Suez/India and other services

Mooltan • liner • 1861-80 • 106.28 x 11.91m (348.8ft x 39.1ft) • 2,257grt • Hull iron • Pass. 112 first class, 37 second class • Crew n/a • Cargo n/a • Mach. tandem compound inverted double-acting steam engine, 1,734ihp, 1 propeller, 12.0knots • Built Thames Ironworks and Shipbuilding Co., Blackwall, UK • Employment Southampton/Alexandria and Calcutta/Suez

Victoria • liner • 1887-1909 • 141.93 x 15.84m (465.8ft x 52.0ft) • 6,091grt • Pass. 230 first class, 156 second class • Crew 238 • Cargo 5,111 cubic metres (180,512 cubic feet) • Mach. triple-expansion steam engines, 7,000ihp, 1 propeller, 16.0knots • Built Caird & Co., Greenock, UK • Employment UK/Australia, Bombay/Far East and trooping

Himalaya • liner • 1892-1916, 1919-22 • 141.86 x 15.9m (465.6ft x 52.2ft) • 6,898grt • Pass. 265 first class, 144 second class • Crew 249 • Cargo 4,177 cubic metres (147,537 cubic feet) • Mach. triple-expansion steam engines, 10,000ihp, 1 propeller, 18.0knots • Built Caird & Co., Greenock, UK • Employment UK/Australia later UK/India and UK/China

Moldavia • liner • 1903-16, 1917-18 • 158.62 x 17.76m (520.6ft x 58.3ft) • 9,500grt • Pass. 348 first class, 166 second class • Crew 327 • Cargo 5,871 cubic metres (207,352 cubic feet) • Mach. triple-expansion steam engines, 12,000ihp, 2 propellers, 16.5knots • Built Caird & Co., Greenock, UK • Employment UK/Australia mail service

Salsette • intermediate liner • 1908-17 • 134.06 x 16.21m

(440.0ft x 53.2ft) • 5,842grt • Pass. 140 first class, 121 second class • Crew 238 • Cargo 1,710 cubic metres (60,411 cubic feet) • Mach. quadruple-expansion steam engines, 10,000ihp, 2 propellers, 20.0knots • Built Caird & Co., Greenock, UK • Employment express service Aden/Bombay

Ballerat • emigrant liner • P&O Branch Line 1911-17 • 152.38 x 19.14m (500.1ft x 62.8ft) • 11,120grt • Pass. 302, permanent, 750 temporary • Crew n/a • Cargo 16,980 cubic metres (559,740 cubic feet) • Mach. quadruple-expansion steam engines, 9,000ihp, 2 propellers, 14.0knots • Built Caird & Co., Greenock, UK • Employment UK/Australia emigrant service via the Cape of Good Hope

Ballerat • emigrant liner • P&O Branch Line 1921-35 • 158.37 x 19.56m (519.8ft x 64.2ft) • 13,033grt • Pass. 491, permanent, 758 temporary • Crew 290 • Cargo 16,443 cubic metres (580,750 cubic feet) • Mach. quadruple-expansion steam engines, 9,500ihp, 2 propellers, 13.5knots • Built Harland & Wolff Ltd, Greenock, UK • Employment UK/Australia emigrant service via the Cape of Good Hope

Ranpura • liner • 1925-44 • 167.06 x 21.72m (548.3ft x 71.3ft) • 16,601grt • Pass. 305 first class, 282 second class • Crew 357 • Cargo 9,744 cubic metres (344,144 cubic feet) • Mach. quadruple-expansion steam engines, 15,000ihp, 2 propellers, 16.5knots • Built R & W Hawthorn, Leslie & Co. Ltd, Newcastle-upon-Tyne, UK • Employment London/Bombay mail service

Viceroy of India • liner • 1929-42 • 186.56 x 23.22m (612.3ft x 76.2ft) • 19,648grt • Pass. 415 first class, 258 second class • Crew 413 • Cargo 6,165 cubic metres (217,752 cubic feet) • Mach. steam turbo-electric, 17,000ihp, 2 propellers, 19.0knots • Built Alexander Stephen & Sons Ltd, Glasgow, UK • Employment UK/Bombay mail service and cruising

Strathnaver • liner • 1931-62 • 194.61 x 24.44m (638.7ft x 80.2ft) • 22,547grt • Pass. 498 first class, 670 tourist class • Crew 487 • Cargo 12,500 cubic metres (441,000 cubic feet) • Mach. steam turbo-electric, 28,000ihp, 2 propellers, 21.0knots • Built Vickers-Armstrong Ltd, Barrow-in-Furness, UK • Employment UK/Australia and cruising

Soudan • general cargo liner • 1948-70 • 159.63m x 20.48m (523.9ft x 67.2ft) • 9,080grt • Pass. 10 • Crew 101 • Cargo 16,473 cubic metres (581,813 cubic feet) • Mach. Doxford diesel, 13,600bhp, 2 propellers, 17.0knots • Built Barclay, Curle & Co. Ltd, Glasgow, UK • Employment UK/Far East

Maloja • tanker • 1959 Charter Shipping Co., P&O 1959-76 • 170.40m x 21.81m (559.2ft x 71.6ft) • 19,948 dwt, 12,763grt • Pass. nil • Crew 65 • Cargo 26.130 cubic metres (922,926 cubic feet) • Mach. two double-reduction geared steam turbines, 8,250shp, 1 propeller, 14.5knots • Built Smith's Dock Co. Ltd, Middlesbrough, UK • Employment carriage of refined petroleum products

Oriana • liner • 1960-86 • 244.97m x 29.61m (804.0ft x 97.1ft) • 41,915grt • aluminium alloy superstructure • Pass. 638 first class, 1,496 tourist class • Crew 899 • Cargo 4,749 Cubic metres (172,500 cubic feet) • Mach. Pametrada double-reduction geared steam turbine, 65,000shp, 2 propellers, 27.5knots • Built Vickers-Armstrong (Shipbuilders) Ltd, Barrow-in-Furness, UK • Employment UK/Australasia and Pacific also cruising

Canberra • liner • 1961-97 • 249.39m x 31.24m (818ft x 102.5ft) • 45,720grt • aluminium alloy superstructure • Pass. 538 first class, 1,650 tourist class • Crew 900 • Mach. steam turbo-electric, 85,000shp, 2 propellers, 27.5knots • Built Harland & Wolff Ltd, Queen's Island, Belfast, Northern Ireland • Employment UK/Australia and cruising

Orama • tanker • P&O subsidiary Trident Tankers Ltd. 1964-74 • 236.14m x 32.3m (775.0ft x 106.0ft • 65,972 dwt, 38,767grt • Pass. nil • Crew n/a • Cargo 78,888 cubic metres (2,786,327 cubic feet) • Mach. B&W diesel, 20,700shp, 1 propeller, 16.75knots • Built Lithgowa Ltd, Port Glasgow, UK • Employment chartered to Texaco Panama to supply its Pembroke refinery

Strathardle • general cargo liner • 1967-79 • 171.6 x 24.32m (563.0ft x 79.8ft) • 12,539grt • Pass. n/a • Crew n/a • Cargo 21,765 cubic metres (768,630 cubic feet) • Mach. SCSA B&W diesel, 20,700bhp, 1 propeller, 21.0knots • Built Mitsui Zosen, Tamano, Japan • Employment UK/Far East

Norwave • roll-on/roll-off vehicle-passenger ferry • P&O subsidiary North Sea Ferries Ltd 1965-87 • 108.78m x 18.94m (357.0ft x 62.1ft) • 4,306grt • Pass. 247 (including 187 berthed, 28 air seats and 20 couchettes) • Crew 50 • Cargo 65 trailers + 70 cars or 200 cars • Mach. NV Smit en Bolnes diesel, 5,200bhp, 2 propellers, 15.0knots • Built AG 'Weser' Seebeck Werft, Bremerhaven, West Germany • Employment Hull/Rotterdam later hull/Zeebrugge overnight service

Wahine • roll-on/roll-off vehicle-passenger ferry • P&O subsidiary Union Steam Ship Company of New Zealand Ltd 1966-68 • 149.01m x 22.16m (488.9ft x 72.6ft) • 8,944grt • Pass. 931 • Crew n/a • Cargo 200 cars and trailers • Mach. steam turbo-electric, 18,000shp, 2 propellers, 19.0knots • Built Fairfield Shipbuilding & Engineering Co. Ltd, Govan, UK • Employment Wellington/Lyttleton express service

Dragon • roll-on/roll-off vehicle/passenger ferry • P&O subsidiary General Steam Navigation Company Ltd 1967-85, P&O European Ferries 1987-92 • 134.57m x 21.86m (441.7ft x 71.8ft) • 6,141grt • Pass. 850 (including 276 berthed, 156 reclining seats and 244 couchettes) • Crew n/a • Cargo 65 trailers + 250 cars (510 lane-metres) • Mach. SEMT-Pielstick diesel, 9,467bhp, 2 propellers, 19.0knots • Built Dubigeon Normandie SA, Nantes, France • Employment Southampton/Le Havre later Cairnryan/Larne

Nevasa • troopship later used for educational cruising • P&O Subsidiary, British India Steam Navigation Company Ltd 1956 P&O Passenger Division 1972-75 • 185,65m x 23.86m (609.3ft x 78.3ft) • 20,527grt • Pass. In trooping service 220 first, 100 second, 180 third, 69 NCOs, 931 troops • Crew 409, for educational cruising from 1965, 308 cabin passengers, 1,090 schoolchildren • Mach. Pametrada steam turbine, 18,400bhp, 2 propellers, 18.0knots • Built Barclay, Curle & Co. Ltd, Glasgow, UK • Employment trooping 1856-62 educational cruises 1965-75

Moreton Bay • container ship • P&O subsidiary Overseas Containers Ltd (OCL) 1969-90 • 227.22m x 30.55m (745.8ft x 100.2ft) • 26,876grt • Pass. nil • Crew n/a • Cargo 1,563 teu • Mach. double-reduction geared steam turbine, 32,000shp, 1 propeller, 21.5knots • Built Blohm & Voss AG, Hamburg, West Germany • Employment UK and Europe/Australia

Ardtaraig • supertanker • P&O subsidiary Trident Tankers Ltd. 1969-79 • 324.17m x 48.12m (1,063.9ft x 157.9ft • 214,128 dwt, 119,666grt • Pass. nil • Crew 39 • Cargo 256,262 cubic metres (9,051,200 cubic feet) • Mach. double-reduction geared steam turbine, 28,000shp, 1 propeller, 16.0knots • Built Mitsui Zosen, Chiba, Japan • Employment Gulf/Europe, Japan 'shuttle' services, long-term charters to oil companies

Dwarka • cargo/passenger liner • P&O Subsidiary, British India Steam Navigation Company Ltd 1947, P&O General and Deep Sea Cargo Divisions 1971-82 • 121.48m x 16.7m (398.7ft x

54.8ft) • 4,851grt • Pass. 20 first, 32 second, 534 berthed deck, 533 un-berthed deck • Crew 130, • Cargo 6,013 cubic metres (212,384 cubic feet) • Mach. SCSA Doxford diesel, 4,200bhp, 1 propeller, 13.5knots • Built Swan Hunger & Wigham Richardson Ltd, Newcastle-upon-Tyne, UK • Employment India and Pakistan/Persian Gulf

Uganda • liner later used for educational cruising • P&O Subsidiary, British India Steam Navigation Company Ltd 1952, P&O Passenger Division 1971-86 • 164.47m x 21.76m (539.8ft x 71.4ft) • 14,430grt • Pass. In line service 167 first, 133 tourist • Crew 287, for educational cruising from 1967, 306 cabin passengers, 920 schoolchildren • Mach. Parsons steam turbine, 12,300shp, 2 propellers, 16.0knots • Built Barclay, Curle & Co. Ltd, Glasgow, UK • Employment UK/East Africa 1952-67 educational cruising 1968-83

Eagle • roll-on/roll-off vehicle/passenger ferry • P&O subsidiary General Steam Navigation Company Ltd, 1971, P&O Short Sea Shipping Ltd 1971-75 • 141.79m x 22.61m (465.2ft x 74.2ft) • 11,609grt • Pass. 750 • Crew n/a • Cargo 200 cars • Mach. SCSA SEMT-Pielstick diesel, 20,400bhp, 2 propellers, 23.0knots • Built Dubigeon Normandie SA, Nantes, France • Employment Southampton/Lisbon/Tangier

Norland • roll-on/roll-off vehicle/passenger ferry • P&O subsidiary North Sea Ferries Ltd 1974-2002 • 153.0m x 25.2m (501.9ft x 82.7ft) • 12,988grt • Pass. 1,072 • Crew 98 • Cargo 179 12-metre (40-ft) trailers or 500 cars • Mach. Stork-Werkspoor diesel NV, 18,000bhp, 2 propellers, 18.0knots • Built AG 'Weser' Seebeck Werft, Bremerhaven, West Germany • Employment Hull/Rotterdam passenger and freight service

Jetferry One • high-speed hydrofoil passenger ferry • P&O Ferries Ltd 1980-82 • 30.1m x 9.5m (98.8ft x 31.2ft) • 329gt • Hull aluminium • Pass. 250 • Crew n/a • Cargo nil • Mach. GM Detroit gas turbine, 7,400hp, 2 propellers, 43.0knots • Built Boeing Marine Systems, Seattle, USA • Employment London/Ostend.

Spirit of London • cruise ship • P&O Passenger Division 1972-89 • 164.46m x 24.81m (539.8ft x 81.4ft) • 17,370grt • Pass. 736 • Crew 328 • Mach. Fiat SCSA diesel, 18,000bhp, 2 propellers, 19.0 • Built Cantieri del Tirreno e Riuniti, Riva Trigoso, Italy • Employment USA West Coast-based cruising

Pacific Princess • cruise ship • P&O Passenger Division 1975-2001 • 168.74m x 24.64m (553.61ft x 80.84ft) • 20,636grt • Pass. 644 • Crew 317 • Mach. Fiat SGM diesel, 18,000bhp, 2 propellers, 19.0 • Built Rheinstahl Nordseewerke, Emden, West Germany 1970 as *Sea Venture* for Norwegian Cruiseships A/S, Oslo, Norway • Employment USA West Coast-based cruising, featured in US television series 'Love Boat'

Elk • roll-on/roll-off cargo ferry • P&O Ferries Ltd 1977-2000 • 155.99m x 21.67m (511.8ft x 71.1ft) • 5,463gt • Pass. 12 • Crew 21 • Cargo 142 12-metre (40-ft) trailers + 2 15-metre (50-ft) trailers • Mach. SEMT-Pielstick diesel, 15,600bhp, 2 propellers, 18.0knots • Built Ateliers Reunis du Nord et de l'Ouest, Dunkerque, France • Employment Middlesbrough/Gothenburg

Royal Princess • cruise ship • P&O Passenger Division 1984-2009 • 230.89m x 29.42m (757.52ft x 96.52ft) • 44,348grt • Pass. 1,260 • Crew 500 • Mach. SCSA Pielstick diesel, 31,543bhp, 2 controllable-pitch propellers, 22.0knots • Built OY Wärtsilä Ab, Helsinki, Finland • Employment USA-based cruising

Pride of Dover • roll-on/roll-off vehicle/passenger ferry • Townsend Car Ferries Ltd 1987, P&O European Ferries Ltd 1987-2006 • 169.6m x 28.27m (556.4ft x 92.7ft) • 26,433gt • Pass. 2,290 • Crew 137 • Cargo 650 cars or 100 15-metre (50-ft) freight units • Mach. Sulzer CCM diesel, 31.500bhp, 3 controllable-pitch propellers, 22.0knots • Built Schichau Unterwesser AG, Bremerhaven, West Germany • Employment Dover/Calais passenger and freight service

Norsea • roll-on/roll-off vehicle/passenger ferry • P&O subsidiary North Sea Ferries Ltd 1987-2006 • 179.2m x 25.4m (587.9ft x 83.3ft) • 31,785gt • Pass. 746 berthed, 504 un-berthed • Crew 107 • Cargo 2,200 lane metres (850 cars) • Mach. Sulzer diesel, 26,100bhp, 2 controllable-pitch propellers, 18.5knots • Built Govan Shipbuilders Ltd, Glasgow, UK • Employment Hull/Rotterdam passenger and freight service

Oriana • cruise ship • P&O Cruises 1995- • 260.0m x 32.2m (853.0ft x 103.6ft) • 69,153gt • Pass. 1,975 • Crew 760 • Mach. MAN-B&W diesel, 47,750kW, 2 propellers, 24.0knots • Built Meyer Werft, Papenburg-Ems, West Germany • Employment UK-based cruising

Grand Princess • cruise ship • P&O subsidiary Princess Cruises Inc. 1998- • 289.51m x 40.20m (949.8ft x 131.9ft) • 108,806gt • Pass. 2,600 • Crew 1,137 • Mach. diesel-electric, 69,600kW, 2 fixed-pitch propellers, 22.5knots • Built Fincantieri Cantieri Navali Italiana SpA, Monfalcone, Italy • Employment cruising for Princess Cruises

Pride of Rotterdam • roll-on/roll-off vehicle/passenger ferry • P&O subsidiary North Sea Ferries Ltd 2001- • 215.44m x 31.85m (706.83ft x 104.5ft) • 59,925gt • Pass. 1,360 • Crew 141 • Cargo 3,355 lane metres (1,380 cars) • Mach. Wärtsilä diesel, 51,394bhp, 2 propellers, 22.0knots • Built Fincantieri Cantieri Navali Italiana SpA, Marghera, Italy • Employment Hull/Rotterdam passenger and freight service

Ventura • cruise ship • P&O Cruises Inc. 2008- • 289.6m x 36.0m (950.15ft x 118.11ft) • 113,000gt • Pass. 3,572 • Crew 1,076 • Mach. diesel-electric, 2 azimuthing pods, 21.7knots • Built Fincantieri Cantieri Navali Italiani SpA, Monfalcone, Italy • Employment UK-based cruising

Spirit of Britain • roll-on/roll-off vehicle/passenger ferry • P&O Ferries 2011- • 212.97m x 30.8m (698.73ft x 101.05ft) • 47,592gt • Pass. 2,000 • Crew 200 • Cargo 2,741 lane metres • Mach. MAN-B&W diesel, 2 propellers, 22.0knots • Built STX Finland, Rauma, Finland • Employment Dover/Calais passenger and freight service

P&O FERRIES FLEET 2012

The following ships constitute the current P&O fleet in service at the time or this book's publication apart from the passenger tonnage operated by Carnival Corporation under the Princess and P&O Cruises brands.

European Causeway • 2000 • 159.5m x 23.4m (523.3ft x 76.8ft) • 20,646gt • Pass. 410 • Cars 315 • Trailers • Lane metres 1,771 • Speed 22.5knots • Employment Cairnryan/Larne

European Endeavour • 2000 • 180.0m x 25.0m (590.6ft x 82.0ft) • 22,152gt • Pass. 366 • Lorries 120 • Lane metres 1,950 • Speed 22.5knots • Employment Dover/Calais later Liverpool/Dublin

European Highlander • 2002 • 162.7m x 23.4m (533.8ft x 76.8ft) • 21,128gt • Pass. 410 • Cars 315 • Trailers 84 • Lane metres 1,771 • Speed 22.5knots • Employment Cairnryan/Larne

European Seaway • 1991 • 179.7m x 27.8m (589.6ft x 91.2ft) • 22,986gt • Pass.200 • Lorries 120 • Lane metres 1,925 • Speed

21.0knots • Employment Dover/Calais

European Trader • 1978 • 176.2m x 20.6m (578.1ft x 67.6ft) • 17,068gt • Pass. 12 • Trailers 194 • Lane metres 2,723 • Speed 17.0knots • Employment Teesport/Rotterdam

Express • 1998 • 91.3m x 26.0m (299.5ft x 85.3ft) • 5,902gt • Pass. 868 • Cars 195 • Speed 42.0knots • Employment Larne – Cairnryan/Troon

Norbank • 1993 • 166.7m x 23.4m (546.9ft x 76.7ft) • 17,464gt • Pass. 114 • Trailers 125 • Lane metres 2,040 • Speed 21.5knots • Employment Liverpool/Dublin

Norbay • 1992 • 166.7m x 23.4m (546.9ft x 76.7ft) • 17,464gt • Pass. 114 • Trailers 125 • Lane metres 2,040 • Speed 21.5knots • Employment Liverpool/Dublin

Norking • 1980 • 170.9m x 23.0m (560.7ft x 75.5ft) • 17,884gt • Pass. 12 • Trailers 155 Lane metres 2,100 • Speed 17.5knots • Employment Tilbury/Zeebrugge

Norqueen • 1980 • 170.9m x 23.0m (560.7ft x 75.5ft) • 17,884gt • Pass. 12 • Trailers 155 Lane metres 2,100 • Speed 17.5knots • Employment Tilbury/Zeebrugge

Norsky • 1999 • 180.0m x 25.2m (590.6ft x 82.7ft) • 19,992gt • Pass 12 • Trailers 194 • Lane metres 2,630 • Speed 20.0knots • Employment Teesport/Zeebrugge

Norstream • 1999 • 180.0m x 25.2m (590.6ft x 82.7ft) • 19,992gt • Pass 12 • Trailers 194 • Lane metres 2,630 • Speed 20.0knots • Employment Teesport/Zeebrugge

Pride of Bruges • 1987 • 179.0m x 25.3m (587.3ft x 83.0ft) • 31,598gt • Pass. 1,050 • Cars 310 • Trailers 185 • Lane metres 2,230 • Speed 18.0knots • Employment Hull/Zeebrugge

Pride of Burgundy • 1992 • 179.7m x 27.8m (587.3ft x 83.0ft) • 28,138gt • Pass. 1,420 • Cars 465 • Lorries 120 • Lane metres 1,925 • Speed 21.0knots • Employment Dover/Calais

Pride of Calais • 1987 • 169.6m x 27.8m (556.4ft x 91.2ft) • 26,433gt • Pass. 2,290 • Cars 585 • Lorries 85 • Lane metres 1,545 • Speed 22.0knots • Employment Dover/Calais

Pride of Canterbury • 1991 • 179.7m x 27.8m (589.6ft x 91.2ft) • 30,635gt • Pass. 2,000 • Cars 537 • Lorries 120 • Lane metres 1,900 • Speed 21.0knots • Employment Dover/Calais

Pride of Dover • 1987 • 169.6m x 27.8m (556.4ft x 91.2ft) • 26,433gt • Pass. 2,290 • Cars 585 • Lorries 85 • Lane metres 1,545 • Speed 22.0knots • Employment laid up at time of writing

Pride of Hull • 2001 • 215.4m x 31.5m (706.7ft x 103.3ft) • 59,925gt • Pass. 1,360 • Cars 205 • Trailers 263 • Lane metres 3,348 • Speed 22.0knots • Employment Hull/Rotterdam

Pride of Kent • 1992 • 179.7m x 27.8m (589.6ft x 91.2ft) • 30,635gt • Pass. 2,000 • Cars 537 • Lorries 120 • Lane metres 1,900 • Speed 21.0knots • Employment Dover/Calais

Pride of Rotterdam • 2001 • 215.4m x 31.5m (706.7ft x 103.3ft) • 59,925gt • Pass. 1,360 • Cars 205 • Trailers 263 • Lane metres 3,348 • Speed 22.0knots • Employment Hull/Rotterdam

Pride of York • 1987 • 179.0m x 25.1m (587.3ft x 82.3ft) • 31,785gt • Pass. 1,050 • Cars 310 • Trailers 185 • Lane metres 2,230 • Speed 18.0knots • Employment Hull/Zeebrugge

Spirit of Britain • 2011 • 212.0m x 30.8m (695.5ft x 101.0ft) • 47,592gt • Pass 2,000 • Cars 194 • Lorries 180 • Lane metres 2,741 • Speed 22.0k • Employment Dover/Calais

Spirit of France • 2011 • 212.0m x 30.8m (695.5ft x 101.0ft) • 47,592gt • Pass 2,000 • Cars 194 • Lorries 180 • Lane metres 2,741 • Speed 22.0k • Due for employment Dover/Calais 2012

REFERENCES

1 Friedrich Engels, 'The Conditions of the Working Class in England', The Great Towns, online edition.
2 David Howarth and Stephen Howarth, The Story of P&O, Weidenfeld & Nicolson, London, 1986, p.16.
3 David Howarth and Stephen Howarth, The Story of P&O, Weidenfeld & Nicolson, London, 1986, p.27.
4 David Howarth and Stephen Howarth, The Story of P&O, Weidenfeld & Nicolson, London, 1986, p.25.
5 William Makepeace Thackeray, Notes of a Journey from Cornhill to Grand Cairo, online document.
6 William Makepeace Thackeray, Notes of a Journey from Cornhill to Grand Cairo, online document.
7 'The Bentinck', The Illustrated London News, 12 August 1843, p.108.
8 'The *Bentinck*', The Illustrated London News, 12 August 1843, p.108.
9 R.R. Palmer, Joel Colton and Lloyd Kramer, A History of the Modern World, McGraw-Hill, New York, 2006, p.642.
10 Letter from P&O to Messrs Zulueta & Co., Cadiz, 27 January 1845.
11 'On the way to India', The Graphic, 27 November 1875, pp.524-526.
12 Stephen Rabson and Kevin O'Donoghue, P&O: A Fleet History, World Ship Society, London, 1989, pp.18-19.
13 Stephen Rabson and Kevin O'Donoghue, P&O: A Fleet History, World Ship Society, London, 1989, pp.20-21.
14 'A Voyage to China', The Illustrated London News, 9 November 1872, pp.436-438.
15 'On the way to India', The Graphic, 27 November 1875, pp.524-526.
16 Malcolm R. Gordon, From *Chusan* to *Sea Princess*: Australian Services of the Peninsular and Oriental and Orient Line, Harper Collins, London, 1986, p.20.
17 Malcolm R. Gordon, From *Chusan* to *Sea Princess*: Australian Services of the Peninsular and Oriental and Orient Line, Harper Collins, London, 1986, p.21.
18 Stephen Rabson and Kevin O'Donoghue, P&O: A Fleet History, World Ship Society, London, 1989, p.19.
19 Malcolm R. Gordon, From *Chusan* to *Sea Princess*: Australian Services of the Peninsular and Oriental and Orient Line, Harper Collins, London, 1986, pp.21-22.
20 'The Suez Maritime Canal', The Illustrated London News, 13 March 1869, p.265.
21 Stephen Rabson and Kevin O'Donoghue, P&O: A Fleet History, World Ship Society, London, 1989, p.77.
22 'The Indian Mail at Venice', The Illustrated London News, 31 August 1872, p.198.
23 Stephen Rabson and Kevin O'Donoghue, P&O: A Fleet History, World Ship Society, London, 1989, p.77.

24 K.T. Rowland, Steam at Sea, David & Charles, Newton Abbott, 1970, pp.119-120.
25 'Peninsular and Oriental Company's Steam-ship *Mooltan*', The Illustrated London News, 3 August 1861, p.106.
26 'The New Steam-ship *Australia*', The Illustrated London News, 19 November 1892, p.653.
27 Malcolm R. Gordon, From *Chusan* to *Sea Princess*: Australian Services of the Peninsular and Oriental and Orient Line, Harper Collins, London, 1986, p.46.
28 Michael Fry, The Scottish Empire, Birlinn, Edinburgh, 2001, pp.255-264.
29 'The British India Steam Navigation Company Ltd deck-passenger trade,' The Mariner's Mirror, Volume 97, No. 2, 2011, p.72.
30 Stephen Rabson and Kevin O'Donoghue, P&O: A Fleet History, World Ship Society, London, 1989, p.84.
31 David Howarth and Stephen Howarth, The Story of P&O, Weidenfeld & Nicolson, London, 1986, p.114.
32 Stephen Rabson and Kevin O'Donoghue, P&O: A Fleet History, World Ship Society, London, 1989, p.169.
33 Malcolm R. Gordon, From *Chusan* to *Sea Princess*: Australian Services of the Peninsular and Oriental and Orient Line, Harper Collins, London, 1986, pp.50-51.
34 Stephen Rabson and Kevin O'Donoghue, P&O: A Fleet History, World Ship Society, London, 1989, p.170.
35 Malcolm R. Gordon, From *Chusan* to *Sea Princess*: Australian Services of the Peninsular and Oriental and Orient Line, Harper Collins, London, 1986, pp.152-3.
36 Stephen Rabson and Kevin O'Donoghue, P&O: A Fleet History, World Ship Society, London, 1989, p.172.
37 Stephen Rabson and Kevin O'Donoghue, P&O: A Fleet History, World Ship Society, London, 1989, p.173.
38 See John K. Galbraith, The Great Crash 1929, Penguin, London, 1954 for a detailed description of the circumstances leading to and consequences of the Wall Street Crash.
39 R.R. Palmer, Joel Colton and Lloyd Kramer, A History of the Modern World, McGraw-Hill, New York, 2006, pp.798-799.
40 David Howarth and Stephen Howarth, The Story of P&O, Weidenfeld & Nicolson, London, 1986, p.151.
41 Jim Davis, You and Your Ships, The Memoir Club, Stanhope, 2006, p.39.
42 David L. Williams and Richard P. de Kerbrech, Damned by Destiny, Teredo Books, Brighton, 1982, pp.269-270.
43 Stephen Rabson and Kevin O'Donoghue, P&O: A Fleet History, World Ship Society, London, 1989, p.170.
44 Jim Davis, You and Your Ships, The Memoir Club, Stanhope, 2006, pp.66-67.
45 Philip Dawson, *Canberra*: in the Wake of a Legend, Conway, London, 1997, p.59.
46 Interview with Jim Davis, former P&O Lines director, by Bruce Peter at The Baltic Exchange, London, 8 August 2011.
47 See Ewan Corlett, The Ship: The Revolution in Merchant Shipping, National Maritime Museum, London, 1981 for a more detailed account of these issues.
48 A.B. Marshall, Taking The Adventure, Michael Russell, Norwich, 1999, pp.51-59.
49 See Brian J. Cudahy, How Container Ships Changed the World, Fordham University Press, New York, 2006 for a detailed account of the reasoning behind the container revolution.
50 Jim Davis, You and Your Ships, The Memoir Club, Stanhope, 2006, p.72.
51 Brian J. Cudahy, How Container Ships Changed the World, Fordham University Press, New York, 2006, pp.25-41.
52 Bruce Peter and Philip Dawson, The Ferry: A Drive-through History, Ferry Publications, Ramsey, 2010, pp.98-99.
53 '*Norwave*: Hull-Rotterdam service inaugurated by twin-screw roll-on/roll-off ferry', Shipping World & Shipbuilder, January 1966, pp.78-80.
54 David Fairhall, 'New Generation of Steamers', The Manchester Guardian, 7 January 1967, p.9.
55 David Howarth and Stephen Howarth, The Story of P&O, Weidenfeld & Nicolson, London, 1986, pp.173-174.
56 Interview with David Trevor-Jones, former P&O and BI Educational cruise passenger, by Bruce Peter, London, 26 September 2011.
57 Interview with David Trevor-Jones, former P&O and BI Educational cruise passenger, by Bruce Peter, London, 26 September 2011.
58 Bruce Peter and Philip Dawson, The Ferry: A Drive-through History, Ferry Publications, Ramsey, 2010, pp.157-158.
59 Stephanie Gallagher, True North: About the career of Knut Utstein Kloster, iUniverse, Bloomington, 2009, pp.6-12.
60 Jim Davis, You and Your Ships, The Memoir Club, Stanhope, 2006, p.78.
61 Interview with Sandy Stirling, former P&O Lines director, by David Trevor-Jones, 14 March 2009.
62 Stephanie Gallagher, True North: About the career of Knut Utstein Kloster, iUniverse, Bloomington, 2009, pp.10-11.
63 Interview with Sandy Stirling, former P&O Lines director, by David Trevor-Jones, 14 March 2009.
64 Jim Davis, You and Your Ships, The Memoir Club, Stanhope, p.78.
65 Interview with Jim Davis, former P&O Lines director, by Bruce Peter at The Baltic Exchange, London, 8 August 2011.
66 A.B. Marshall, Taking The Adventure, Michael Russell, Norwich, 1999, pp.71-131.
67 '*Dwarka* London: An Arabian Voyage', BBC TV, 1979.
68 Bruce Peter, Knud E. Hansen A/S: Ship Design through Seven Decades, Forlaget Nautilus, Frederiksvaerk, 2007, pp.197-202.
69 Philip Dawson, *Canberra*: In the Wake of a Legend, Conway, London, 1997, pp.99-119.
70 David Howarth and Stephen Howarth, The Story of P&O, Weidenfeld & Nicolson, London, 1986, pp.195-199.
71 Philip Dawson, Cruise Ships: An evolution in design, Conway, London, 2000, pp.154-159.
72 Interview with Kai Levander, former Project Manager for Wärtsilä Shipbuilders, by Bruce Peter, London, 25 January 2010.
73 Philip Dawson, Cruise Ships: An evolution in design, Conway, London, 2000, pp.160-164.
74 David Howarth and Stephen Howarth, The Story of P&O, Weidenfeld & Nicolson, London, 1986, p.202.
75 David Howarth and Stephen Howarth, The Story of P&O, Weidenfeld & Nicolson, London, 1986, pp.204-210.

76 Stephen Rabson and Kevin O'Donoghue, P&O: A Fleet History, World Ship Society, London, 1989, p.474.
77 John Hendy, Ferry Port Dover, Ferry Publications, Staplehurst, 1997, pp.54-56.
78 John Hendy, The Short-Sea Route Dover-Calais, Ferry Publications, Ramsey, 2009, pp.74-77.
79 David Howarth and Stephen Howarth, The Story of P&O, Weidenfeld & Nicolson, London, 1986, p.213.
80 Bruce Peter, Knud E. Hansen A/S: Ship Design through Seven Decades, Forlaget Nautilus, Frederiksvaerk, 2007, pp.275-276.
81 Maurizio Eliseo, The Sitmar liners & The V Ships, Carmania Press, London, 1998, pp.107-140.
82 Maurizio Eliseo, The Sitmar liners & The V Ships, Carmania Press, London, 1998, pp.141-149.
83 Philip Dawson, Cruise Ships: An evolution in design, Conway, London, 2000, pp.226-232.
84 Interview with John McNeece, McNeece Design, by Bruce Peter, Edinburgh, 16 May 2008.
85 Interview with Paul Woodbury, former manager P&O Ferries Portsmouth, by Bruce Peter, Glasgow, 3 June 2010.
86 John Hendy, The Short-Sea Route Dover-Calais, Ferry Publications, Ramsey, 2009, p.76.
87 John Hendy, The Short-Sea Route Dover-Calais, Ferry Publications, Ramsey, 2009, pp.79-88.
88 Terry Macalister, 'P&O turns back to the sea with plan to float Bovis', The Guardian, 24 March 1999.
89 See *Aurora*: Dawn of a New Era, P&O, London, 2000 for a detailed description of the vessel's design, construction and outfitting.
90 See Fulvio Roiter, *Grand Princess*, Fincantieri, Trieste, 1999 for a detailed illustrated record of the vessel's construction and outfitting.
91 Ralf Schröder and Michael Thamm, AIDA: Die Erfolgsstory, Delius Klasing Verlag, Bielefeld, 2008, pp.96-101.
92 'P&O sells 50% of ABC to Eurotower', The Independent, 28 December 2000.
93 www.prnewswire.co.uk/cgi/news/release?id=113061 P&O Completes Exit from Bulk Shipping.
94 Niels Lunde, Hr. Mollers Nye Mand: Nils Smedegaards revolution på Esplanaden – og på Carlsberg, Jyllands-Postens Forlag, Copenhagen, 2008, pp.141-142.
95 Maurizio Eliseo, *Queen Elizabeth*: More than a ship, Fincantieri, Trieste, 2010, pp.72-79.
96 See Andrew Sassoli-Walker and Sharon Poole, *Artemis*: The Original Royal Princess, Amberley Publishing, Stroud, 2010 for a detailed study of this vessel's career.
97 '*Dwarka* London: An Arabian Voyage', BBC TV, 1979.
98 www.nti.org/e_research/e3_75.html, Randall Beisecker, Research Assistant, Monterey Institute of International Studies and, James Martin, Center for Nonproliferation Studies, DP World and U.S. Port Security, March 2006.
99 See Designs 2011, ShipPax, Halmstad, 2011 and John Hendy, Two New Ships, One New Era: P&O Ferries' *Spirit of Britain* and *Spirit of France*, Ferry Publications, Ramsey, 2011 for detailed descriptions of these vessels.
100 P&O Heritage Collection exists to preserve the history, archive and collections of P&O and is supported by P&O's owners, DP World.
101 P&O Cruises' vessels fly the P&O flag under licence.

*The **Chakla** was purchased by the British India Steam Navigation Co. Ltd in 1964. (FotoFlite)*

Interviews

Interview with Jim Davis, former P&O Lines director, by Bruce Peter at The Baltic Exchange, London, 8th August 2011.
Interview with Kai Levander, former Project Manager for Wärtsilä Shipbuilders, by Bruce Peter, London, 25 January 2010.
Interview with John McNeece, McNeece Design, by Bruce Peter, Edinburgh, 16 May 2008.
Interview with Sandy Stirling, former P&O Lines director, by David Trevor-Jones, 14th March 2009.
Interview with David Trevor-Jones, former P&O and BI Educational cruise passenger, by Bruce Peter, London, 26 September 2011.
Interview with Paul Woodbury, former manager P&O Ferries Portsmouth, by Bruce Peter, Glasgow, 3rd June 2010.

Books

Aurora: Dawn of a New Era, P&O, London, 2000.
Corlett, Ewan, The Ship: The Revolution in Merchant Shipping, National Maritime Museum, London, 1981.
Cudahy, Brian J., How Container Ships Changed the World, Fordham University Press, New York, 2006.
Davis, Jim, You and Your Ships, The Memoir Club, Stanhope, 2006.
Dawson, Philip, *Canberra*: in the Wake of a Legend, Conway, London, 1997.
Dawson, Philip, Cruise Ships: An evolution in design, Conway, London, 2000.
Donovan, Arthur and Bonney, Joseph, The Box That Changed The World. Fifty years of container shipping – an illustrated history, Commonwealth Business Media, East Windsor, New Jersey, 2006.
Elphick, Peter, Liberty: The Ships that Won the War, Chatham Publishing, Chatham, 2001.
Eliseo, Maurizio, The Sitmar liners & The V Ships, Carmania Press, London, 1998.
Eliseo, Maurizio, *Queen Elizabeth*: More than a ship, Fincantieri, Trieste, 2010.
Fry, Michael, The Scottish Empire, Birlinn, Edinburgh, 2001.
Galbraith, John K., The Great Crash 1929, Penguin, London, 1954.
Gallagher, Stephanie, True North: About the career of Knut Utstein Kloster, iUniverse, Bloomington, 2009.
Gordon, Malcolm R., From *Chusan* to *Sea Princess*: Australian Services of the Peninsular and Oriental and Orient Line, Harper Collins, London, 1986.
Greenway, Ambrose, Cargo Liners: An Illustrated History, Seaforth Publishing, Barnsley, 2009.
Guthrie, John, A History of Marine Engineering, Hutchison, London, 1971.
Hendy, John, Ferry Port Dover, Ferry Publications, Staplehurst, 1997.
Hendy, John, The Short-Sea Route Dover-Calais, Ferry Publications, Ramsey, 2009.
Hendy, John, Two New Ships, One New Era: P&O Ferries' *Spirit of Britain* and *Spirit of France*, Ferry Publications, Ramsey, 2011.
Howarth, David and Howarth, Stephen, The Story of P&O, Weidenfeld & Nicolson, London.
Hviid, Søren Lund (ed.), Dansk Illustreret Skibsliste 2009, Sea Press, Århus, 2008.

*Passengers take in the air on the **Caledonia**'s promenade deck. (Ferry Publications Library)*

Jennings, Eric, Cargoes: A Century Story of the Far Eastern Freight Conference, Meridian Communications, Singapore, 1980.
Johnston, Ian, Ships for a Nation: John Brown & Company Clydebank 1847-1971, Dunbartonshire Libraries & Museums, Clydebank, 2000.
Levinson, Marc, The Box: How the shipping container made the world smaller and the world economy bigger, Princeton University Press, Princeton and Oxford, 2006.
Lunde, Niels, Hr. Mollers Nye Mand: Nils Smedegaards revolution på Esplanaden – og på Carlsberg, Jyllands-Postens Forlag, Copenhagen, 2008.
Marshall, A.B., Taking The Adventure, Michael Russell, Norwich, 1999.
Palmer, R.R., Colton, Joel, and Kramer, Lloyd, A History of the Modern World, McGraw-Hill, New York, 2006.
Peter, Bruce, Knud E. Hansen A/S: Ship Design through Seven Decades, Forlaget Nautilus, Frederiksvaerk, 2007.
Peter, Bruce and Dawson, Philip, The Ferry: A Drive-through History, Ferry Publications, Ramsey, 2010.
Rabson, Stephen and O'Donoghue, Kevin, P&O: A Fleet History, World Ship Society, London, 1989.
Roiter, Fulvio, *Grand Princess*, Fincantieri, Trieste, 1999.
Rowland, K.T., Steam at Sea, David & Charles, Newton Abbott, 1970.
Sassoli-Walker, Andrew and Poole, Sharon, *Artemis*: The Original Royal Princess, Amberley Publishing, Stroud, 2010.
Sawyer, L.A. and Mitchell, W.H, The Liberty Ships: The History of the 'Emergency' Type Cargo Ships Constructed in the United States During World War Two, Lloyd's of London Press, London, 1985.
Schröder, Ralf and Thamm, Michael, AIDA: Die Erfolgsstory, Delius Klasing Verlag, Bielefeld, 2008.
Tolerton, Nick, Reefer Ships: The Ocean Princesses, Willson Scott, Christchurch, 2008.
Williams, David L. and de Kerbrech, Richard P., Damned by Destiny, Teredo Books, Brighton, 1982.

Journals

Designs
Designs 2011, ShipPax, Halmstad, 2011.
The Mariner's Mirror
'The British India Steam Navigation Company Ltd deck-passenger trade', Volume 97, No. 2, 2011, p.72.
Shipping World & Shipbuilder
'*Norwave*: Hull-Rotterdam service inaugurated by twin-screw roll-on/roll-off ferry', January 1966, pp.78-80.

Newspapers

The Guardian
Terry Macalister, 'P&O turns back to the sea with plan to float Bovis', The Guardian, 24 March 1999.
The Graphic
'On the way to India', 27 November 1875, pp.524-526.
The Illustrated London News
'The *Bentinck*', 12 August 1843, p.108.
'A Voyage to China', 9 November 1872, pp.436-438.
'The Suez Maritime Canal', 13 March 1869, p.265.
'The Indian Mail at Venice', 31 August 1872, p.198.
'Peninsular and Oriental Company's Steam-ship *Mooltan*', 3 August 1861, p.106.
'The New Steam-ship *Australia*', 19 November 1892, p.653.
The Independent
'P&O sells 50% of ABC to Eurotower', 28 December 2000.
The Manchester Guardian

*The **Chusan** leaving Southampton. (John Hendy)*

David Fairhall, 'New Generation of Steamers', 7 January 1967, p.9.

Online documents

Engels, Friedrich, 'The Conditions of the Working Class in England', The Great Towns, online edition.
Thackeray, William Makepeace, Notes of a Journey from Cornhill to Grand Cairo, online document.
www.prnewswire.co.uk/cgi/news/release?id=113061 P&O Completes Exit from Bulk Shipping.
www.nti.org/e_research/e3_75.html, Randall Beisecker, Research Assistant, Monterey Institute of International Studies and, James Martin, Center for Nonproliferation Studies, DP World and U.S. Port Security, March 2006.

Other sources

Letter from P&O to Messrs Zulueta & Co., Cadiz, 27 January 1845.
'*Dwarka* London: An Arabian Voyage', BBC TV, 1979.

*The **Lion** in the Dover Strait following her opening the Dover-Boulogne link in April 1977. (FotoFlite)*

A'Rosa Blu see Crown Princess
Achilles 22
Adonia 162, **163,** 174
Aida (Aida vita) 160
Aida aura 160
Aida Blu see Crown Princess
Aida cara 160
Alcantara 45
Anco Charger 118
Antelope, HMS 121
Arabia 35
Arcadia (1888) 33
Arcadia (1954) 7, 64, **68–69, 70, 72,** 73, **100,** 113, 116
Arcadia (1997) see Star Princess
Arcadia (2005) **170,** 173
Ardlui 91
Ardshiel 91
Ardtaraig 91, 183–184
Ardvar 91
Arkona 160
Arrow 22
Artemis see Royal Princess
Asturias 45
Atfeh 16
Athena 143
Atherstone 93
Atlantic Conveyor 121
Aurora 10, **155,** 156, **157,** 173, 174
Aurora Australis 104
Australia 30, **31, 32,** 33, 35
Azura **171, 172, 173,** 174

Ballarat (1911-1914) 37
Ballarat (1921) 44
Ballerat (1911-17) 183
Balmoral 136
Balranald 44
Banala 37
Baradine 44
Barrabool 44
Baudouinville see Cathay (1961)
Beltana 37
Benares 27
Bendigo 44
Bentinck **17,** 17–19, 182
Berrima 37
Birka Queen 133
Bombay 26, 182
Borda 37, 40, 43
Botany Bay 97
Braganza 22
Bretagne 143
Britannia 33
Buccleuch 93

Caen Express **165**
Cairo 16–17
Caledonia **188**
Canberra 7, 10, 16, 67, **72–79,** 73–78, 81, 87, 91, **97,** 98, **100,** 100–101, 108, 109, 113, 117–123, **119,** 133–136, 137, **137,** 141–143, 183
Candia **27**
Cannanore 59
Canterbury, POSL **153**
Canton (1848) **15**
Canton (1939) 60, **61**
Cardigan Bay 97
Carinthia see Fair Princess
Carla C. (Princess Carla) 114, 116
Carnivale 168
Carthage 33, **61**
Cathay (1925) **42,** 45, 56
Cathay (1961) 87, 100
Chakla **187**
China 35, 43
Chitral (1925) 45, **45, 56,** 60
Chitral (1961) 87, 100
Chusan (1852) 25–26, 182
Chusan (1949) 7, **62–63,** 64, **64–67,** 73, **73,** 100, 174, **189**
Clan Macintyre 37
Comet 6, 9
Commonwealth 36
Comorin 45
Corfu **60**
Coromandel 33, 59
Cotswold 93
Crown Odyssey 136
Crown Princess 133, 143, 160, 161, **162, 163**

Dara **91**
Dawn Princess (1957) 132, **132,** 133
Dawn Princess (1996) **142,** 143, 156
Delhi 30
Devanha 43
Devonia (1939 Devonshire) **101,** 102
Discovery see Island Princess
Discovery Bay **96,** 97
Don Juan 11–12, 13, 21, 182
Dorset **95**
Dover, POSL see Pride of Dover
Dragon **98,** 99, **125,** 129, 183
Dreamward 136
Dulhallow 93
Dumra 113–114
Dunera 102
Dwarka 113–114, 177, 184

Eagle 104–105, **106,** 184
Eckerö 151
Egypt 35
Elk 117, 118, 121, 184
Emeu 27
Empire Paragon 59
Empress of Britain 168
Empress of Canada 168
Encounter Bay 97
Eston 56
Estonia 144
Etretat see Pride of Le Havre
European Ambassador 151, 168
European Causeway 151, **151,** 184
European Clearway **127, 153**
European Endeavour **128,** 184
European Highlander 151, **177,** 184
European Highway see Pride of Kent (2003)
European Mariner 184
European Pathfinder see European Clearway
European Pathway 144, **166**
European Seaway 144, **167, 176,** 184
European Trader 184–185
Europic Ferry **129**
Express 185

Fair Princess 132, **132,** 133
FairMajesty see Star Princess
Fairsea see Dawn Princess (1957)
Fairsky 123, 132, **133, 135**
Fairstar 117, 132, 133, **134**
Festivale 170
Flandre (Princess Carla) 114, 116
Flinders Bay 97
Floristan **93**
Flying Princess 105–107, **107**
Formosa 26
France see Norway
Free Enterprise V **127**

Garonne 87
General Belgrano 118–119
Gneisenau 56
Golden Princess (1993) 133
Golden Princess (1999) 156, 160, **160**
Grand Princess **156,** 156–160, **158, 159,** 184
Great Liverpool 13, **13,** 14, 18, 182
Gwalior **32**

Haddington 22, 24, 182
Hauraki **92**
Herald of Free Enterprise **127,** 129–130, 131
Himalaya (1854) **19**
Himalaya (1892) **31, 32,** 33, 35, 40, 182
Himalaya (1949) 7, 64, **66, 67, 71,** 73, 100
Hindostan 17–18, 182
HMS Antelope 121
HMS Medea 11
HMS Sheffield 119
Homeric 136
Honfleur see Pride of Portsmouth

Iberia (1844) 15
Iberia (1954) 7, 64, **71,** 73
Ideal X 95
Ile de France 56
India 35, **36**
Island Princess 114–116, **115,** 123, 175
Island Venture see Island Princess
Isle of Innisfree 143, **166**
Isle of Lewis 152
Italia 108, 114

Jadotville see Chitral (1961)
Jamaica Queen 168
Jervis Bay 97

Jetferry One 107, 184
Jetferry Two 107

Kaisar-I-Hind 32, **39**
Kalyan 43
Kalypso 143
Karanja **114**
Karmala 43
Kashgar 43
Kashmir 43
Kent, POSL **147**
Kenya **4,** 100, 102
Khyber 43, **57**
Koningin Beatrix 130
Kowloon Bay 97
Kungsholm see Sea Princess (1979)

Lady Mary Wood 15, 22, 23, 182
Lahore **42**
Leopard 99, 129
Lincoln 64–66
Lion 104, **105,** 127–129
Liverpool (1840) see Great Liverpool
Liverpool Bay **96,** 97
Lotus 16–17

Macedonia 35, **38,** 40
Madras 26, 182
Maersk Madrid **164**
Maloja 44, 47, 60, 73, 183
Malwa 35
Mantua 35, 40, 73
Maori 98
Mardi Gras 168
Marmora 35, **38**
Max Mols **165**
Medea, HMS 11
Medina 6, 35, **36,** 54
Minerva 175
Moldavia (1903) 35, 182–183
Moldavia (1922) **41,** 43, 54
Mongolia (1865) **28**
Mongolia (1903) 35
Mongolia (1923) **40, 41, 42,** 43, 54
Mooltan (1861) **30,** 31–32, 182
Mooltan (1905) 35, 43
Mooltan (1923) 44, **44, 57,** 60
Morea 35
Moreton Bay 97, 183
Mulbera **113**
Munster 121

n.f. Panther see St Sunniva
n.f. Tiger **120,** 129
Naldera **40, 41,** 43
Narkunda **41, 42,** 43, 56
Narrung 36
Nevasa 102, **102,** 103, 117, 183
Nieuw Amsterdam 123
Nili 168
Noordam 123
Norbank 147, 151, 185
Norbay 147, **147,** 151, 185
Norking 185
Norland 105, **107, 118,** 118–121, 131, 184
Norna 26
Norqueen 185
Norsea 130–131, **131,** 146, 147, 184, 185
Norsky 185
Norstar 105, **128,** 131
Norstream 185
Norsun 130–131, 146, 147, **153, 168,** 185
Norwave 98–99, 105, 183
Norway 121, 132
Norwind 98–99, **99,** 105
Nubia 30

Ocean Princess **142,** 156, 159, 162, **163,** 174
Ocean Village see Star Princess
Ocean Village II see Crown Princess
Oceana (1887) 33
Oceana (2002) see Ocean Princess
Olau Britannia see Pride of Portsmouth
Olau Hollandia see Pride of Le Havre
Olympia see Pride of Bilbao
Oneida 26
Opawa 91
Orama 91, 183
Orbustus see Oriana
Orcades 72, 73, **85, 86,** 101, **112, 191**
Oriana **4,** 7, 67, 73, 78–81, **78–83,** 87, 91, 97, **97,** 100, 108, 113, 117, 121, **135,** 136–141, **137–141,** 143, 156, 173, 174, **175,** 183, 184
Orient 16
Oriental 13, 14, 15, 97, 182
Orion **48,** 72
Orissa 91
Oronsay 73, **84, 86,** 101, **112**
Orpheus 121

*The P&O liner **Orcades** outward bound from Tilbury. (FotoFlite)*

Orsova 73, **85, 86, 88–89**
Osaka Bay 97
Osiris **37**
Ottawa 91
Oxfordshire *see* Fairstar

P&O Nedlloyd Kobe **164**
Pacific Dawn *see* Crown Princess
Pacific Pearl *see* Star Princess
Pacific Princess **114, 115,** 116, 117, 123, 184
Padua 43
Panther, n.f. *see* St Sunniva
Panther, SF 105, **106**
Pasteur 56
Peninsular Bay **164**
Perim 43, 59
Persia 35, **35, 36,** 43
Peter Pan *see* SF Panther
Piako **113**
Pinjarra 59
Poonah **29,** 30, **30**
POSL Canterbury **153**
POSL Dover *see* Pride of Dover
POSL Kent **147**
Pottinger 22, 182
Pride of Bilbao 143, **145, 146, 151,** 166
Pride of Bruges (1987) *see* Norsun
Pride of Bruges (1988) **128**
Pride of Burgundy **144,** 144–145, **146,** 185
Pride of Calais **124,** 130, **130,** 180, 185
Pride of Canterbury 185
Pride of Cherbourg 143, **166**
Pride of Dover **127, 129,** 130, **148–149,** 180, 184, 185
Pride of Hull 146, 147, **150,** 185
Pride of Kent (1987) **147**
Pride of Kent (2003) 144, **146, 166, 179,** 185
Pride of Le Havre 143, 166
Pride of Portsmouth 143, **144,** 166
Pride of Rotterdam 146, 147, **150,** 184, 185
Pride of Winchester **18,** 143
Pride of York *see* Norsea
Princess Carla 114, 116
Princess Patricia 114
Pundua **93**

Queen Elizabeth 2 108, 109, 110, 119, 121, 132, 133, 173
Queen Mary 2 173
Queen Victoria *see* Arcadia (2005)

R Eight (Adonia) 162, **163,** 174
Rajputana 44
Ranchi **43,** 44, 60
Rangatira 98
Rangitoto 100
Ranpura 44, 183
Ravenna 32
Rawalpindi 44, 56
Red Dragon 12
Redcar 56
Regal Princess 132, 133, **134,** 143
Repulse 12
Rohilla 32–33, 43
Rome 16, 33
Rosetta 32–33
Rotterdam 123
Royal Iris *see* Eagle
Royal Princess **121, 122,** 123, 132, 135, 136, 174, 184
Royal Viking Sky 133
Ruahine **92**

Salmara **94**
Salsette (1858) 27
Salsette (1908) 35, 54, 183
Salsette (1956) **58**
Sapphire Princess **161**
Sardinia 35
Scharnhorst 56
Sea Princess (1979) **115, 116,** 116–117, 132, 136, **136,** 174
Sea Princess (1998) 156, 162 *see also* Adonia
Sea Venture *see* Pacific Princess
Sea-Land Maclean 97
SF Panther 105, **106**
Shanghai 26
Sheffield, HMS 119
Shenzhen Bay **164**
Shillong 59
Sicilia 35, 43
Simla 27
Singapore 59
Sitmar FairMajesty *see* Star Princess
Sky Princess *see* Fairsky
Skyward 108
Socotra 59
Somali 35, **58,** 59
Song of America 123
Song of Norway 108
Soudan (1901) 35, 43
Soudan (1948) 59, 183
Southern Cross 73
Southward 109
Sovereign of the Seas 132
Spirit of Britain **178, 180,** 180–181, **181,** 185
Spirit of France 180–181, 185
Spirit of Free Enterprise **147**
Spirit of London **109,** 109–110, **110, 111, 112,** 114, 116, 123, 184
St Clair (1975) 105, **106**
St Clair (1992) 151
St Ola 151
St Sunniva **128,** 129, 151, **152**
Star Aquarius 143
Star Pisces 143
Star Princess 132, 133, **134,** 137, 161, **161, 163, 169, 170**
Starward 108
Stathconnon **93**
Stena Fantasia **153**
Stena Nordica 151, 168
Strathaird **48, 52–53,** 54, 56, 87
Strathallan 55, **55,** 56
Strathardle 94, 183
Strathbrora 94
Strathconon 94
Stratheden **49, 50, 51, 54,** 55, 60, **60, 61, 87**
Strathewe 118
Strathmore **48,** 55, 64
Strathmost *see* Canberra
Strathmuir **113**
Strathnaver **6–7, 48, 52–53,** 54, 60–64, **61,** 183
Sumatra 24, **28**
Sun Princess (1974) *see* Spirit of London
Sun Princess (1995) **142,** 143, 156
Sunda **58,** 59, **59**
Sunward 108, 168
Surat 59
Svea Scarlett 151
Sylvania *see* Dawn Princess (1957)
Syria 35, 43

Tagus 11, **11,** 15, 16, 182
Talamba 78
Talamba **91**
Taupo **94**
Tiger, n.f. **120,** 129
Tokyo Bay 97
Tor Baltica *see* Elk
Travemünde 151
Treloske **92**

Uganda 102–103, **103, 104, 118,** 118–119, 121, 184
Ullswater **162**
Ulster Prince 104
Ulster Queen 104, **105**
United States (1840) *see* Oriental

S.A. Vaal 170
Valetta 33
Vectis (1881) 35
Vectis (1904) 16, 33
Ventura **171,** 174, 184
Viceroy of India 45–47, **46, 47,** 48, 54, 56, 183
Victoria (1887) 33, 182
Victoria (1995) *see* Sea Princess (1979)
Viking Venturer **126**
Volkerfreundschaft 160

Wahine **97,** 97–98, 183
Wakool 36
Waratah 37
Wilcannia 36
William Fawcett 10, 182
Windward 136